Beyond the Pale

BEYOND THE PALE

Reading Ethics from the Margins

Edited by
Stacey M. Floyd-Thomas and Miguel A. De La Torre

WESTMINSTER
JOHN KNOX PRESS
LOUISVILLE · KENTUCKY

© 2011 Westminster John Knox Press

First edition
Published by Westminster John Knox Press
Louisville, Kentucky

11 12 13 14 15 16 17 18 19 20—10 9 8 7 6 5 4 3 2 1

Portions of chapter 24 ("Stanley Hauerwas on Church") appeared previously in *Latino/a Social Justice: Moving Beyond Eurocentric Moral Thinking,* by Miguel A. De La Torre, and are used here by permission of Baylor University Press.

Book design by Sharon Adams
Cover design by Lisa Buckley
Cover illustration © Ekeley/Vetta Collection/Getty Images

Library of Congress Cataloging-in-Publication Data
Beyond the pale. Reading ethics from the margins / Miguel A. De La Torre and Stacey M. Floyd-Thomas, editors.—1st ed.
    p. cm.
    Includes bibliographical references (p.   ).
    ISBN 978-0-664-23680-9 (alk. paper)
    1. Christian ethics. 2. Theologians. 3. Liberation theology. 4. Postcolonial theology. I. De La Torre, Miguel A. II. Floyd-Thomas, Stacey M., 1969– III. Title: Reading ethics from the margins.
    BJ1275.B49 2011
    241—dc23

                                                            2011023666

To those who came before us and
carved out a space in the academy for
our discourse

To those who are with us in the struggle to
move from the margins to the center of
our own realities

To those who follow in the hopes that they will
continue to forge beyond the pale for the sake of liberating
our communities

If in this book harsh words are spoken about some of the greatest among the intellectual leaders of mankind, my motive is not, I hope, the wish to belittle them. It springs rather from my conviction that, if our civilization is to survive, we must break with the habit of deference to great men. Great men may make great mistakes; and as the book tries to show, some of the greatest leaders of the past supported the perennial attack on freedom and reason. Their influence, too rarely challenged, continues to mislead those on whose defence [sic] civilization depends, and to divide them. The responsibility of this tragic and possibly fatal division becomes ours if we hesitate to be outspoken in our criticism of what admittedly is a part of our intellectual heritage. By reluctance to criticize some of it, we may help to destroy it all. . . . Although the book presupposes nothing but open-mindedness in the reader, its object is not so much to popularize the questions treated as to solve them.

—Karl Popper[1]

Contents

Contributors

Ilsup Ahn is Carl I. Lindberg Associate Professor of Philosophy in Applied Ethics and faculty fellow for Asian studies at North Park University, where he teaches philosophy, theology, and ethics. He holds a doctorate (religious ethics) from the Divinity School of the University of Chicago. He is the author of *Position and Responsibility: Jürgen Habermas, Reinhold Niebuhr, and the Co-Reconstruction of the Positional Imperative* (2009) and has been published in journals such as *Journal of Religious Ethics*, *The Heythrop Journal*, and *Cooperation and Conflict*.

Victor Anderson is the Chancellor Chair, Oberlin Theological School, and Professor of Christian Ethics, Religious Studies, and African American and Diaspora Studies in the College of Arts and Sciences. He is author of three books: *Beyond Ontological Blackness: An Essay on African American Religious and Cultural Criticism* (1995), *Pragmatic Theology: Negotiating the Intersections of an American Philosophy of Religion and Public Theology* (1998), and *Creative Exchange: A Constructive Theology of African American Religious Experience* (2008).

Edward Antonio teaches theology, social theory, and African studies and serves as Iliff School of Theology's Associate Dean of Diversities. He has published a number of scholarly articles in these areas and is currently working on two book projects. He has also taught at the University of the Witwatersrand in Johannesburg, South Africa, where he served as the treasurer of the South African Academy of Religion and as a consultant for the World Council of Churches project on Ecumenical Hermeneutics.

Elias K. Bongmba holds the Harry and Hazel Chavanne Chair in Christian Theology and is also Professor of Religious Studies at Rice University. His book *The Dialectics of Transformation in Africa* won the Frantz Fanon Prize from the Caribbean Philosophical Association. He is also author of *Facing a Pandemic: The African Church and Crisis of AIDS.*

Alejandro Crosthwaite, OP, is Professor of Catholic Social Teaching, Social and Political Ethics, and Media Studies at the Faculty of Social Sciences, Director of the Ethical Leadership in Business and Politics Program, and Vice-Rector for Public Relations at the Pontifical University of Saint Thomas Aquinas (Angelicum) in Rome. He is the author of lectures and articles on the social and political thought of St. Thomas Aquinas, Ethical/Servant Leadership studies, Latin American and Latino/a social ethics, and Media studies.

Keri Day is Assistant Professor of Theological and Social Ethics and Director of the Black Church Studies Program at Brite Divinity School. She received her BS in political science with a minor in economics from Tennessee State University. She earned an MA in religion and ethics from Yale University Divinity School and received her PhD in religion from Vanderbilt University (with a graduate certificate in women's and gender studies). Her research sits at the intersections of critical social theory, Black religion, womanist theology, and ethics and poverty studies.

Miguel A. De La Torre has authored numerous articles and over twenty books, including the award-winning *Reading the Bible from the Margins* (2002), *Santería: The Beliefs and Rituals of a Growing Religion in America* (2004), and *Doing Christian Ethics from the Margins* (2004). He presently serves as Professor of Social Ethics at Iliff School of Theology in Denver. Within the academy he is a director of the American Academy of Religion, past director of the Society of Christian Ethics, and President of the Society of Christian Ethics (2012). Additionally, he is the editor of the *Journal of Race, Ethnicity, and Religion* (www .raceandreligion.com).

Valerie Elverton Dixon, PhD, is an independent scholar and lecturer. She is founder of JustPeaceTheory.com. She taught Christian Ethics for nearly ten years at the United Theological Seminary in Dayton, Ohio, and at Andover Newton Theological School in Newton Centre, Massachusetts. While working at Andover Newton, she was a faculty member of the ethics PhD seminar at

Boston College. She blogs at *God's Politics* and the *Tikkun Daily* Blog. She is a *Washington Post on Faith* panelist.

Stacey M. Floyd-Thomas is Associate Professor of Ethics and Society at Vanderbilt University Divinity School and Graduate Department of Religion. She is the author of *Mining the Motherlode: Methods in Womanist Ethics* (2006), *Deeper Shades of Purple: Womanism in Religion and Society* (2006), *Black Church Studies: An Introduction* (2007), and *Liberation Theologies in the United States: An Introduction* (2010). As a proponent of bridging the gap that exists between the academy and the church, Floyd-Thomas serves as the cofounder and CEO of the Black Religious Scholars Group (BRSG), and is also the executive director for the Society of Christian Ethics (SCE).

Rodolfo J. Hernández-Díaz is a PhD candidate in religious and theological studies, concentrating in religion and social change, at University of Denver and Iliff School of Theology. He is the author of a number of entries in *Hispanic American Religious Cultures* (2009) and the *Dictionary of Scripture and Ethics* (*DSE*) (forthcoming). He currently serves on the steering committee of the Latina/o Critical and Comparative Studies Consultation and the Latina/o Religion, Culture, and Society Group at the AAR. He also serves as coconvener of Latino(a) Working Group of the Society of Christian Ethics.

Robyn Henderson-Espinoza is a joint doctoral student at the University of Denver and at the Iliff School of Theology, pursuing a degree in social ethics with a graduate certificate in Latina/o studies. Robyn's academic work seeks to shape the existing discourse concerning social ethics and Latina/os, and her primary academic interest is the mestizaje body, moral subjectivity, and queer theories and epistemologies. The lenses of the Christian agnostic and queer-mestizo shape her pursuit of justice and ethical analysis. Robyn is a doctoral fellow for the Hispanic Theological Initiative and was selected as a Human Rights Campaign Fellow.

Ada María Isasi-Díaz is Professor Emerita of Ethics and Theology, Drew University, where she taught from 1991 to 2009. A native of Cuba, she received her PhD in 1990 from Union Theological Seminary, New York. Since 1987 Isasi-Díaz has elaborated a mujerista theology based on the religious understandings and practices of USA Latinas. She is coauthor with Yolanda Tarango of *Hispanic Women: Prophetic Voice in the Church*, the first USA Latina theology book. Her other books are: *En La Lucha—In the Struggle*, *Mujerista Theology*, and *La Lucha Continues*. She has coedited several books and has published articles in countless books and journals.

James Samuel Logan was born in Harlem and raised in the South Bronx. At Earlham College he is Associate Professor of Religion and Associate Professor and Director of African and African American Studies. Logan is the author of *Good Punishment? Christian Moral Practice and U.S. Imprisonment* (2008) and "Liberalism, Race, and Stanley Hauerwas," *CrossCurrents* (Winter 2006). He is coeditor (with Marcia Riggs) of *Ethics That Matters*, a volume of contemporary African, Caribbean, and African American essays on religious social ethics (2011).

Anthony B. Pinn is the Agnes Cullen Arnold Professor of Humanities and Professor of Religious Studies at Rice University. He is the author or editor of twenty-six books addressing a variety of issues related to religious aesthetics, liberation theologies, religion and popular culture, and humanism. He is the founding director of the HERE Project, a program fostering better relationships between Houston and Rice through creative research collaborations and innovative pedagogical approaches. Pinn is also the director of research for the Institute for Humanist Studies, and a member of the Meadville Lombard Theological School Board of Trustees.

Rosetta Ross teaches religious studies at Spelman College in Atlanta. Her research and writing explore the role of religion in Black women's activism, focusing particularly on the civil rights movement. She is author of *Witnessing and Testifying: Black Women, Religion, and Civil Rights,* which examines religion as a source that helped engender and sustain activities of seven Black women civil rights leaders. Ross has also written many articles examining religion in Black women's activism.

Ben Sanders III is currently a PhD student in Religion and Social Change (Social Ethics) in the PhD program at the Iliff School of Theology and the University of Denver. He earned a BA in religion from Hope College (Holland, Mich.) and an MDiv with a focus in Christian theology and social ethics from Union Theological Seminary, New York. His research engages the roles of race and religion in the construction of moral and political systems in the United States, with the aim of imagining and constructing new social possibilities from the grassroots level.

Angela Sims is Assistant Professor of Ethics and Black Church Studies at Saint Paul School of Theology in Kansas City, Missouri. Her oral history research has been supported by the Ford Foundation, the Womanist Scholars Program at the Interdenominational Theological Center, the Louisville Institute, the Wabash Center for Teaching and Learning in Theology and Religion, and the Institute for Oral History at Baylor University. She is the author of *Ethical Complications of Lynching: Ida B. Wells's Interrogation of American Terror* and the coeditor, with Katie Geneva Cannon and Emilie Townes, of *Womanist Theological Ethics: A Reader.*

Andrea Smith is an associate professor of Media and Cultural Studies at the University of California–Riverside. She is the author of numerous works, including *Native Americans and the Christian Right: The Gendered Politics of Unlikely Alliances* (2008), *The Revolution Will Not Be Funded* (2007), and *Conquest: Sexual Violence and American Indian Genocide* (2005). She is the U.S. coordinator for the Ecumenical Association of Third World Theologians (EATWOT). Dr. Smith is also the cofounder of INCITE! Women of Color against Violence and the Boarding School Healing Project.

George (Tink) Tinker is Professor of American Indian Cultures and Religious Traditions at Iliff School of Theology (Denver). He is the author of numerous books, including *Missionary Conquest: The Gospel and Native American Cultural Genocide* (1993) and *American Indian Liberation: A Theology of Sovereignty* (2008). Tinker's writings, speeches, and activism bring attention to the liberation efforts of American Indians and critique the colonialism perpetuated against American Indians. Tinker has served as director of Four Winds American Indian Survival Project in Denver and president of the Native American Theological Association.

Asante U. Todd is a doctoral candidate in the Graduate Department of Religion at Vanderbilt University in the Ethics and Society program. He holds degrees from the University of Texas at Austin (BA) and Austin Presbyterian Theological Seminary (MDiv). Todd's research, under the rubric of political theology, is located at the intersection of African American cultural studies and theological ethics. At Vanderbilt, Todd is also a member of the Theology and Practice program, which emphasizes critical thought on issues of theological education and Christian ministry.

Darryl Trimiew is the chair of the Department of Philosophy and Religion at Medgar Evers College, Brooklyn, New York. He holds a PhD from Emory University and a JD from Rutgers School of Law, Newark. He is on the board of *The Journal of Law and Religion* and is a past president of the Society of Christian Ethics. His best-known publications are *God Bless the Child That's Got Its Own: The Economic Rights Debate* (1997), *Voices of the Silenced: The Responsible Self in a Marginalized Community* (1993), and an edited collection of sermons, *Out of Mighty Waters* (1994).

Traci West is Professor of Ethics and African American Studies at Drew University Theological School in Madison, New Jersey. She is the author of *Disruptive Christian Ethics: When Racism and Women's Lives Matter* (2006) and *Wounds of the Spirit: Black Women, Violence, and Resistance Ethics* (1999). She is also the editor of *Our Family Values: Religion and Same-sex Marriage* (2006) and has published several articles on justice issues in church and society.

Preface and Acknowledgments

The genesis of this book can be traced to when the editors first met: in a doctoral class being taught by the fearless liberationist ethicist Dr. Katie Geneva Cannon at Temple University during the mid-1990s. Influenced by her wisdom, the experiences of being marginalized throughout our lives, and having the scholarship that our communities conduct dismissed within the academy led us, and many other scholars of color, to read the dominant culture with a healthy dose of hermeneutical suspicion. Although we are not interested in simply discarding the formative ethical or theological thinkers of the dominant culture, we are propelled to seriously consider how their works consciously or unconsciously contribute to the disenfranchisement and dispossession of marginalized communities of color. Regardless of how progressive their words may sound, their unexamined social location influences their thinking in ways that are life-denying to the communities existing on their underside.

We are keenly aware that subalterns are seldom allowed to speak for themselves, let alone critique the scholarship and wisdom of those accustomed to speaking for the subalterns. To do so runs the risk of being labeled "angry colored folk," so that what is being said can easily be dismissed. Yet it is crucial, for the sake of academic excellence, not only to find our own voices, but also to use those voices to unmask and uncover how the moral and theological reasoning of the dominant culture perpetuates the continued marginalization of communities of color.

For these reasons, we are deeply grateful for all of our colleagues, our sisters and brothers, who chose to stand in solidarity with us. Their individual voices have created a collective witness concerning how the thinking of the dominant culture has been normalized and legitimized within the academy—to our detriment. We are also grateful to Jon Berquist, former editor at Westminster John Knox, who believed in our mission from the start. Special thanks must also be given to Jacob G. Robinson, a doctoral student at Vanderbilt Divinity School, who spent countless hours assisting in editing this manuscript. And finally we thank our soul mates, Juan M. Floyd-Thomas and Deborah De La Torre, who have been faithful in love and unrelenting *en la lucha*.

Introduction

Beyond the Pale: Reading Ethics from the Margins

Liberation ethics is debunking, unmasking and disentangling the ideologies, theologies and systems of value operative in a particular society, by analyzing the established power relationships that determine the cultural, political and economic presuppositions and by evaluating the legitimating myths which sanction the enforcement of such values, in order to become responsible decision-makers who envision structural and systematic alternatives that embrace the well-being of us all.

—Katie Geneva Cannon[2]

Embedded within the liberationist ethical process is the fundamental query: *How do we resurrect the ethical realities and concerns of those from the underside of history?* Attending to the underside of history is a bold, audacious, and willful act. As marginalized ethicists continue to push from margin to center in their presence, perspectives, and publications, the foundational truths of our discipline must shift to allow room for the ethical realities of *all* people as those who are not only endowed with the "unalienable rights . . . [of] life, liberty and pursuit of happiness," but also were "made in the image and likeness of God." Such work makes marginalized Christian ethicists not only adept scholars but also liberationists who wrest marginalized ethical realities from the death-dealing grips of what womanist ethicist Katie Cannon calls the "false, objectified conceptualities and images that undergird the apparatuses of systemic oppression" that threaten to obliterate the truth of history and those caught within it.[3] Thus the mandate of this work is to attend to an ethical historiography that unearths the ethical realities of people of color and the two-thirds world from the pervasive as well as perpetually conjoined gazes of White supremacy: the purpose is to illustrate how the oppressed were silenced and have suffered, survived, and subverted those gazes throughout history. It is the uncovering of normative, oppressive ideologies and the recovering of liberationist analysis that drives this work. This is especially vital as it furthers the liberationist task, as womanist ethicists claim, of *wanting to know more and in greater depth than that which has been considered "good" and "true."*

To be sure, liberation ethics in the United States has matured, gaining both the attention of the publishing world and a solid place in the curriculum of undergraduate and graduate institutions of higher learning. While attention has been given to the genealogy of various forms of liberation theological ethics, much of this revolves around introductory texts that treat each modality in isolation. However, the study of the field of Christian ethics has been two-tiered: (1) normative ethics discussed about and by White males, and (2) marginalized ethics written by and for minoritized people and those who are curious. Rarely does the study of the field's genealogy include the centered perspectives and sustained critiques of those who forever seek to move from the margin of Christian ethics to the center of its study. Even surveys that seek to present a cross-range of liberation ethics tend to understand these forms of ethics within the context of a general liberal religion framework. In so doing, the unique theoretical and resource framework of constructive ethics—such as womanist ethics or Latina/o ethics—is lost to a general ethos that theoretically privileges the dominant liberal/neo-orthodox framework. This is problematic because progressive ethics such as feminist ethics and those previously named develop as a way to jettison the rather rigid and status-quo concerns of the dominant ethical paradigms in the United States. The very structural logic of most texts in Christian ethics frames "introductory readings in Christian Ethics" in a way that privileges the (almost exclusively) White and (predominantly) male traditions of moral thought: liberationist views of ethics are not presented in a way that best highlights their connections to important challenges of the dominant ethical traditions. Mindful of this, several liberationist scholars have long noted the need for a foundational text that seeks to liberate Christian ethics from its stronghold of Eurocentric heteropatriarchal normativity. To accomplish this, *Beyond the Pale* is a reader that offers liberationist critiques of the fathers of Christian ethics and their concepts that serve as presuppositions and legitimating myths limiting the human flourishing of people of color.

The expression "beyond the pale" typically refers to any action regarded as outside the limits of "normal" behavior that might be construed as unacceptable or improper. A prime example of this primary usage is found in the British novelist Charles Dickens's *The Pickwick Papers* (1837): "I look upon you, sir, as a man who has placed himself *beyond the pale* of society, by his most audacious, disgraceful, and abominable public conduct" (emphasis added). The two words "pale" appear as two homonyms, with tricky etymological roots: one root refers to matters of color and is from the Latin verb *pallere*, "to be pale"; the second root is from *palus*, meaning "a stake." Turning our attention toward the double entendre allows us to grapple with two concepts of "pale." On the one hand, we clearly address "pale" as an adjectival reference for something approaching whiteness in color in both a literal as well as a figurative sense. As scholars of color, we strive to envision theological education and academic discourse writ large in ways that can freely criticize and thoroughly deconstruct the hegemonic stranglehold of the White normative gaze. On the other hand, when "pale" is taken in the sense of an enclosure or a limited space beyond which it is not permissible to go, our discussion of the pale also means an old name for a pointed stake driven into the ground (our modern word "pole" is derived from the same source). By an obvious extension, this use of "pale" suggests the creation of a fence made of such stakes as a means of marking territory and claiming ground that is one's exclusive property or domain. As such, the relevance of our current endeavor is focused on the pale as a realm of activity, a branch of study, or a body of knowledge in much the same way we use the notion of academic "field" nowadays, with an implicit notion that civilization effectively stops at its fixed and definite boundary. Toward this end, our operative notion of the pale as an enclosed sphere of influence has grown out of this particular sense. Ultimately, those of us who strive to move beyond the pale do not share dominant values, beliefs, or social customs; thus we yearn to exist outside the parameters of the academy's normalizing effects by delving more deeply into the full range of our experiences and consciousness.

Having said all this, the purpose of the book is to read formative ethical thinkers from the social location of marginalized communities—as a means by which to interrogate the Eurocentrism ensconced within the canon of Christian ethics. Within these pages, some of the leading liberation ethicists, who have been significantly involved in the academic success and ongoing development of liberation thought in the field, have chosen to critique those classic theorists at the center from the margins of society, with the goal of a more thoroughgoing liberation ethics in mind. Twenty-four scholars address this need by providing the following in each essay:

- A historical backdrop for the development of a normative ethical thinker who has shaped the philosophical or social tradition of Christian ethics
- A description of the thinker's role in a given moral camp
- Reference to marginalized sources for engaging the thinker's form of ethics
- Theoretical and methodological considerations at work
- Ongoing issues of concern within that moral tradition

Throughout the modern era, people of color have had proof texts of philosophical and religious ethical thinking imposed upon them.[4] In order to justify racialized oppression in the modern world, everything from biblical teachings to pseudo-scientific research to governmental public policy has been used to fabricate a sense of identity and history that not only rationalized the misery of racial-ethnic minorities but also mandated that White patriarchal supremacy was God's only ordained plan for all humanity. Debunking, unmasking, and disentangling these normative ideologies is not simply *revisionism*; it also is actually *revivification*. For liberation ethicists, an interrogation of the history of Christian ethics is a constant and ongoing attempt to right the wrongs of our field, in an effort to undo the damage that a flawed and incomplete rendition of history has already done. This is so that the lives and thoughts of those who have been silenced and denigrated may become the indigenous sources that might not only rescue the oppressed from "the Western metaphysic of rationalization that dispirits the world in favor of power and hierarchy," but will also further the real work of human flourishing and communal accountability.[5]

Of course, no single scholarly act can single-handedly erase the legacy of oppression that the marginalized face, but such intentionality makes a vital difference in the case of informing the future direction of a field while instituting an ethic of accountability and self-reflexivity for the work of all scholars. So much of the experience of oppressed peoples has been portrayed as a series of inevitabilities. When viewed in this manner, the perennial crises facing marginalized communities are justified by the fact that people of color in this country are the descendants of denigrated and dispossessed peoples who were ostensibly reviled by Western culture. Consequently, it has been nearly impossible to imagine escape from the strongholds of such disdain, let alone redeem any sense of *the good*. What does it mean to have some sense of selfhood and moral agency as a person of color in America? How does one gain a positive sense of self in society while trying to wrestle with a historical context that has systematically denied these men, women, and children the basic elements of human regard and self-determination?

The challenge now is not only to tell the general public about what happened in the past, in accord with the radical truth-telling provided by the crisis caused by the history of Christian ethics, but to also inform them about why it matters. As it embraces the mandate of a liberative ethic, the overarching concern in the case of this emergent field is to challenge the prevailing sense of apathy that so often accompanied by the perennial question "So what?" We need a liberationist historiography such as this text that will challenge what we presently and naively take for granted as true concerning the most marginalized among us. In such a critique of our historical horizon, Christian ethicists become moral agents who have the responsibility to identify the so-called normative aspects of religious, social, political, cultural, and economic typologies. Typologies that have reproduced justifications for oppression, conditions for slavery, laws for apartheid, and frequently state-sanctioning of genocide have perennially invoked a divine sanction and scholarly rationale for declaring that God has ordained the natural order this way. By propping up the status quo in this fashion, we witness the codification of grave injustices done in the name of a religion that is supposed to liberate the oppressed. Even worse, this process of co-opting an otherwise liberating faith for the purposes of perpetuating oppressive power structures and unequal human relationships further destroys the moral agency of those of us on the margins; in turn, it makes us complicit in reproducing the same rationales and conditions that thwart the prospects of meaningful life and human flourishing.

Beyond the Pale is an effort to move beyond traditionalist modes of normative Christian ethics. It is an unapologetic and unashamed act to address the fictive truth of the status that people of color have as an oppressed class, as expressed and enacted by a Eurocentric project to dehumanize them. As Charles Long declares, this is "their second creation": the discovery of their own autonomy and agency to reveal the myths and tell the truth about "their first creation."[6] Indeed, the moral impetus for this project is to dehistoricize the myth-making and delegitimize death-dealing components of normative Christian ethics for the sake of creating a new discourse and new form of humanity—one that is no longer based on the master-slave or center-margins dialectic. This is done in order to help reeducate the world that people are not the sum total of their history, but rather that the course of scholarship is to write a history that is the sum total of a people. In so doing, the goal of this text is to actually reveal a "hidden history" of sorts that has been shared by both the oppressed and the oppressor but never articulated as such. The White patriarchal supremacy of Western culture has reinforced the logic that controlling the history of a people through canonical literature results in the absolute control of the people themselves. Conversely, a people in search of their own history move from being victims of circumstance to becoming agents of change. The appeal of the history-making work of liberation ethics is that it offers a consistent and insistent challenge to capture the rich essence of the experience of those who have had a worm's-eye view of the world, from its foundation to the foreground of a brighter future.

In sum, *Beyond the Pale* embraces this historical approach to liberation ethics not only to demonstrate how individual lives come to represent vital generational changes. It also elevates the importance of the momentous decisions that frame moral formation within the Western imagination and American community. The interrogation of a normative history and the incorporation of a truer one illuminate how marginalized ethical perspectives and concerns have been overlooked for centuries. This work attempts to bring the fullness and richness of an ethical and liberative agenda in the hopes of serving as a thoroughgoing corrective.

Notes

1. Karl R. Popper, *The Open Society and Its Enemies* (London: Routledge & Sons, 1945), preface to the first edition.
2. Katie Cannon, "Wheels in the Middle of Wheels," *Journal of Feminist Studies in Religion* 8, no. 2 (Fall 1992): 125–32.
3. Ibid., 125.
4. For a critical analysis of this phenomenon, see Anthony Pinn, *African American Humanist Principles: Living and Thinking Like the Children of Nimrod* (New York: Palgrave, 2004).

5. In womanist metaethics, the answering of the "So what?" question is the linchpin for satisfying the why-crisis of any moral problem. The answer to this question must take into account the pathos (feelings), logos (reason), ethos (values), and theos (ultimate concern) of an otherwise apathetic audience who must be logically persuaded and morally compelled to use their agency to address and resolve a moral problem in which they have been complicit.

6. Charles Long, *Significations: Signs, Symbols, and Images in the Interpretation of Religion* (Aurora, CO: The Davies Group, 1995), 184.

PART ONE
PHILOSOPHICAL
TRADITION

1

Plato on Reason

STACEY M. FLOYD-THOMAS

The safest general characterization of the European philosophical tradition is that it consists of a series of footnotes to Plato.
—Alfred North Whitehead[1]

Plato is philosophy, and philosophy, Plato—at once the glory and the shame of mankind, since neither Saxon nor Roman have availed to add any idea to his categories. No wife, no children had he, and the thinkers of all civilized nations are his posterity, and are tinged with his mind.
—Ralph Waldo Emerson[2]

HISTORICAL BACKDROP

Plato was born into an aristocratic family circa 427 BCE and lived in Athens, a city that served as home to scores of scientists, artists, mathematicians, and those considered to be "lovers of wisdom." Athens was a leading city of cultural achievement and scientific advancement and was regarded then, as now, as the cradle of Western civilization. Even though it was a sizable and significant city-state, Athens was still relatively small enough that everyone who was anyone knew each other. Despite his disheveled appearance and curious personal habits, Plato's teacher Socrates was a popular figure among the young upper-class Athenians. This was especially true with Plato, who along with his peers considered the philosopher Socrates to be a charismatic guru, due to his unconventional wisdom and courage to challenge traditional beliefs. Plato was drawn particularly to Socrates' dialectical irony and thought-provoking dialogue, which consisted of a quirky method of asking basic questions about various concepts and abstract ideals such as "What is the good life?" Like the Sophists, Socrates rejected the idea that tradition alone justifies conduct. Unlike them, however, he deemed morality not merely to be a convenience, but also a path chartered by the impetus to guide conduct by the means of reason. For Socrates, reason alone could bring about true self-knowledge.

Socrates maintained that neither morality nor philosophy could be taught because the life of the mind is a way of life rather than a body of knowledge. Thus he insisted that his pupils—among whom Plato claimed to be chief—engage in dialectical dialogue as an effort to override ignorance as the cause of evil, and take up reason as their life's calling because "the unexamined life is not worth living." According to Plato, until the final days leading up to his execution, Socrates maintained that "God orders me to fulfil [*sic*] the philosopher's mission of searching into myself and other men."[3] Plato found it difficult to live in Athens after the death of Socrates and as the city declined under the dominance of Sparta; he gave up his political aspirations and philosophical ponderings and left the cradle of his motherland and his father figure.

Sometime around 387 BCE, the homesick yet headstrong Plato returned to Athens as a man on a mission—to resurrect the classical soul of Athens and the spirit of Socrates. Although his professional résumé was distinguished by his experience as an aristocrat, philosopher, mathematician, and descendant of royalty and lawmakers, it was his founding of the Academy that enabled him to make a profession out of his mentor's way of life. With the power from this position, Plato created what was to become the first institution of higher learning in the Western world (where his star pupil, Aristotle, would later become the father of ethics); he did this by using the fiscal capital provided by his familial inheritance and by laying claim as the rightful inheritor of the cultural capital and legacy of the great philosopher Socrates.

Socrates is considered to be the architect of Western philosophy, yet so far as we know, he never wrote a word because he believed in the superiority of oral argument over writing. It is Plato's account of his mentor's conversations and debates that serves as our primary source for the words and thoughts of the historical Socrates—an account that functions as the very cornerstone of the field of Western philosophy. Thus it is actually Plato's original institutionalization of this philosophy that forms the foundation of how the academy and Western civilization study normative ethics and define and measure reason. Since Plato is regarded as both a beguiling and imaginative writer, historians of Western philosophy have observed that "it is very hard to judge how far Plato means to portray the historical Socrates and how far he intends the person called 'Socrates' in his dialogues to be merely the mouthpiece of his own opinions."[4] With the heft of the Academy, the fundamental history of Socratic thought, and his aristocratic clout, Plato helped to lend credibility to the saying "Knowledge is power." Consequently Plato is regarded as having written the blueprint for how to conceive of moral reasoning in modern ethics. Moreover, his ambition established philosophy as the root of ethics, which uses reason as a means to persuade people and order society.

As he established the Academy and compiled and codified Socrates' philosophy in his own hand, Plato tried to develop a coherent and sound answer to the Socratic question "What is the good life?" Preferring perfection to life, however, Plato did not feel that the question of the good could or should be answered through the radicality of Socrates' way of living. Instead, Plato felt that efforts to define the good life needed to be systematic, comprehensive, and persuasive. It had to become a school of thought that could only be explored and grasped within the process of schooling itself. Plato's motivating concern regarding reason was one of ethics. When systemized academically, Plato held that one could appreciate ethics as a philosophical system, but when employed systemically in society, it could also become public truth. Therefore Plato's ethics were interested not only in the *personal* pursuit for the good life but more importantly to establish a *political* system that would govern how people conducted their lives for the greater purpose of "civilizing" them.[5] Plato sought to develop a hierarchy of persons who would both exemplify and allow others to understand what it means to live the good life, to be civilized. Foregrounding ethics in the pursuit of the good and truth was, in fact, Plato's faulty way of expressing and solving the problem of justice, faulty in that his rationale was founded on the presumption that injustice could be righted by the intellectual rigor of those who possessed the highest skills of reason and by the obedience of everyone else to devote their role in life and society according to what these intellectual elites *reasoned* to be truly good. To achieve his goal, however, Plato required a means of ethical analysis that explained why people do what they do, in order to inform what they *ought* to do. To this end, Plato introduced readers to the Theory of the Soul.

THE THEORY OF THE SOUL

Drawing upon Socrates' ideas, Plato conceptualized the soul as the definitive essence of human beings, which helps determine their behavior. However, he realized that the intricacies and inner workings of the soul were difficult, if not impossible, to understand. So Plato utilized the analogy of the state as a clearly delineated entity, in order to extrapolate from it insight into the soul. In his most regarded text, the *Republic*, which served as the basic framework and foundation for his entire philosophy, Plato outlined his Theory of the Soul and of the society as the individual soul writ large. By correlating its function with that of the larger society, Plato set the course for what, how, and why reason is essential for the soul's quest in search of the good in both microcosmic and macrocosmic terms. Simply put, he argued that a person's conduct is analogous to the social systems wherein people display the same features, functions, and forces that city-states do. Just as a society is made up of different characters, so too the individual is made up of distinct characteristics. Likewise, whether as a citizen or city, people experience conflict when they are forced to make a choice about how to conduct themselves when their inclinations pull them in different directions. Plato thought the most reasonable path was to distinguish among the elements and interests of the soul, along with the virtues that relegate them and the classes that represent them, and thus one could come to understand the soul in its own right.

Plato's Theory of the Soul has three elements, with three corresponding interests, classes, and virtues. First, the *appetite* is the base and most common element of the soul, driven as it is by the basic desires of people to stay alive (via hunger and thirst) as well as by the unduly desires in which people often indulge (via overeating and excessive sex). The appetite is most dominant among the working class (the commoners and laborers), for whom moderation is the ultimate virtue because it compels their right behavior and ensures the good of their soul and livelihood. Next, the *spirit* is the element of the soul that seeks honor and victory—the responsibilities of the auxiliary/military class (soldiers and warriors), who rely on the virtue of courage to defend and protect the citizen, the city, and civilization. Last but not least, *reason* is the rational part of the soul, which is driven by the pursuit of the truth and is the sole domain of the guardian class, the philosophers, whose virtue of wisdom is not only necessary to rightly divide the truth but also to use truth as a dividing line to limit the spirit and appetite of the soul/state and keep the lust of the masses and the violence of the military in check.

Within the Theory of the Soul, one finds what Karl Popper has called the "spell of Plato," by which he suggests that Plato used his spokesman Socrates to lead his readers down a dubious road of Socratic dialogue.[6] What began as a pursuit in philosophical humility culminated in an ominous ontological ordering of human beings, wherein the specific functions of the soul via the separate, three factions of society must conform to this hegemony in order for individuals to live the good life and for the establishment of a just society. Individually, members of society were valued only in accordance with their specialization and natural impulse, inasmuch as they worked on behalf of the common good by attending to their constitutive character. The ideal state could be realized only if and when there was a rigid ethic governed by reason and everyone acted according to their purpose.

THEORY OF FORMS AND DUALISM

Plato's Theory of the Soul is situated within a larger dualistic world of forms, in which philosophers regarded reason as being independent of the senses (forms) and prioritized mind over matter (dualism). Since morality or virtue have universal, ephemeral, and fleeting qualities in Plato's world of forms, it is not necessary to define morality or virtue with absolute precision, but rather to seek and search for their essence. Likewise, his Theory of Dualism insists that the universe is divided into two irreducible realms, wherein abstraction trumps reality, sacred is separate from secular, and transcendence is dissociated from immanence. Plato's privileging of one reality over and against another in this manner maintains a hierarchical categorization of entities in which normative manners of reason and intelligence override all other forms of knowledge. When taken together, forms and dualism create a soul and state whose ideal existence is independent of a "sensible" world. Referred to as *apatheia* by the Stoics, this notion of being spiritually free from emotion privileges conceptual power via reason as the vehicle through which justice emerges and develops within the formation of an ideal society.

According to womanist theologian Kelly Brown Douglas, this theoretical trinity of state, forms, and dualism represents the problematic theological core of what she calls the "heretical nature of Platonized Christianity."[7] Plato's reasoning purports to protect the integrity of the soul and society by creating a social hierarchy, privileging the surreal over the real, as well as separating the mind from the body; yet in essence it undermines and is at odds with the very mission of Christian ethics. Thus the trinity of state, forms, and dualism has created ongoing issues toward making this field of inquiry unusable for those who are on the margins or underside of the hierarchical divide.

ONGOING ISSUES

The Power of the Elect

In that his philosophical pursuit forms the very basis of the political ideology of the Western world, Plato's moral reasoning also represents a sophisticated, Western cosmology. His notion of reason has become the divine law—in effect the Logos—of the Western world. Regarding this reality, English philosopher John Locke declared, "*Reason* must be our last Judge and Guide in every Thing."[8] A crucial question in this respect is, To whom does the sovereign domain of reason belong in this world? According to Platonic reasoning, it is only the philosopher who is able to reason and therefore discern the good. In Plato's cosmos, all of society should listen to and follow the philosopher-kings, and any activity or opinion that runs counter to them is regarded as unreasonable. As they fulfill their roles as philosophical guardians of the soul, the philosophers become a class of kings and thus the only ones capable of defining, meting out, and commanding justice. However, the fact remains that where there are kings, there is no democracy.

Plato's principles leave little doubt as to the role reason plays in establishing the sovereign ability of the philosopher-kings to control and discipline the proletariat—in direct opposition to the ideals of an open society or true democracy. In the second passage from *Laws,* Plato states:

> The greatest principle of all is that nobody, whether male or female, should ever be without a leader. Nor should the mind of anybody be habituated to

letting him do anything at all on his own initiative, neither out of zeal, nor even playfully. But in war and in the midst of peace—to his leader he shall direct his eye, and follow him faithfully. And even in the smallest matters he should stand under leadership. For example, he should get up, or move, or wash, or take his meals . . . only if he has been told to do so. . . . In a word, he should teach his soul, by long habit, never to dream of acting independently, and to become utterly incapable of it. In this way the life of all will be spent in total community. There is no law, nor will there ever be one, which is superior to this, or better and more effective in ensuring salvation and victory. . . . *And in times of peace, and from the earliest childhood on*, should it be fostered—this habit of ruling others, and of being ruled by others. And every trace of anarchy should be utterly eradicated from *all the life of all the men*, and even of the wild beasts which are subject to men.[9]

Platonic reason actually draws us to the problematic theological core of orthodox Christianity. With the hierarchy of society and the sovereignty of the philosopher-kings, the notion of an elect class—propagated since the time of Paul—became a driving force for scores of theologians who proclaimed a form of Christianity that implicitly used Platonic thought to provide a theological justification for claims that God had preordained certain people to govern the affairs, lives, and bodies of others. Chief among these theologians was John Calvin, who made use of Platonic reason to create a doctrine of election. Commonly referred to as the doctrine of predestination, Calvinist orthodoxy sought to articulate the method by which the "elect" were "eternally adopted" as "sons of God." In Calvin's own words, "God's eternal decree, by which he compacted with himself what he willed to become of each man. For all are not created in equal condition; rather eternal life is foreordained for some, eternal damnation for others."[10] Such systematic theology and Calvinist orthodoxy gave way to the theological foundation and assertions that deemed Black people as cursed ("The Hamitic Curse") and saw little irony in the fact that the first British ship that carried enslaved Africans as chattel across the Atlantic was nicknamed "The Good Jesus." Platonized hierarchy is intertwined in Christianity to such a degree that many deem them as synonymous. Platonized Christianity is so inherently compatible with institutionalized systemic oppression that some of the worst atrocities known to humanity (such as Native American genocide, the Atlantic slave trade, and the Jewish Holocaust) have not only been deemed rational but also justified as preordained and carried out in accordance with the will of God by God's very elect themselves.

The culmination and most comprehensive impact of Plato's principles is Platonized Christianity, seen today in the vestiges of Calvinist orthodoxy. Taking Plato's cue that we search for the good, Calvin argues that we are incapable of apprehending the good if left to our own impulsive and divisive devices; our only hope of salvation (from ourselves or by God) is to be found in the power of the sovereign. God's sovereignty is the good and determines the will. There is no other power of salvation. But immediately, the philosophical or theological question arises: If living the good life or seeking the power of salvation is only possible by the power of the sovereign and is independent in any respect from human free will, how is it then that some people are saved and others are not? The answer to this question is found in the decree of election: the adjudicating divine principle that a person's moral worth is determined by one's ability to reason and thus to rule. Thus the elect in this sense are those who live apathetic lives, refusing to concern themselves with the matters of the world.

The Pretense of Enlightenment

Plato's most famous passage, the Allegory of the Cave, provides an effective snapshot of the role that human knowledge (reason) plays in framing and understanding both reality and the human condition. In it, Socrates describes a big dark cave, shrouded in darkness and hidden from the world. Inside it, people stand next to each other with their backs to the exit and their necks, limbs, and feet bound so that none can see either each other or a way out. Shadows are cast by a fire behind their backs, and echoes of voices can be heard resounding through the cave. All they can see on the wall facing them are projected reflections, images, and shadows of people walking back and forth while talking and transporting things on their heads. The only things these prisoners ever perceive or experience throughout their subterranean existence are these shadows and echoes: this alone is their perceived "reality." If a prisoner should somehow become free from his chains, he would initially find himself entirely confounded as a result of being held entirely hostage by the darkness of the cave. Upon exiting the cave, he would at first be blinded by the light and fearful for his freedom. Upon returning to the cave, he would once again be blinded by its darkness. The outside reality that he experienced would be unintelligible and impossible to share with the other prisoners, whose knowledge and range of experience extended no further than the reality of the shadows and the echoes of the cave. The moral of the Allegory of the Cave is that the mind and ability of humans to reason are trapped in their bodies. Save for those few elected to be enlightened, most people are equally imprisoned and incapable of discerning their real selves, their own reality, and the realities of others. In other words, for most people the experience of reality is nothing more than projected images and echoes of reality that resound in their minds.

The Allegory of the Cave is a crystallization of everything that Platonic philosophy represents. It is familiar to nearly all who count themselves among the educated, general public, and it is virtually impossible to understand the discourse of the Enlightenment without it. This allegory has also served as the prevailing narrative of Eurocentric, White cultural ideology, as well as the means through which Platonized Christianity gives birth to the religious racism via Eurocentric heteropatriarchal normativity.

However much Plato's writings are considered to be preracist in the modern sense of that term, they were still elitist and eventually pressed into the service of the modern forms of racism that the Enlightenment philosophies spawned and fostered. As two prime examples, Cartesian thought (*Cogito ergo sum*, "I think, therefore I am") and Kantian thought (*Sapere aude*, "Dare to know") were philosophical projects that not only were complicit in the dehumanization of African peoples, but also disposed pre-Enlightenment Platonic thought into an organized, comprehensive, and classified system of Western knowledge that continues to be influential to the present day. Chief among the champions of its Americanized version was Thomas Jefferson, who clearly wielded both his pen and power in the dissemination of Enlightenment discourse and the rationalization of religious racism. Many of our contemporary practices and perspectives regarding criminalization, enslavement, impoverishment, eroticization, demonization, and second-class citizenship of African Americans are heavily dependent on Jeffersonian thought based on Platonic and Enlightenment perspectives of reason. In his *Notes on the State of Virginia*, Jefferson shares his views on African Americans:

> We will consider [Blacks] here, on the same stage with the whites, and where the facts are not apocryphal on which a judgment is to be formed. It will be right to make great allowances for the difference of condition, of education, of conversation, of the sphere in which they move. . . . Most of them indeed have been confined to tillage, to their own homes, and their own society: yet many have been so situated, that they might have availed themselves of the conversation of their masters. . . . In general, their existence appears to participate more of sensation than reflection. . . . Comparing them by their faculties of memory, reason, and imagination, it appears to me that in memory they are equal to the whites; in reason much inferior. . . . Their love is ardent, but it kindles the senses only, not the imagination. . . . Though for a century and a half we have had under our eyes the races of black and of red men, they have never yet been viewed by us as subjects of natural history. I advance it therefore as a suspicion only, that the blacks, whether originally a distinct race, or made distinct by time and circumstances, are inferior to the whites.[11]

As if giving an eighteenth-century rendition of Plato's fifth-century-BCE myth, Jefferson's republic is the United States, and his allegory alludes to the systematic chattel enslavement of African Americans. He supports that all people (Blacks and Whites) are created by God; yet simply because of conditions or unforeseen circumstances, those who are enlightened and freed from the same bondage as other human beings are deservedly masters of reason. If they should, perhaps, be willing to facilitate the cultivation of their lesser counterparts, they would ultimately be unable to do so due to their counterparts' lack of reason, and thus inferior state. This resounds with Kelly Brown Douglas: "The underlying assumption is that white people are the quintessence of rationality."[12] Consequently, twenty-first-century politics, ethics, metaphysics, rhetoric, the art of reasoning, and the division of the social sciences are all heavily dependent on this line of reasoning made possible via Platonic thought. Even more, Plato's philosophy becomes the impetus and thesis not only of scientific racism but also of the racist ideologies that limit the social welfare, educational opportunity, and equal rights of people of color who are subject and held hostage to the Enlightenment forms of government, which dictate the legislative, judicial, and administrative functions of their private and public life.

The Problem of Embodiment

The fact that Plato never admitted the category of slavery into his Theory of the Soul or his model state (which he acknowledged existed in his day) itself proves that much of his moral reasoning is founded upon the invalidation of other epistemologies or functional wisdom. According to his reasoning, "We have different natural aptitudes, which fit us for different jobs,"[13] and this too, in Plato's ideal republic, had to find its damaging and dualistic end. It only served to reason that the ideal form of the philosopher-king and enlightened individual also be examined.

In our final analysis, Platonism is most damaging in terms of how it deals with the materiality of the body. While the metaphors of the philosopher-king as the elect or the enlightened master of the races are powerful and pretentious, it is in the relationship between God and the world that Platonism lends its final blow by denigrating not only matter and the senses but also the body. In so doing, Platonism provides no notion for communion with God through the embodiment of humankind, especially as it relates to women and people and color.

Taken as a whole: the Theory of the Soul relegates both the lowest class of society and the most depraved part of humanity to the realm of sensory perception, which lends itself to hypersexuality and gluttony (to name only two of its vices); the Theory of Forms claims that the existence of soul within the body renders it tainted by the "nonsensible" world of forms; and the Theory of Dualism mandates that the mundane, material world of matter is inferior and should be dominated by the rational capacity of the mind. The culmination of this rational equation (as we can readily see with the Elect and the Enlightened) is that a certain class of people are marked by the bodies they inhabit and are subject to the whims of their senses. As such, they are unable to be entrusted or endowed with the power of reason.

Among the many subsequent understandings of Neoplatonic thought, Augustine's construction of sexuality is first and foremost. In the course of Western, European history, a blend of Greek and Christian hierarchical and patriarchal concepts fostered a pattern of ideas, expectations, and institutions that were available to the church during the Middle Ages. Augustine of Hippo adapted Plato's reasoning about the good and the soul into a Christian legacy of control that views sexuality specifically as a problem. When coupled with Judeo-Christian understandings of the fall (Gen. 3), Plato's reasoning suggests not merely that the body must obey the soul, but also that the fall itself represents the impulsive power of lust leading to the soul's loss of control over the body. The result is humanity's sin against and separation from God. In his Platonized reasoning, Augustine also argues that there is an essential human sexual nature that includes two sexes, male and female, and two genders, masculine and feminine: in each set the two features correspond to and are opposite to each other. Sex is an undisciplined result of a body overtaking its soul—a powerful force that drives men more than it does women, yet one nonetheless caused by women. Since the mind should control the body, sexual activity should be controlled as well.

The man/woman hierarchy, therefore, is reflective and synonymous to the soul/body relation. Interrelated patterns of sexism follow suit, for as kings and warriors, men are superior and must guard both their bodies and those of women who are subject to a "strict watch." When men rape women, it is because women have used their bodies to ensnare the soul of men. As a result, misogyny is rational and heterosexism is a virtue. Likewise, sexual activity should be severely restricted for women of the same social and economic class as the men whose sexual needs are so powerful and demanding, but it is nonetheless allowed and encouraged for men with "lower-class" women (women outside the circle of dominant-class men).

Taken one step further, when Neoplatonized constructions of sexuality find a common cause with expressions of religious racism, Platonized Christianity portends a catastrophic crisis for people of color. In the American scene, Blacks serve as the baseline for how this unfortunate partnership plays out. In effect, the genocide, raping, lynching, forced sterilization, medical butchering, state-sanctioned violence, police brutality, and human trafficking of Black, Latino/a, Asian, and Native bodies all serve as the sacrificial offerings of White racists, which both fulfill their mimetic desires to absolve their guilt, shame, and existential angst, and also uphold the sanctification and enactment of their flawed reasoning. The price for restoring order is often the price of colored flesh, and the rationale for their bodies as sacrifice becomes a religious rite. One need look no further than to the numerous accounts in U.S. history when the lynching of Black bodies was seen as a religiously sanctioned ritual enacted by White Christians, sometimes after Sunday services and during the course of family picnics:

> 2,000 people watched as [Sam] Hose was burned to death. But "before the torch was applied to the pyre, the Negro was deprived of his ears, fingers and other portions of his body with surprising fortitude. Before the body was cool, it was cut to pieces, the bones were crushed into small bits and even the tree upon which the wretch met his fate was torn up and disposed of as souvenirs. The Negro's heart was cut in several pieces, as was also his liver. Those unable to obtain the ghastly relics directly, paid more fortunate possessors extravagant sums for them." Ritual remains were often displayed, . . . turned into jewelry worn with pride, like a family heirloom, . . . as if to "signify" on the threat of blacks' presence and to pronounce white control over the enemy within.[14]

With Plato as the heir apparent of Socrates, mentor to Aristotle, prime mover to Augustine, role model to Calvin, and progenitor of Enlightenment—it is clear for all to see what one man hath wrought. Plato's ethics and theories for reason may have unified intellectual concepts, but they also created a greater, more-tragic, unfathomable distancing between human beings. His contribution to how modern society grapples with the ethical and philosophical realities of the world looms large. The great, ongoing challenge now is to reconcile that which Plato has torn asunder.

Notes

1. Alfred Whitehead, *Process and Reality* (New York: MacMillan Press, 1929), 63.
2. Ralph Waldo Emerson, "Plato; or, The Philosopher," in *Representative Men: Seven Lectures*, with text established by Douglas Emory Wilson (Cambridge, MA: Belknap Press of Harvard University Press, 1996), 21.
3. Plato, *The Dialogues of Plato*, trans. Benjamin Jowett (New York: Random House, 1937), 412.
4. Bertrand Russell, *A History of Western Philosophy* (1945; repr., New York: Simon & Schuster, 2007), 84.
5. Howard Alexander Slatte, *Plato's Dialogues and Ethics* (New York: University Press of America, 2000), 88.
6. Karl R. Popper, *The Open Society and Its Enemies*, vols. 1–2 (London: Routledge & Kegan Paul, 1945).
7. Kelly Brown Douglas, *What's Faith Got to Do With It? Black Bodies / Christian Souls* (Maryknoll, NY: Orbis Books, 2005), 71–103.
8. John Locke, *An Essay Concerning Human Understanding* (Philadelphia: Kay & Troutman, 1847), 456.
9. Plato, *Laws*, trans. Benjamin Jowett (Amherst, NY: Prometheus Books, 2000), emphasis added.
10. John Calvin, *Institutes of the Christian Religion* (Library of Christian Classics edition), 3.21.5.
11. Thomas Jefferson, "On the Differences between the Races," in *Notes on the State of Virginia* (London: J. Stockdale, 1787), Query 14.
12. Douglas, *What's Faith Got to Do With It?* 117.
13. Plato, *The Republic* (New York: Penguin Classics, 2003), 2.2.57.
14. The lynching of Sam Hose in 1899 as cited in Anthony Pinn, *Terror and Triumph: The Nature of Black Religion* (Minneapolis: Fortress Press, 2003), 74.

2

Aristotle on Politics

EDWARD P. ANTONIO

I set out to describe some of Aristotle's basic views on slavery.[1] I suggest that
whatever place is accorded them in the Aristotelian corpus, they are central to
his understanding of both politics and ethics. There are two basic approaches
to these views. First, some see them as either containing logical inconsistencies
in an otherwise admirable body of work or are embarrassed by them and regard
them as outdated, indefensible, and expressive of Aristotle's inability to transcend
the ideology of his society. Second, others more or less defend Aristotle's comments on slaves. One of the striking features of this second group is the manner
in which its representatives simply take it for granted that there is something
defensible in slavery or at least in Aristotle's account of it.[2] I shall avoid getting
involved in these debates, tempting though it is. My goal here is to offer a brief
and relatively straightforward and focused description of some of the basic elements of Aristotle's defense of natural slavery without engaging in criticism of the
secondary literature. I shall also, for the most part, avoid arguing with Aristotle
himself. The point is to let his views speak for themselves. Anyone acquainted
with the horrors of slavery in modernity will not fail to see just how troubling and
ethically untenable slavery (ancient and modern) is, whatever good *theoretical*

arguments can be made on its behalf. I focus, then, on description. Such a description is needed because there are not many places students of theology, religion, and ethics can go to find a concise statement of Aristotle's views.

HISTORY

Aristotle is one of the major founding figures in the history of Western thought. He was born in 384 BCE in Stagira, Macedonia, north of Greece (ancient Hellas); Stagira was just northwest of the Aegean Sea. His father, Nicomachus, was a physician to Amyntas III, grandfather of Alexander the Great and king of Macedonia. As a teenager, Aristotle left Stagira for Athens, where he joined Plato's Academy and became the latter's student. He remained there until he was about forty. After Plato's death in 348/347, Aristotle began extensive travel around Asia Minor and the Aegean islands, then returned to Macedonia in 343, where King Philip II invited him to become the tutor to his son Alexander the Great. In 336 Philip died and Alexander became king, and in 334, with Aristotle's encouragement, Alexander invaded Persian-ruled Asia Minor. Aristotle returned to Athens in 335, where he founded the Lyceum, a school that rivaled Plato's Academy. One of his many achievements included dividing knowledge into various disciplinary areas such as physics, psychology, poetics, logic, and rhetoric. He wrote widely on a large variety of topics, and the influence of his thought on Western thought has been enormous. After Alexander's death in 323, anti-Macedonian sentiment flared in Athens, so Aristotle retreated to his mother's family estate in Chalcis, where he died a year later.

Since I will be writing about Aristotle's views on politics, there are several things worth noting about his biography. First, he clearly was born to privilege. This is attested by his father's position at the court of Amyntas. Second, he moved in powerful and influential circles. As tutor to the king's son, he had the means to open the Lyceum at Athens. Third, much of his thinking and writing took place in the context of empire (the expanding Macedonian Empire, under Philip II and then Alexander the Great). These facts are important because they provide some of the background against which Aristotle justifies slavery and the subordination of women.

Aristotle believed that some human beings are slaves by nature and others are masters by nature. Slaves by nature are human beings to whom the question of justice applies as a matter of natural right. Natural slavery is expedient and right.[3] In this essay I discuss what Aristotle meant in making this claim. My goal is to show that Aristotle's idea of "natural slaves" is, appearances notwithstanding, crucial for understanding a range of important organizing concepts in his thought as represented in two of his major influential works: *Politics* and *Nicomachean Ethics* (with a title based on his father's name). Specifically, I argue that whatever the extent of their development in his corpus, as articulated in *Politics*, Aristotle's views of slavery are an important part of his understanding of concepts

such as human nature, justice, family, gender, the state, various types of government, and human association or society. Taken to their logical conclusion, his
views of women and slaves are politically dangerous and should be rejected.

Aristotle's comments on slavery must be put in the wider context of the practice of slavery in the ancient world. Slavery existed in both ancient Greece and
Rome, and the Babylonians and other ancient nations practiced it before them.
This point is important for two reasons. The first is that Aristotle's defense of
slavery takes place in the context of the actual existence of slavery. In other words
he was not just speculating about an imagined social reality. This contradicts the
view of some modern commentators who seek to absolve Aristotle by saying that
his discussion of slavery was hypothetical. Placing Aristotelian views in the general framework of ancient slavery also allows us to see the persistence, scale, and
impact of the problem he was addressing. Without suggesting that Aristotle was
a representative spokesperson for all the different patterns of slavery that existed
in the ancient world, I observe that the widespread nature of the phenomenon
itself may account for Aristotle's views or at least for what he saw as the need for
justifying slavery as a fundamental form of rule.

To characterize slavery in terms of nature is on the face of it to deny that it
is merely a function of custom or convention.[4] It is to affirm its necessity[5] and
to deny that it is accidental.[6] So the first step in understanding what Aristotle
means in asserting the existence of natural slavery is to investigate what he means
by "nature."

ARISTOTLE ON NATURE

Since Aristotle rejects slavery by war and through convention as unjust and argues
that only natural slavery is just, it is important to understand what he means by
"nature." The best place to start is with his own fivefold definition of nature,
found in book 5, section 4, of *Metaphysics*. He characterizes the first aspect of this
definition as "the genesis of growing things."[7] Both components of this definition (genesis and growth) are relevant to Aristotle's understanding of nature and
how nature is a source of slavery. We shall see later that, among other things,
slavery has its genesis in birth, climate, and so forth, and that it represents part
of the evolution and growth of both an individual's virtuous character through
praxis, custom, and education as well as the growth of the human community
from family, through village, to the state. Furthermore, growth is important in
that it is a feature of the teleological structure of Aristotle's thought. Second, he
says nature is "the primary element in a thing from which its growth proceeds."
Third, nature is "the source from which the primary movement in each natural
object is present in virtue of its own essence." There are several terms in this
statement worth highlighting: source, primary, movement, object, and essence.
He explains slavery in various places in *Politics* by using these terms. Fourth, Aristotle asserts that "nature is the primary matter of which any non-natural object

consists or out of which it is made, which cannot be modified or changed from its own potency." Finally, "nature is the substance of natural objects, as with those who say that nature is the primary mode of composition."

"CAUSES" OF NATURAL SLAVERY

It is important to understand how, for Aristotle, slaves become slaves and how nature is implicated in that process. What are the causes of natural slavery? Aristotle posits several causes, including (1) birth; (2) otherness; (3) lack of reason or the possession of impaired reason; (4) lack of the capacity for deliberation; (5) climate; (6) psychological imbalance constituted by excessive *thymos* (passion, spiritedness, or the capacity for excitement); and (7) the type of body that the slave has.

Let me briefly address each of these. First, Aristotle thinks that some people are destined to be slaves from the moment they are born.[8] In this case natural slavery is not the result of one's actions: it is simply a fact of biology. Second, otherness stands in Aristotle's thought as a sign of natural slavery. Several of his examples of natural slavery have to do with foreigners. Aristotle denies that there is anything like a natural ruler among "barbarians." Indeed, from the Greek poets he approvingly quotes the view that the Hellenes have the right to rule over the "barbarians."[9]

In book 2 Aristotle says that foreigners are more servile than Hellenes, and Asiatics are more servile than Europeans. Foreign populations are not able to resist the tyrannical rule under which they live because they are slaves by nature. In *Nicomachean Ethics* Aristotle imagines or describes as brutish "foolish people . . . who by nature are thoughtless and live by their senses alone, . . . like some races of the distant foreigners."[10] This brings me to my third point regarding the causes of slavery, the allegation that some people naturally lack reason and that those who do are slaves by nature. The reference to thoughtless races that live by the senses alone describes a lack of reason, though Aristotle is ambiguous on this point. In one place he says slaves can understand reason or can participate in it,[11] yet he also describes natural slaves as bereft of reason even though they are capable of excellence. However, this should not be taken to mean that they are like their masters, for the excellence of which the master is capable is essentially different from that of the slave. There is difference not of degree but of kind, which Aristotle explains in terms of reason by distinguishing between the excellence of the rational and that of the irrational. The ambiguity is dealt with by the claim Aristotle makes that natural slaves share in reason only in the rational principle but do not have reason as such.[12]

The fourth point that qualifies a slave as a "natural" slave is one's lack of deliberative capacity. Aristotle makes this claim categorically. The slave, unlike a woman or child, has no such capacity at all. A woman has it but lacks authority, and the child has it but is simply immature. Reason and deliberation are important to the good life, which is the telos, or purpose, of every form of human association, its goal or final end, the reason for which it ultimately exists. The good life itself is a life of virtue. Any true description of properly ordered human relationships necessarily entails describing its telos. To understand what Aristotle means by this, we need to recall several aspects of his view of rationality. First, according to Aristotle, the human capacity for the virtuous life is speech, or logos (λόγος). "Logos" stands for speech as well as reason. Only humans have speech and reason. This is what distinguishes them from the beasts. The importance of logos for Aristotle lies in its being the capacity through which we are able to identify and deliberate about "the expedient and the inexpedient," "the just and the unjust," and good and evil. Second, Aristotle distinguishes between *technē* (τέχνη) and *phronēsis* (φρόνησις). *Technē* stands for a kind of rationality oriented toward production, craftsmanship, or with activities that lack intrinsic value. *Phronēsis*, on the other hand, describes practical wisdom and is evinced in praxis (πρᾶξις), or action that is intrinsically meaningful, which for Aristotle amounts to the practice of virtue.[13]

Third, the virtuous life is one of moral choices motivated not by some external phenomenon but by their inherent value: the good is chosen for its own sake. Choice or *prohairesis* (προαίρεσις) is crucial to Aristotle's understanding of the good life since it is connected on the one hand with the human capacity to reason and on the other with the source of moral character.

The connection between practical wisdom and virtue is important because it explicates a particular aspect of the relationship between slave and master. Slaves cannot think for themselves, cannot explore alternative forms of life and choose among them, and cannot give reasons for their actions and choices (such as they are). This amounts to saying that the slave is incapable of the good life (*eudaimonia*, εὐδαιμονία), which cannot be achieved without the ability and the exercise of the capacity for deliberation. Aristotle's theory of the good life is developed in his book *Nicomachean Ethics*. Lack of deliberative capacity means lack of freedom. Aristotle argues that this lack is natural and not the result of being enslaved through war or by convention.

I now move to the fifth point in terms of which Aristotle explains the basis of natural slavery: climate. The way in which Aristotle uses environmental determinism (the idea that climate determines behavior and identity) to justify natural slavery is linked to the connection he makes between slavery and otherness, as indicated earlier. Those who live in cold climates, like Europeans who enjoy relative freedom, are full of *thymos* (θυμός), or spirit, and thus lack intelligence. This means that they cannot rule over others. By contrast, Asians are intelligent and resourceful but lack *thymos* and thus are prey to perpetual slavery. Aristotle places the Hellenes between these two races and claims that their character and temperament are measured and balanced, "being high-spirited and also intelligent." This being so, they are not only free; they are also the best governed among the nations and have the potential to rule the world.[14] The short passage in *Politics* where Aristotle makes these remarks is important because it brings together race, psychology, the question of rule or government, slavery, and rationality. Here Aristotle racializes slavery.

The sixth cause of slavery is *thymos*, as we have just seen in the case of the Asians. While *thymos* is hard to define, Aristotle describes it in terms of passion or spiritedness and links it to fear and anger.[15] In *Politics* it is described as passion and channels affective expressions of injustice and affront,[16] love and fondness.[17] In addition, Aristotle says that *thymos* is relevant to the question of rule and freedom.[18] As Malcolm Heath has put it, "*Thymos* underpins a set of dispositions which are fundamental to maintaining the dynamic stability of a social network."[19]

Finally, slavery is due to the type of body a slave has. The bodies of slaves obey passion and not reason; they are meant for use or to be used in the service of others; since they cannot do better, they therefore make one a natural slave.[20]

The important point to note in all of this is that Aristotle's description of the "causes" of slavery is also by and large his description of the identity of a slave. Thus if we ask who is a slave, Aristotle's answer will be something like this: (1) in a addition to being someone's possession, a slave is a foreigner;[21] (2) a slave is a person who does not have rationality; (3) a slave is a person whose character (which qualifies one to be slave) is determined by one's environment; (4) a slave is one who can never rule but is destined by nature to be ruled.

THE POLITICS OF "RULE" AND NATURAL SLAVERY

Aristotle's definition not only makes slavery a natural condition; it also both makes it necessary to politics and politicizes nature or the "natural."[22] To see this, let us return to the opening of book 1 of *Politics*, where he puts forward his account of slavery. *Politics* opens with a discussion of four kinds of human association or communities and the government or forms of rule appropriate to each. Aristotle places these communities in hierarchical and evolutionary order: the state is the highest and most perfect expression of human association, and the family, or household, is the lowest. This is the most basic unit from which other institutions such as the village emerge as the family itself becomes larger and internally more diversified. The village, following a similar process of growth and variation, gives rise to consociations of villages which, in turn, create the state.[23] Aristotle explains the necessity of these institutions in teleological terms. Thus the family is produced by nature for the purpose of meeting human needs.[24] The state on the other hand, like the family, originates in the "bare needs of life" and comes to exist "for the sake of good life."

Aristotle's history of institutions is premised on the idea that all communities tend toward some good and that a state, which Aristotle calls a political community, is inaugurated by nature in order to achieve and promote the highest good because it represents and recapitulates the development of all previous and extant communities. The manner in which Aristotle sets up the relationship between the household and the state is particularly interesting. He begins his description of political reality by analyzing the composition of the household. In addition to the wife and children (over whom the husband rules, albeit in different ways), the ideal household will also be made up of several other particular features among which slaves, masters, property, and the means by which wealth is produced and acquired are the most distinctive. In *Politics* the slaves have the status of property (a living possession) and are also an instrument (a living instrument) for sustaining life. A slave is wholly owned and thus part of the master's wealth.[25]

There is one important observation to make in connection with this. By subsuming the history of the development of the household and the village and its growth into consociations of villages under the state, Aristotle politicizes human associations, which at first he describes as natural. This is consistent with his claim that a human being is a "political animal."

The fact that Aristotle places his understanding of slavery in the context of hierarchy must be seen in terms of the relation between hierarchy and various kinds of government or modes of rule. In a sense, hierarchy structures these modes of rule, and they in turn give hierarchy its political content. Aristotle thought of this hierarchy as natural. The importance of hierarchy can be seen first in the way in which it defines different forms of social institutions, and second in how it orders and organizes human relationships within those same institutions. The idea that hierarchy is natural follows from the place it occupies in Aristotle's teleology. Here hierarchy is understood in terms of both movement and growth. Again, growth is a linear process from the lower to the higher, better, and excellent. But hierarchy is also represented in terms of the good. As is well known, the good is the essence of the telos. Aristotle characterizes the political aspect of this teleology in several ways.

First, it is described in terms of the evolutionary process, the process of becoming through which the state—the most developed form of rule or human association—acquires its perfection. Second, Aristotle defines teleology in terms of the goal and ends of human relationships. The unfolding of these relationships in history and society is meant to foster and promote virtue. This is not a matter of happenstance but rather a function of the particular ways in which the relationships are politically organized to reflect the state as the realized or embodied telos of human relationships, which are ordered in terms of the idea of rule or government. Aristotle approaches this question directly in terms of whether or not there is anyone who is intended by nature to be a slave. He is trying to answer the question "Isn't slavery a violation of nature?" He thinks the answer to this question is straightforward and can be ascertained on the basis of both fact and reason.

The idea of rule, as Aristotle understands it, is natural and thus necessary. It can be found in animate as well as in inanimate things. Again, the idea of rulers and the ruled derives from the whole of nature. Aristotle gives several examples of how the notion of rule works in its expression of "the intentions of nature." First, let us imagine a person whose being represents the most perfect body and soul (an elemental division in living creatures).[26] In this situation the soul by nature rules the body. Moreover, the soul does this despotically. A related example is that of the rule of the intellect over the appetites, which Aristotle describes as constitutional and royal. A fundamental part of Aristotle's argument is that the division between ruler and ruled excludes two things: it excludes equality, and it excludes the inferior ever being in a position of ruling.

Second, Aristotle gives the example of how humans rule over domesticated animals. These animals are better than their wild counterparts precisely because they are ruled. Being ruled is better for them because it preserves them. A third illustration of the political ordering of human relationships through naturalized hierarchy derives from gender. Aristotle states it thus: "Again, the male is by nature superior, and the female inferior; and the one rules and the other is ruled; this principle, of necessity, extends to all mankind."[27] Here one is struck by the fact that women and animals are put next to each other and are consigned to inferiority, with no distinction or qualification. It is as though women are just another breed of animals. If this is not the meaning that Aristotle intends to be attached to his view of women, it is one he attaches to his view of slaves, for he clearly declares that there is no distinction between the use made of domestic animals and that made of slaves. Their bodies are ordained to serve life.[28] In a sense Aristotle would have no problems with this since he considers humans to be political animals, and women are political animals in the sense of being politically qualified as subjects of rule. Clearly, natural slaves are placed in the same category.

Thus far I have discussed three examples of how human relationships are organized through two fundamental categories: hierarchy and rule. Both of these categories are important for understanding Aristotle's idea of politics. In the political arena are ontological inequalities: men rule over women and children, Greeks rule over barbarians, and masters rule over slaves. Human relationships are organized through the concept of rule, which is understood in terms of hierarchy, with hierarchy itself understood as the expression of nature. A state is well ordered and represents its true telos to the extent that it maintains these inequalities. What Aristotle has managed to do here is to raise the fundamental questions of race and nation, politics and economics, gender and the state, identity and ethics—and then organize them around the notion of natural slavery. Hence we see that slavery has a central place in Aristotle's political order.

Notes

1. Although ancient and outdated, Aristotle's views on slavery merit attention today for several important reasons. Aristotle's writings continue to be studied in colleges and universities; his views on slavery continue to be a subject of serious debate among scholars, with some expressing embarrassment and others defending them; and important aspects of the culture of ancient Greece that Aristotle represented continue to be influential and to anchor much of Western culture today. Think here of the role of the classics in education and other cultural expressions. The Western cultures of Europe and America have, in the

recent past, been slaveholding cultures. The role of Aristotle's thought in justifying Western practices of slavery is, therefore, an important part of our history that we need to understand. Finally, Aristotle's views on slavery involve a whole philosophical anthropology, a theory of human nature worth investigating in its own right.

2. See William W. Fortenbaugh, *Aristotle on Emotion*, 2nd ed. (London: Duckworth, 2002); idem, "Aristotle on Slaves and Women," in *Articles on Aristotle*, ed. Jonathan Barnes, Malcolm Schofield, and Richard Sorabji, vol. 2, *Ethics and Politics* (London: Duckworth, 1977); Nicholas D. Smith, "Aristotle's Theory of Natural Slavery," in *A Companion to Aristotle's Politics*, ed. David Keyt and Fred D. Miller Jr. (Oxford: Blackwell Publishing, 1991); Darrel Dobbs, "Natural Right and the Problem of Aristotle's Defense of Slavery," *The Journal of Politics* 56, no. 1 (1994): 69–94.

3. Aristotle, *Pol.* 1.5a1–1255. I follow the standard method of citing Aristotle's work and have used *The Complete Works of Aristotle: The Revised Oxford Translation*, ed. Jonathan Barnes, 2 vols. (Princeton, NJ: Princeton University Press, 1984). I refer to *Politics* as *Pol.*, to *Nicomachean Ethics* as *Eth. Nic.*, and to *Metaphysics* as *Metaph.*

4. Aristotle, *Pol.* 1.6, 1255a1–1255b15.

5. On necessity as that which cannot be otherwise, see Aristotle, *Metaph.* 6.2, 1026b15–30.

6. On the notion of the "accidental," see *Metaph.* 6.30, 1025a15–30.

7. Aristotle, *Metaph.* 5.4, 1014b–1015a19.

8. Aristotle, *Pol.* 1.4, 1254a22–23.

9. Ibid., *Pol.* 1.2, 1252b5–9; 1.6, 1255a.28–b2; 3.14, 1285a19–21.

10. Aristotle, *Eth. Nic.* 7.5, 1149a9–11

11. Aristotle, *Pol.* 1.5, 1254.20–23.

12. Ibid., 1.5, 1254b20–23; 1.13, 1259b27–28.

13. Aristotle, *Eth. Nic.* 2.4, 1105a31–2; 6.3, 1144a18–20; 10.6, 1176b6–10.

14. Aristotle, *Pol.* 7.7, 1327b18–31.

15. Aristotle, *Topics* 4.5, 126a8–10.

16. Aristotle, *Pol.* 7.7, 1328a1–16; *Eth. Nic.* 7.6, 1149a32.

17. Aristotle, *Pol.* 7.7, 1327b36–8a1.

18. Ibid., 7.7, 1328a6–15.

19. Malcolm Heath, "Aristotle on Natural Slavery," *Phronesis* 53 (2008): 255–56.

20. Aristotle, *Pol.* 1.5, 12541b15–1255a1.

21. Ibid., 1.4, 1254a5–15.

22. Jill Frank, "Citizens, Slaves, and Foreigners: Aristotle on Human Nature," *American Political Science Review* 98, no. 2 (2004): 95.

23. Aristotle, *Pol.* 1.1–8.

24. Ibid., 1.2, 1252b1, 10–20.

25. Ibid., 1.3, 1253b1–4, 1253b25–1254a1, 5–15.

26. Aristotle wants to imagine such a perfect being because he believes that it represents the intentions of nature whereby the soul rules the body. In a corrupted and deviant being, the body will appear to rule the soul. This is unnatural.

27. Aristotle, *Pol.* 1254b10–15.

28. Ibid., 1.5, 1254b1–1255a1.

3

Augustine on Just War

VALERIE ELVERTON DIXON

In the West, it took nearly three hundred years for the Roman Empire to slowly decline and pass into the afterlife of history, after centuries of domination.[1] Augustine, Bishop of Hippo (354–430), was born into this weakened, fragile, dying world, which was under attack from within and from without. He articulated ideas about the justice of war based on the concept that the ruler of the state holds power because of the will of God, and therefore has a divine obligation to use that power to resist invasion, maintain order, and enforce Christian orthodoxy. The marginal, the oppressed, those who wanted liberation from both the power of orthodoxy and the power of the state—these were subject to state violence, with the blessing of Augustine and his ideas of justice. When we rethink Augustine's just-war ideas, the questions become, Where does justice live? Does justice necessarily require violence?

THE ROMAN EMPIRE

The history of the Roman Empire is a remarkable story of organization, discipline, government, war, and more. For more than a thousand years—through both republican and imperial government—human beings in Italy built an ordered life of politics, economics, engineering, music, art, sport, and religion that, because of the skill of its army, spread and conquered the Mediterranean world and beyond. The founding mythology connects it to the Troy of Homer's epic poetry. Aeneas, son of the goddess Aphrodite, survived the destruction of Troy, made his way to Italy, and founded a line that produced a daughter whose beauty caused the god Mars to love her and to give her twin sons. Rather than obey the usurper Amulius's order to kill the babies, his servants placed their cradle in the Tiber River. All of nature cooperated in their rescue. The waters delivered them safely to land. A she-wolf found them and suckled them. Romulus and Remus grew to manhood, killed the usurper, and then founded Rome.[2]

The Roman population divided along class lines: patricians, businesspeople, plebeians, and slaves. A republic ruled Rome during the sixth century BCE, and Rome made a career of conquest. Victory in war supplied Rome with slaves. At this moment in history, slavery was considered to be an act of mercy; defeat in war no longer automatically meant death. Slaves came from all walks of life. They could earn money, buy their freedom, and join the ranks of the plebeians.[3] Class rivalry was ubiquitous and would be for all the history of the empire. There were times when the plebs and the debtors refused to work or to fight. Patricians who were willing to give aid to the poor were sometimes killed for attempting to become kings. However, the plebs demanded secular and written law, and the result was the Twelve Tables. These laws, along with their organization and structures of government, made Rome important to human history. Law, politics, contracts with businesspeople for public works, and wars all helped to unify an expanding nation.

Military conquest was important to Rome in many respects. Conquered peoples supplied slaves. Conquered territory created space for an expanding population, yielded food for the cities, and provided markets. Thus the army was vital, and its success was built on strict and brutal discipline. According to historian Will Durant, "Rome remained great as long as she had enemies who forced her to unity, vision and heroism. When she had overcome them all, she flourished for a moment and then began to die."[4] And as Rome weakened, Romans began to question their gods.

The Romans worshiped thirty thousand gods. The goddess Vesta was the divinity of the sacred flame of every household. She symbolized the continuity of the family. Keeping her flame lit was a sacred obligation. The Roman gods were spirits: "sometimes they were abstractions like Health, Youth, Chastity, Concord, Victory, or Rome."[5] The state appropriated the gods for its own purpose of creating national unity. Thus Vesta became a national goddess with a group of women, vestal virgins, charged with keeping the national flame. The national gods often fused with the gods of conquered peoples. The Romans would bring the statue of the foreign gods to Rome, and in the minds of some people, the statue itself was the god. The Romans believed they won wars because of their gods. When they lost, in order to placate the gods, they increased their devotion and offered more sacrifices, including human sacrifice.

It was not long before alien gods along with alien philosophies conquered the conquerors. The Greek goddess Cybele, the Great Mother, came to Rome. Every April, Rome celebrated her feast with both sorrow and joy. "For Cybele was a vegetarian deity, and legend told how her son Attis, symbol of autumn and spring, had died and gone to Hades, and then had risen from the dead." The cults of Dionysus-Bacchus and Orpheus with Eurydice gave believers a resurrected god and a promise of eternal life.[6]

Greek Stoicism and Epicureanism influenced the Roman philosophers Lucretius and Seneca.[7] The Greek philosophers also brought skepticism and doubt to Rome. This disturbed some Roman officials to the point of having Greek ambassadors sent home. It was too late.[8] The Greek Stoic Panaetius taught that the individual "is part of a whole and must cooperate with it—with his family, his country, and the divine Soul of the World."[9] This thinking influenced the Roman philosopher Cicero. He wrote that all men are brothers and the world ought to be understood "as the common city of gods and men." Centuries later, Augustine would read Cicero and make the common city as two: the city of man and the city of God. Morality for Cicero is "loyalty to this whole."[10]

This loyalty to the whole did not exist in reality. Class struggle was a prominent feature of the Roman world, and leaders rose and fell with the measures they took to appease this or that class. Slave uprisings were always a concern. Spartacus, one of the most renowned and successful slave leaders, raised an army of 120,000, intending to march north to the Alps and to freedom. However, his army splintered. Some plundered towns in north Italy. In response, the Roman Senate sent armies to subdue the rebels. Durant writes:

> Half the slaves of Italy were on the verge of insurrection, and in the capital no man could tell when the revolution would break out in his very home. All that opulent society, which had enjoyed every luxury slavery could produce, trembled at the thought of losing everything—mastery, property, life.[11]

The rebels were defeated in battle. Spartacus died on the battlefield, hacked into unrecognizable pieces. Sixty thousand were crucified; their bodies were left hanging for months "so that masters might take comfort, and all slaves take heed."[12] Yet the revolt of the lower classes against a rich, powerful, and corrupt government that favored the rich and powerful continued; the clash opened the door for the Caesars.

Jesus of Nazareth was born into the Roman world of the Caesars. He lived a short life and died the horrific death of crucifixion. During his life, he preached a revolutionary message: The last would be first, and the first would be last. He walked people through the Jewish law and on to a place of more-authentic relationships. After returning from Egypt as a young child, history leaves no record of him living anywhere other than the dry, dusty province of Palestine, among poor people oppressed by Roman tribute, provincial taxes, and temple tithes. He saw the economic hardships of his community and thus encouraged radical generosity, debt relief, and aid to the sick, prisoners, the hungry, and the naked. His closest disciples were of the lower rungs of society. Some were outcasts. He endured criticism for eating with those on the margins of society, yet this itinerant Jewish rabbi also taught nonviolence and reconciliation. His moral imperative was a command to love even one's enemies. His call was to a mature, complete, radical love. He expected a kingdom of God to come on earth through the offices of this radical living love. He demonstrated an alternative authority.

The Roman Empire stood because of its willingness to employ brutality against those who would undermine its authority. Moreover, the authority and the power of the state were understood to be given by the gods. Jesus came and said that there was another realm, one more powerful and more eternal than Rome. He taught his followers to fear only those who could destroy both body and soul. By teaching a fearless love in a world governed by fear, he was a threat to both the Jewish temple authorities and to the empire itself. He had to die.[13] After his death, a split gradually developed between his followers and what became rabbinic Judaism, and his story absorbed into itself some myths and symbols of antecedent gods and religions.[14]

Christianity spread throughout the Roman Empire via workers' *collegia*. In these organizations members were brothers and sisters. Slaves and freeborns shared a table. These associations were social, economic, and political. "In the end, they became vehicles through which Christianity entered and pervaded the life of Rome."[15] As Christianity grew, the power of Rome began to crumble. Its own excesses, economic disparity, and moral laxity demonstrated in part by bloodthirsty entertainment were symptoms of its fatal final illness. At the same time, tribes from the north began to descend upon a weak Rome.

When Rome lost its wars, people believed that the gods were displeased with the worship of this new god: Christ. Christians who refused devotion to the Roman gods were persecuted, especially beginning in 64 CE after the burning of Rome. Early Christians saw the conflation of the worship of the gods with the worship of the state as polytheism and idolatry. Although early Christians were imprisoned, beaten, exiled, and sent to the mines, contrary to popular perception, they were rarely killed. The emperor Diocletian (ruled 284–305) persecuted them, burning books and confiscating property, and some church officials avoided further persecution by giving up sacred texts to Roman authorities. This act would be the source of the Donatist schism. At first the majority of the common people opposed the Christians. However, as the persecution continued and Christians faced martyrdom with courage, the pagan population sympathized with the Christians. They saw a god who could give believers the strength to stand for their faith in spite of brutality. The Romans witnessed an undefeated god. This witness gave the pagans the courage to speak out against Rome's brutality.[16]

And then the emperor Constantine (ruled 306–337) saw a cross in the sky. The next day he went to war with the symbols of Christianity on his soldiers' shields. The defeat of opposing pagan armies marked the beginning of Christianity being conflated with the power of the state. The unity of state and religion required the unity of religious belief. However, now as in every epoch of Christianity's existence, there were many sects with different theologies. The Manicheans believed in a brand of Gnosticism that posited a dualistic world. In the Manichean world were paired opposites: light against dark, spirit against matter, good against evil. The soul that shares the nature of God has fallen into an evil material world. The Donatists believed that any priest who had surrendered Christian books to be burned during the Diocletian persecution was not fit to administer the sacraments. They believed in a separation of church and state and a strict moral rigor, especially for church leaders. They also took the side of the lower classes in North African society. Violent conflicts broke out between the Donatists and the branch of the church supported by the state. This schism would remain a feature of North African life until the rise of Islam. The Pelagians believed with Pelagius that there is no such thing as original sin. He argued against the notion of innate human depravity, claiming that good works have their own saving power. A Pelagian morality taught, "If I ought, I can."[17] Meanwhile, Arianism questioned the doctrine of the Trinity. It held that Jesus was neither consubstantial nor coeternal with God.

AUGUSTINE OF HIPPO

Augustine was born into this political and theological maelstrom in 354. After living in a loving relationship with a woman for years, fathering a son who would precede him in death, studying and teaching rhetoric, and becoming a Manichean, he later converted to Christianity and rose to the office of bishop in North Africa. He understood argument as a kind of warfare: Like a trained rhetorician, using etymological and exegetical skill, he argued against the celebration of the pagan gods in poetry and theater. He considered their mythological stories morally shameful.[18] His polemics against paganism were intended to send the thirty thousand Roman gods back to the limitless realm beyond being, where the philosophers' gods live, or to oblivion. He did not see that Christianity had rendered them oblivious.

Working through a Neoplatonic ontology, Augustine believed that the one true God of Christianity was not unlike the Supreme Good in Neoplatonism.[19] Augustine believed that the one true God was of a different substance than human beings, but that God could bring humanity into its substantial unity through its own gracious will. God would share God's beneficence with humanity when human beings worshiped God in truth and with love.[20] This blessedness for Augustine was the source of happiness and true peace. The fellowship of the true God with the church as represented by the orthodoxies of Roman Catholicism was the city of God. Thus for Augustine, no matter what one's class or station in life was, no matter the sufferings one endured, one ought to accept it all with humility and allow God to be all in all through "fidelity of affection."[21] God orders all things according to God's will.

Thus for Augustine, those who hold authority do so because of God's will. Augustine could not escape Manichean dualism. Binary oppositions and hierarchical relationships explained the world. Light over dark, spirit over flesh, sovereign over subject, man over woman, adult over child, master over slave—these hierarchies ordered the natural way of the world in Augustine's mind. Only the sovereign of the state had just authority to wage war, and every subject of the sovereign was obliged to fight in the wars.[22] For Augustine, Christian pacifism had no place in this world, where the Roman Empire was facilitating the birth of the Roman Catholic Church. He advocated violence to compel people to worship according to the orthodoxy agreed upon at the Council of Nicaea in 325 CE.

Arguing the necessity for discipline and that the state is the instrument of God's discipline, Augustine called for Roman authorities to intervene in the conflict with the Donatists. He not only wanted an intervention to stop the violence between the parties of the schism, but he also wanted to enforce theological orthodoxy. He saw the adoption of Christianity as Rome's state religion as a fulfillment of prophecy and thus gave the state compelling power. He wrote, "Consequently, she cannot only invite others to embrace what is good, but also compel them."[23] He believed that once people were forced into orthodoxy, they would then embrace it willingly. But, is this justice?

Justice is that which is rightly due to an individual or group. It is respect for the dignity of the Other. It is due regard. It is sustenance and joy. Where does justice live? Does it live in the emperor's palace, in the halls of the senate, a business enterprise, in a meeting of workers, in a family home, or in a slave's quarters? Does justice organize a slave rebellion and then die a bloody death on a battlefield? Does it eat a last supper with a radical rabbi condemned to die? Justice, like power, is everywhere; like faith and doubt, the solid and shadow of each other, justice and injustice exist together. The problem with the just-war theory as expressed by Augustine and others before and after him is the privilege it grants to those who hold state authority. By giving the requirement that a just war can only be a war that is declared by a legitimate authority and that authority is necessarily a state authority, people who do not hold such authority, but who may be acting for the sake of justice, cannot be considered as fighting a just war. The rebellion led by Spartacus, for example, could never be considered a just war.

Current just-war theorists are working on this deficiency.[24] One problem today is that given the global character of warfare, can a war be legitimately fought without the authorization of an international body? However, a further problem to consider is the question of whether or not justice requires physical violence. Violence has many forms and faces: it is structural, symbolic, personal, and societal.[25] Political economies often create disparities that make violent conflict inevitable. Such was the situation in South Africa during apartheid.[26] So the question now becomes, How do moral agents correct injustice, even when that means defying the given order and orthodoxy?

The ethics of liberation says that justice may not necessarily live in the accepted order and orthodoxy. An ethics of liberation calls for a new ontology, one where being is not understood in hierarchical binary relationships, but rather where a kaleidoscopic absolute existence brings the truth and the beauty of those at the margins into the center, where everyone participates in a unity whose substance is radical fairness. An ethics of liberation says that each individual is a moral agent whose obligation is to tend the fires of truth and respect for the Other, in such a way that this quality of living brings about a security rooted and grounded in righteous relationships. These relationships include the natural world, the waters, and the wolves. This is justice. And justice exists to make just-war theory and war itself obsolete. It exists to place violent conflict forever beyond the pale.

Notes

1. Will Durant, *The Story of Civilization*, vol. 3, *Caesar and Christ* (New York: Simon & Schuster, 1944), 665. In the East, by contrast, the empire endured until 1453, when it was conquered by the Ottomans.
2. Ibid., 13.
3. Ibid., 22.
4. Ibid., 33.
5. Ibid., 59.
6. Ibid., 94.
7. Ibid., 95.
8. Ibid., 96.
9. Ibid., 97.
10. Ibid., 165.
11. Ibid., 137.
12. Ibid., 138.
13. See Valerie Elverton Dixon, "Torture, Terror, War, and the End of Bloodshed Sacrifice," http://justpeacetheory.com/files/Torture_Terror_War_and_the_End_of_Bloodshed_Sacrifice.pdf.
14. Durant writes: "Greek mysteries passed down into the impressive mystery of the Mass. Other pagan cultures contributed to this syncretistic result. From Egypt came the ideas of a divine family, the Last Judgment, and a personal immortality of reward and punishment; from Egypt the adoration of the Mother and child, and the mystic theosophy that made Neoplatonism and Gnosticism, and obscured the Christian creed; there too Christian monasticism would find its exemplars and its source. From Phrygia came the worship of the Great Mother; from Syria the resurrection drama of Adonis; from Thrace, perhaps, the cult of Dionysus, the dying and saving god. From Persia came millenarianism, the 'ages of the world,' the 'final conflagration,' the dualism of Satan and God, or Darkness and Light; already in the Fourth Gospel Christ is the 'Light shining in the darkness, and the darkness has never put it out.' The Mithraic ritual so closely resembled the Eucharistic sacrifice of the Mass that Christian fathers charged the Devil with inventing these similarities to mislead frail minds. Christianity was the last great creation of the ancient pagan world." Durant, *Caesar and Christ*, 595.
15. Ibid., 335.
16. Ibid., 652.
17. Will Durant, *The Story of Civilization*, vol. 4, *The Age of Faith* (New York: Simon & Schuster, 1950), 69.

18. Augustine, *City of God* (New York: Penguin Books, 2003), 236, 304–5.
19. Ibid., 311.
20. Ibid., 375.
21. Ibid., 875.
22. John Mark Mattox, *Saint Augustine and the Theory of Just War* (New York: Continuum, 2006), 74–84. Augustine's just-war criteria are the following: to defend the state from outside invasion; to defend the safety and honor of the state; to avenge injury and punish a nation for failing to bring to retributive justice its members who have committed wrong; to gain the return of something wrongfully taken; to obey a divine command. Once war commences, violence ought to be limited to military necessity; only the state's warriors are justified in using violence; mercy is to be shown to captives and noncombatants; promises made to the enemies ought to be kept; ruses are permissible.
23. Augustine, *Political Writings*, ed. E. M. Atkins and R. J. Dodaro (Cambridge: Cambridge University Press, 2001), 157.
24. See, e.g., Nicholas Fotion, *War and Ethics: A New Just War Theory* (New York: Continuum, 2007); and Valerie Elverton Dixon, "From Just War to a Just Peace Paradigm," http://justpeacetheory.com/files/From_Just_War_to_a_Just _Peace_Paradigm.pdf.
25. See Slavoj Žižek, *Violence: Six Sideways Reflections* (New York: Picador, 2008).
26. See Nelson Mandela, *Long Walk to Freedom: The Autobiography of Nelson Mandela* (New York: Little, Brown, 1994).

4

Thomas Aquinas on Servitude

ALEJANDRO CROSTHWAITE

Thomas Aquinas was born in Naples, Italy, in 1224/25; at the age of five he was sent to study at the Benedictine monastery of Monte Cassino. At fifteen he enrolled at the University of Naples, where he became acquainted for the first time with the works of Aristotle. It was in Naples that he joined the Dominicans, much to the opposition of his family. Later he was sent to study at Cologne and Paris under the Dominican scholar Albert the Great. In 1256, he became a professor of theology at the University of Paris, where he taught from 1256 to 1259 and from 1269 to 1272. He also taught at Anagni, Orvieto, Rome, and Viterbo. He died on March 7, 1274, on his way to the Second Council of Lyon (or Lyons). Aquinas was canonized in 1323; in the late nineteenth century, his thoughts and ideas became the official philosophy and theology of the Roman Catholic Church.

Although Aquinas had an extensive positive impact on social, economic, and political thought in the history of humanity, many of his views are unacceptable today (e.g., his view against tyrannicide, his defense of capital punishment for heretics, his attitudes toward Jews, and his belief in the natural inferiority of women), even considering that they were historically conditioned or the result of an uncritical acceptance of Aristotle. One idea that has been particularly detrimental to people and communities of color and justifying of Eurocentric superiority and discriminatory practices is his qualified acceptance of servitude as an institution in society.

SOCIAL LOCATION

Many of the great thinkers of the Middle Ages—Franciscus Accurius, Azo de Bologna, Baldo de Ubaldis, Bartolo da Sassoferrato—as well as influential theologians like Thomas Aquinas and Bonaventure and canonists like Popes Innocent III, Innocent IV, and Gregory IX, grew up in Italy, the home of Roman and canon law. True, "Italy" remained a geographical expression rather than a unified political reality for most of its history; but the cultural experience of being raised and educated and eventually teaching in the Italian peninsula (or, as in the case of some expatriates like Thomas, in Paris), meant that Italian social, political, and economic life shaped these people, who used words that had a wide influence across Europe and later across the globe. The popes who countenanced slavery in the fifteenth century and made a place for Christian slaves in a Christian society were all from the Italian peninsula. The commentators on Roman law at Bologna, who helped to define key concepts like international law and the law of persons, were similarly from what is now Italy. Once one restores the disembodied language of so much intellectual history to its proper Italian context, where slavery was more widespread than most places in Europe, we can see how the language coming from that context affected Thomas Aquinas and later the European encounter with other cultures, especially those of Africa and the Americas.[1]

QUALIFIED ACCEPTANCE OF THE INSTITUTION OF SERVITUS

In both the *Politics* and *Nicomachean Ethics*, Aristotle taught that

> authority [ἄρχων] and subordination [ἄρχεσθαι] are conditions not only inevitable [ἀναγκαίων] but also expedient [συμφερόντων]; in some cases things are marked out from the moment of birth to rule or to be ruled, . . . all men that differ as widely as the soul does from the body and the human being from the lower animal (and this is the condition of those whose function is the use of the body [as opposed to the intellect] and from whom this is the best that is forthcoming)—these are by nature slaves [φύσει δοῦλοι], for whom to be governed by this kind of authority is advantageous [βέλτιον], inasmuch as it is advantageous to the subject things already mentioned. For he is by nature a slave who is capable of belonging to another [ἀλλότριος] (and that is why he does so belong), and who participates in reason [κοινωνῶν λόγου] so far as to apprehend it but not to possess it.[2]

Thus it seems that for Aristotle there is such a thing as "natural slavery" (φύ σει δοῦλοι); however, to determine who concretely is "capable of belonging to another" is not so clear.

Augustine taught that God

> did not wish a rational creature [*rationalem*], made in his own image, to have dominion [*dominium*] save over irrational creatures [*inrationabilibus*]: not man over man, but man over the beasts. . . . Wherefore we do not read of a slave anywhere in the Scriptures until the just man Noah branded his son's sin [*peccatum*] with this word [Gen. 9:25–26—עבד עבדים / παῖς οἰκέτης / *servum servorum* / slave of slaves / houseboy]; so he earned this name by his fault [*culpa*], not by nature [*non natura*].[3]

The ancient consensus, moreover, was that slavery resulted from bad luck and did not necessarily reflect badly on the slave's character. For example, someone might have become a slave through honorable defeat or capture.[4]

Thomas has no general treatise on the subject of servitude (*servitus*). In his *Summa theologica*, in response to the question whether the notion of "state" (*status*) denotes a condition of freedom (*libertas*) or servitude, he answers that

> state, properly speaking, denotes a kind of position [*positionis*], whereby a thing is disposed with a certain immobility in a manner according with its nature [*disponitur secundum modum suae naturae*]. . . . Consequently matters which easily change and are intrinsic to them do not constitute a state among men, for instance that a man be rich or poor, of high or low rank, and so forth. . . . But that alone seemingly pertains to a man's state, which regards an obligation binding his person [*obligationem personae hominis*], in so far, to wit, as a man is his own master or subject to another [*est sui iuris vel alieni*], not indeed from any slight or unstable cause, but from one that is firmly established; and this is something pertaining to the nature of freedom or servitude.[5]

In his study of servitude, Thomas makes no judgment on Aristotle; he simply exposes and systemizes. Evidently certain sympathy toward Aristotle can be observed and may lead us to affirm that Thomas does assume, at least partially, the plausible Aristotelian position on natural servitude. We infer this sympathy from the lack of open or forceful criticism, for Thomas does not generally hesitate to be disagreeable when he needs to be (as in engaging the medieval Muslim philosophers). Still, Aquinas's interpretation of Aristotle is "soft" enough to escape from radical slavery; as to what Thomas's doctrine concerns, it is preferable to speak, in any case, of a natural state of servitude rather than of a natural slavery.[6]

In addition, as Finnis points out, the terms *servitus* and *servus* are not to be automatically translated as "slavery" and "slave":[7] When it is obvious that Thomas means "slavery" for *servitus* and "slave" for *servus*,[8] it is usually in the context of discussing an established institution in many societies, without implying that he considered it morally acceptable; though sadly passing up many opportunities to do so in a forceful way from the testimony of Scripture.[9] Moreover, when he treats the institution (*servitus*) or condition (*servus*) as morally acceptable, it is subject to such severe legal and moral restrictions that it is better translated as servitude or bond service or perhaps serfdom.[10] Slavery was not the vital part of Thomas's economic, political, and social world that it was in antiquity or in the late Roman Empire; Thomas's milieu was that of medieval serfdom.

Thomas's first extended discussion of servitude is in his answer to the question of whether men were equal in the state of innocence and whether in the same state man would have been master over man.[11] He concludes that, although in the primitive state there would have been some inequality, at least regarding gender, age, righteousness, knowledge, as well as bodily disparity due to diet and environment; by nature, however, all people are equal in liberty and ordered to themselves and not to another as an end; hence servitude is not natural but exists by positive law and right. The only sense in which it may be natural is if it is useful [*utile*] for one to be ruled by someone wiser [*sapientiori*], "and to the latter to be helped [*iuvetur*] by the former."[12] The liberty surrendered by those who sell themselves into servitude is a priceless good (*inaestimabile libertatis bonum amittens*);[13] it is wrong to reduce someone to servitude.[14] As an institution, servitude exists only as a result of original sin; it would not have existed in the state of innocence,[15] and was introduced as a penalty for sin (*poenam peccati*).[16] However, Thomas does not challenge the terrible logic whereby, since the fruits of property belong to its owner, the "penalty" of slavery extends, as a matter of human positive law, to the innocent children of female *servae*.[17]

Thomas returns to the topic of servitude in a gloss to the discussion of natural law (*lex naturae*), which does not prohibit some things that are not part of it.[18] For example, it is natural to be naked for "naked I came from my mother's womb, and naked I will depart" (Job 1:21a NIV), but nothing in natural law prohibits the wearing of clothing. In the same way, common ownership of property and liberty are said to be natural, so private property and servitude are not in this sense natural, though not prohibited by natural law. Instead, human reason and positive law and right (*ius positivum, ius civile*) have devised private property and servitude for the benefit of human life, and so God does not condemn either.[19]

In *Summa theologiae*, Thomas also asks if the law of nations (*ius gentium*) is human law (*ius positivum*) or the same as natural law.[20] As part of his answer, Thomas distinguishes two aspects of the natural law—one absolute by necessity and the other by human custom not following absolutely from reason. No natural reason explains why some are free and some are in servitude. Servitude is based on utility and usefulness for human society. Servitude pertains to the *ius gentium* and is natural in the second sense, which is by human agreement on what we would call historical grounds, but not by the first.[21] Here he picks up on, in a qualified manner, Aristotle's thought that

> Both life itself and the good life are impossible without the essentials. . . .
> So a possession is also a tool for the purpose of living, and property is an

assemblage of tools; a slave is a sort of living possession, and every assistant is like a superior tool among tools. For if each tool could perform its own task either at our bidding or anticipating it, and if shuttles shuttled to and fro of their own accord, and puckers played lyres, then master craftsmen would have no need of assistants nor masters any need of slaves.[22]

The *dominus* is owner as well as master of the *servus*, who can be bought and sold. But what is bought and sold is only the service (*servitium*): the *servus* retains morally and legally the right (*ius*) to eat, sleep, marry, perform natural functions, and to practice religion without needing the permission of the *dominus,* notwithstanding opposition. Everything required for a decent marriage and married life prevails over the orders of the master.[23] The state or condition of *servitus* should not deprive anyone of other basic human rights, such as not to be killed, deliberately harmed, raped or used for any extramarital sexual services, lied to, robbed or cheated.[24] Moreover, *servitus* does not extend to the mind or interior life of the *servus.*[25] So it is only precisely in respect of the condition of *servitus* of the *servus* that the relationship of *dominus* to *servus* is not a relationship of justice in the strictest sense but one of *ius dominativum;*[26] in all other respects, it ought to be a relationship governed by justice and mutual rights. Thus Finnis concludes,

> Though falling (we should say) distinctly short of the requirements of human rights, this *servitus* is not the inhuman institution of slavery of republican Rome or the *ante bellum* United States; it differs radically from the "absolute dominion and arbitrary power" of master over slave defended as part of the "right of nature" by John Locke [in his *Second Treatise of Civil Government*].[27]

DETRIMENTAL CONSEQUENCE

In attempting to reconcile two conflicting traditions, Thomas's qualified acceptance of the institution of servitude has had a detrimental effect on the European encounter with other cultures, especially those of Africa and the Americas. On the one hand, Aristotle argued in *Politics* that enslavement of those who are incapable of living a moral life is justified by nature.[28] On the other hand, the fathers of the church, represented by Augustine of Hippo, wrote that all humans are equal by nature and viewed slavery as a consequence of sin.[29] Thomas's answer is to refer to Aristotle's argument, to describe servitude as an "addition" to the natural law "that has been found to be convenient both for the master and servant," and to limit the master's right over his servant in the areas of private and family life as well as the right of sustenance.[30]

"Utility" (*utilitatem humanae vitae*), a word that Thomas uses in much the same way as modern economists, explained why servitude existed, and also the absence of a divine prohibition of it. Thomas was convinced that no one was a serf by defect or sin, and that self-interest impelled any rational person to resist servitude. Liberty was the natural state, and although he accepted a basic human equality, for Thomas the many natural disparities cried out for hierarchy and the need for someone to take command. So the context for criticizing slavery had moved beyond Aristotle's nature and Augustine's sin, but appeals to liberty and equality would not yet carry the day. "The worthwhile life for some still meant, now by human convention's idea of utility, which some people who did not much like it would have to do things that benefited others. Despite slavery's unsavory aspects, its utility outweighed doubt about its ethics."[31]

By the end of the Middle Ages, at least one prominent thinker, Antoninus of Florence, had concluded that divine law itself sanctioned the practice of servitude, and he was prepared to use both Hebrew Scripture and the New Testament to support the legitimacy of slavery in the fifteenth century.[32] Legal commentaries, mainly coming from the University of Bologna in the twelfth and thirteenth centuries, mostly from the pens of Italian scholars, strengthened the reasoning that supported slavery.[33] In the fifteenth century, some of the popes legitimized slavery, at least as a result of war.[34] In 1452 Pope Nicholas V issued the papal bull *Dum Diversas*, which granted Alfonso V of Portugal the right to reduce any "Saracens, pagans, and any other unbelievers" to hereditary slavery. The approval of slavery under these conditions was reaffirmed and extended in his *Romanus Pontifex* bull of 1455. This conclusion, not limited to European servitude, would specifically weigh heavily on the Indians and Africans whom the Europeans encountered in the fifteenth and sixteenth centuries.

And so there was a declension—from bad luck to sin to force—that was evolving, overlapping, even mutually confirming explanations of slavery: "After all, one could easily believe that it was bad fortune for a particular sinner in a world of sin to be coerced into slavery by other sinners."[35] Ethnicity or color came to be a proxy for bad luck. It was bad luck to be a Moor captured in Spain or a Tartar sold to the Genovese in Caffa. In more-complex ways, color also became a proxy for sin itself, as people came to believe that belonging to certain ethnic groups, or even being a particular color, justified enslavement; forgetting that Thomas thought Ethiopians were "White" inasmuch as their teeth were white![36] So, "from bad luck to sin to force to color—the history and language of slavery in a nutshell."[37]

CONCLUSION

Earl Shorris identified three topics—the media, intellectual muggings, and ethnic antagonisms—that can aid our search for ways in which words maintained the forces sustaining slavery.[38] Surely modern and medieval societies profoundly differed in these three matters. The media, as currently understood, did not exist ten centuries ago. News traveled slowly if at all, and the shaping of public opinion relied on talk and the slow diffusion of received truths. If there were a proxy for the modern media in the Middle Ages, perhaps the authoritative statements emanating from the Roman Church and the universities (such as Bologna, Oxford, Paris) gradually persuaded and informed people in ways that created a consensus of opinion on issues. By not straightforwardly condemning the institution and practice of servitude itself, by not using against it the power of words alone (its strongest weapon), Thomas Aquinas, with the church and the universities, buttressed these institutions and eased the consciences of those owning or dealing in slaves for centuries to come.[39]

Notes

1. Steven A. Epstein, *Speaking of Slavery: Color, Ethnicity, and Human Bondage in Italy* (Ithaca, NY: Cornell University Press, 2001), 147.
2. Aristotle, *Politics*, trans. H. Rackham (Cambridge, MA: Harvard University Press, 1998), 13. See also *Pol.* 1.2; and Aristotle, *Nicomachean Ethics* 7.10.4; 7.11.6–7; 10.6.8.
3. Augustine, *City of God*, trans. W. C. Green (Cambridge, MA: Harvard University Press, 2001), 19.15.
4. Epstein, *Speaking of Slavery*, 197.
5. Thomas Aquinas, *Summa Theologica* [*ST*], trans. Fathers of the English Dominican Province (Allen, TX: Christian Classics, 1981), II, q. 183, a. 1, resp. (= book II, question 183, answer 1, response).
6. Hector Zagal, "Aquinas on Slavery: An Aristotelian Puzzle" (paper presented at the International Thomist Congress of the Società Internazionale Tomasso d'Aquino [International Society of Thomas Aquinas], Rome, Italy, September 2003), 5, http://www.e-aquinas.net/pdf/zagal.pdf.
7. John Finnis, *Aquinas: Moral, Political, and Legal Theory* (New York: Oxford University Press, 1998), 184.
8. For example, see Thomas Aquinas, *On Love and Charity: Readings from the Commentary on the Sentences of Peter Lombard*, trans. Peter A. Kwasniewski, Thomas Bolin, and Joseph Bolin (Washington, DC: Catholic University of America Press, 2008), 4.d.28, a. 2; d.32, a. 1–2.
9. Aquinas, *ST* I-II, q. 105, a. 4, obj. 1 & 2 and ad 1–2 (I-II = first section of the second part; obj. = objection; ad = additional).
10. Aquinas, *Commentary on the Sentences* 4.d.
11. Aquinas, *ST* I, q. 96, a. 3–4. Since it is not clear whether Thomas intended "man" to refer to all human beings or just male people, the ambiguous language has been retained.
12. Aquinas, *ST* II-II, q. 57, a. 3 ad 2.
13. Aquinas, *Commentary on the Sentences* 4.d.36, a. 3 ad 1.
14. Aquinas, *On Kingship, to the King of Cyprus*, trans. Gerald B. Phelan, rev. I. Th. Eschmann (1949; repr., Toronto: Pontifical Institute of Mediaeval Studies, 1967), 1.2.
15. Aquinas, *ST* I, q. 96, a. 4c.
16. Aquinas, *Commentary on the Sentences* 4.d.36, a. 1.
17. Ibid., 4.d.36, a. 4.
18. Aquinas, *ST* I-II, q. 94, a. 5 ad 3.
19. Ibid., I-II, q. 94, a. 5 ad 3.
20. Ibid., II-II, q. 57, a. 3.
21. Ibid.
22. Aristotle, *Pol.* 1.
23. Aquinas, *Commentary on the Sentences* 4.d.36.
24. Ibid., 4.d.33, q. 1, a. 3 sol. 1 (sol. = solution).

25. Aquinas, *ST* II-II, q. 104, a. 5c and a. 6 ad 1; q. 122, a. 4 ad 3.
26. Ibid., II-II, q. 57, a. 4 ad 1.
27. Finnis, *Aquinas*, 185.
28. Aristotle, *Pol.* 1.5.
29. Augustine, *City of God* 19.15.
30. Aquinas, *ST* II-II, q. 94, a. 5 ad 3; II-II, q. 104, a. 5.
31. Epstein, *Speaking of Slavery*, 197.
32. Ibid.
33. Ibid., 146.
34. Richard Raiswell, "Nonslaveholders," in *The Historical Encyclopedia of World Slavery*, ed. Junius Rodriquez (Santa Barbara, CA: ABC-CLIO, 1997), 469.
35. Epstein, *Speaking of Slavery*, 197.
36. For example, see Aquinas, *ST* I-II, q. 4, a. 5 ad 3; III, q. 16, a. 8 co., q. 35, a. 5 ad 1.
37. Epstein, *Speaking of Slavery*, 197.
38. Earl Shorris, *New American Blues: A Journey through Poverty to Democracy* (New York: W. W. Norton, 1997), 185, 188.
39. Epstein, *Speaking of Slavery*, 146.

5

Thomas Hobbes
on Human Nature

ASANTE U. TODD

Thomas Hobbes's *Leviathan* (1651), second only perhaps to Niccolo Machiavelli's *The Prince* (1532), is considered one of modern Europe's greatest political treatises. Among Hobbes's writings on law, moral philosophy, physics, optics, and geometry are *A Briefe of the Art of Rhetorique* (1637) and the tripartite corpus of *De cive* (1647), *De corpore* (1655), and *De homine* (1658). Still, *Leviathan* remains of singular importance in modern political theory as well as for the purpose of this short critical essay. Hobbes is most famous or infamous for the doctrines of the sovereign and the social contract as articulated in *Leviathan*. However, this essay focuses on the state-of-nature doctrine, which Hobbes also called the "natural condition," and the manner in which it is deployed to signify people of color. This chapter also takes account of the internalizing effects of this doctrine by people of color. I am interested, albeit in a cursory manner, in the ways people of color often internalize the representational force of stereotypes that circumscribe human beings within the state of nature. Toward the end of this chapter, I will take as an example the contemporary rap group Young Money. The natural condition marks out a space of primitive, irrational, and animal existence that must necessarily be restrained by the *civitas* (civil society, city-state) for the procurement of peace. To critically understand the natural-condition doctrine, I first situate it within Hobbes's own seventeenth-century world. Second, I briefly discuss the anthropological and social aspects of the natural condition and its relationship to the *civitas*. After this, I discuss its significance for the production of the Other, beyond the pale of civil society.

HOBBES AND THE NEW SCIENCE

The son of a minor clergyman in England, the legendary English philosopher Thomas Hobbes had humble beginnings. Born in 1588, he was educated at Oxford and was well acquainted with Anglican politics. I will soon indicate the significance of this connection. His was a time of great political and philosophical upheaval, precipitated by various Renaissance and Reformation movements that circulated throughout early modern Europe. These movements were nothing short of a hermeneutical revolution that destabilized traditional social and political structures of Christendom and medieval scholastic theology. In seventeenth-century England, scientific questioning of these authorities produced such conflicts, forcing Hobbes to flee for Paris in 1640. During the next decade, as an expatriate of a land now raging with civil war, Hobbes penned his magnum opus, *Leviathan*. Characterized by rising death tolls, extensive property damage, an unstable economy, and uneasy alliances, England declined into barbarism and violence. The English Civil War (1641–51) capped nearly a century of such conflicts and served to further the impetus for Hobbes's work.

For Hobbes, religious opinion, based on tradition and authority, was the force behind the political conflicts and must not serve as justification for political authority. In England, Protestants deployed natural law theory, in which everything is governed by universal and necessary laws, to argue for the political right of Calvinist members of Parliament to resist nominalist Anglicans, who supported the crown's supremacy by divine right. This clash resulted in a "war of all against all," a phrase repeated in Hobbes's doctrine of the natural condition. In his writings, Hobbes tries to mediate these warring parties by justifying civil power on scientific grounds rather than religious ones. In turn, this would move political discourse away from the antagonisms between competing religious factions. Unlike traditional religious authorities, scientifically grounded civil power is endowed with unprecedented unity, permanency, and authority. Following Bacon's experimental theory that science is for the amelioration of the human condition, Hobbes's political science was in the service of ameliorating the conditions that brought England into civil war.[1]

The "new science," Baconian empiricism, was thought to be more reliable than religious authority alone. It played a critical role in Hobbes's understanding and interpretation of the social and political world. Science discloses a previously inconceivable natural world, the harmonious diversity of which is orchestrated by natural law. Hobbes refers to nature as a work of art, indeed, "the Art whereby God hath made and governes the World."[2] The new science also offers a method for measuring the highest level of probability in knowledge claims—not only what can be known but also what is known. Bacon's method aimed at mastery over nature through three critical moves. First is the gathering of data from senses and observation. Second is a move from induction to generalizations or abstractions. The third move involves testing generalized conclusions or abstractions by the observations of others, as a critical check against error. Hobbes's approach to politics incorporated these steps, and he was convinced that the findings he collected from available resources at the time provided him with more than enough evidence to draw conclusive judgments about the natural condition of humankind as primitive in relation to advanced civil society. The natural condition, then, is one of Hobbes's critical abstractions from empirical research in his scientific practice.

Hobbes relates this abstraction to politics in order to create a political science that discerns the formal causes of human conflicts and to formulate general and immutable laws that make for a science of politics, whose end is perpetual peace. Such a political science is inspired by Hobbes's understanding of nature as a divine art. The art of nature orders diversity by directing every natural body toward its proper end. *Leviathan* deploys the methods of the natural sciences to enable political mastery over human action in the same way that the sciences enable mastery over other natural bodies. The art by which God has made and governs the world is imitated in the human construction of *Leviathan,* the *civitas* that harmoniously orders and balances diverse human interests.[3] Hobbes was persuaded that the science of politics could simultaneously procure objective rational interests necessary for life, health, and security and produce the conditions necessary for the flourishing of subjective interests by first discerning natural law. The first precept of natural law is to "seek peace, and follow it," and Hobbes conceives of the *civitas* as orchestrating human interests in pursuit of this precept.[4] However, the natural condition exists as the barrier to lasting peace within the *civitas.*

THE NATURAL CONDITION

Recently colonized North America was critical to Hobbes's political science. Reports of so-called new-world savages influenced his empirical lens as he theorized the natural human condition. The distinctive mark of the natural condition is irrationality, characterized by passion, doctrine, and opinion. In this state, few give reasoned attention to consequences of their actions. All are by nature equal, and each possesses the liberty or natural right to use one's natural strength and intellect to get about in the world and pursue irrational ends by any means deemed fit. Hobbes says:

> The Right of Nature . . . is the Liberty each man hath, to use his own power, as he will himself, for the preservation of his own Nature; that is to say, of his own Life; and consequently, of doing any thing, which in his own Judgement, and Reason, he shall conceive to be the aptest means thereunto.[5]

In the natural condition, human beings possess the natural right to anything and are limited only by natural impediments. Much like the sundry aspects of nature disclosed by the sciences of Hobbes's day, the natural condition is also marked by difference in thought, opinion, and doctrine. Good, evil, vice, and virtue are subjectively defined so that a diversity of goods flourishes. Yet, unlike God's art, no mechanism exists in the natural condition that harmoniously governs so wide a range of differences.

As a result of irrational human acts oriented toward the attainment of a diversity of goods, ironically, the natural condition is inclined toward war. It is characterized by primitivism, barbaric passions, and antagonistic relationality. While natural liberty inspires hope for desired ends, competition foils such hopes, and diffidence with respect to goods ascribed to individuals results in war of all against all. Life is plagued by the domination of unchecked power, violence, insecurity, and perpetual war. There is little regard for the natural right or the bodies of others, and life is "solitary, poore, nasty, brutish, and short."[6] Hobbes says:

> The condition of Man . . . is a condition of Warre of every one against every one. . . . It followeth, that in such a condition, every man has a right to every thing; even to one another's body. And therefore, as long as this naturall Right of every man to every thing endureth, there can be no security to any man . . . of living out the time, which Nature ordinarily alloweth men to live.[7]

In a tragic paradox, the exercise of natural right, in the natural condition, is impossible. Unimpeded irrational action is slave to unrestrained appetites and incalculable destruction. Rational interests cannot be secured. Indeed, for Hobbes, this is the case in ungoverned North America, where there reside "savage people in many places, . . . [the] concord whereof dependeth on naturall lust, . . . and [they] live at this day in that brutish manner."[8]

The inevitable violent consequences of the natural condition demonstrate the necessity of the *civitas*, or civil society. In the natural condition, human beings reckon that the preservation of objective interests requires a social contract by which the political community is instituted. The *civitas* preserves the objective interests of citizens by producing or fostering a particular set of relations completely at odds with those in the natural condition. In turn, these relations procure certain ends, such as the good life, the good person, the well-ordered city, or peace. Hobbes's scientific politics procures peace by harmoniously negotiating the interests of all by an overarching rational interest, much as God's art makes and governs the world. In the natural condition beyond the political community, humans enjoy an animal existence in the crudest sense of the words. They are untamed, beastly, and barbaric. From this condition, it follows that social arrangements are disorganized, weak, frequently dysfunctional, and incapable of securing rational interests. Unlike the natural condition, civil society is well-ordered, united, secure, and prosperous. The uncivilized amount to nothing more than brutes, but within the *civitas*, people live qualitatively better lives and become qualitatively better humans. Since the *civitas* is predicated on objective rational interests, Hobbes declares that the head of the *civitas* possesses the power and authority of a "Mortall God."[9] Subjects' sole loyalty is to the head, who alone implements customs and laws. War and peace, judicature and censorship, even right and wrong—all become the prerogative of the sovereign head for the preservation of *Leviathan*.

THE NATURAL CONDITION AND THE PRODUCTION OF THE OTHER

In the absence of viable religious justification of political authority, Hobbes turns to the Baconian empirical method to argue that civil society is necessary for achieving life, health, security, and peace. However, what I call the "natural condition" is an abstraction and not an empirically accurate description of newly encountered societies of Others in the New World. In the following pages, I briefly consider both how this abstraction, having become a stereotype, is internalized by certain Others even today, and how this stereotype still functions to justify the authority of contemporary Leviathans.

The natural condition is irrational, lustful, warring, and premoral. It reduces human beings to essential characteristics and portrays them by a fixed nature. This representational practice of stereotyping is harmful to the production of the Other, and in Hobbes's case, to Native Americans. As a stereotype, the natural condition marks the Other in distinctive ways. First, polarized binaries within the natural condition make it easier to fix its meaning. Although meaning can never be fixed in the truest sense of the word, meaning nevertheless becomes fixed disjunctively as either/or. The natural condition becomes either a place of absolute freedom (natural right) or absolute nonfreedom (a war of all against all), either a state of utter irrationality or a social contract. Second, the natural condition contains a sexual element. As Hobbes puts it, "Concord whereof depends on natural lust." Destructive sexual passions risk the order of civilization. Third, the natural condition is characterized as brutish and childishly irrational, thus emphasizing bodily strength over intellectual capabilities.

In *Leviathan*, we find a representational practice that was not only critical in the production of the Other in Hobbes's times, but also appears internalized in practices signifying the Other in our own times. This is especially true in the U.S. context, where, within broad regimes of representations, African Americans are confined to particular abstractions that echo the natural condition by drawing on one or more of its distinctive marks described above. To show how the internalization of the natural condition works, I focus on one instance: the popular rap group Young Money, formed by the world-renowned rapper and musician Lil Wayne (2009). Here, rap is all too often the straw man and scapegoat for cultural criticism, precisely insofar as it internalizes the Hobbesian natural condition. The genre's unprecedented global appeal forces upon it the "burden of representation," in which rap represents all Black art and consequently all Black people. As a result of this representational burden, rap is expected to show communal, racial, or moral responsibility. It is not my intention to place this unfair burden on rap's shoulders. Rather, my claim is that rap frequently represents African Americans in ways that demonstrate an internalization and presentation of stereotypes found in *Leviathan*'s category of "natural condition." Furthermore, these stereotypes function in much the same manner and for the same purposes as they did in Hobbes's day, namely as legitimating conditions for coercive civil authorities.

I suggest that the natural condition theorized in the seventeenth century is echoed in the twenty-first century's Young Money in at least three ways. First, there are the binaries attributed to the group. As in the natural condition, the group is usually portrayed as lawless, while bound by some natural law or code. Another polarization portrays group members as being both admirably honest (childlike), transparent, and gifted, and at the same time, coldhearted, murderous animals. These binaries create an either/or paradigm, and it becomes easier to fix a meaning to Young Money. They are either extremely honest or murderers, and there exists no possibility outside these meanings. Second, Young Money displays a strong barbaric sexual element. For instance, Lil Wayne frequently uses language that suggests he has literally transformed into a penis. One might even point beyond lyrics to names of members such as "Nikki Minaj." Finally, in self-identifying as "crazy," "goblins," and even "Louisi-animals," Young Money portrays itself as a band of irrational and uncivilized brutes given to animalistic instincts. These traits point to an internalization of *Leviathan*'s natural condition by Young Money.

Meaning can never be permanently fixed, but the meaning of *Young Money* becomes settled when viewed within a nature/culture dialectic. Representing the natural condition, *Young Money* stands contrary to modern Western cultural conceptions of acceptability and normalcy. Such conceptions, found in Hobbes's writings, include cultural values such as self-control, responsibility, refinement, and belief in reason. These cultural values have often been depicted as essential to personal fulfillment and social flourishing. As irrational, sex-crazed, violent animals, Young Money is without culture. Thus the meaning of the group becomes fixed. Young Money becomes representative of both individual instances of nihilism and the decline or complete absence of acceptable social relations. Moreover, when interpreted within a history of representations that privileges a meaning of African Americans as irrational, sexually barbaric, and childish, Young Money contributes to centuries-long processes of "naturing" the Other. The Other is "natured" when aspects of Others are represented so consistently that they are believed to be permanently fixed and natural, rather than culturally produced.

Perhaps most problematically, the prescription for "natured" Others is the same in the twenty-first century as it was in Hobbes's own discourse. Just as the *civitas* delivered humankind from the natural condition then, the great *Leviathan* still operates with similar authority, power, and agenda in contemporary times. For the Others who stand in as representatives for nature—who for purposes of this essay are mostly African Americans in the U.S. context—the results have been disastrous. These populations have been most exposed to the disciplinary and violent power of the *civitas* and thus suffer economic, educational, and health hardships. These populations are also most likely to be treated nihilistically by the policing power of civil society, contributing to frighteningly disparate proportions of African Americans in correctional facilities, jails, and prisons. In the early twenty-first century, the American *civitas*'s remedy for nature is restraint and rapine.

To conclude, just as the "state of nature" or the "natural condition" displays warring interests, which can be remedied only by the authority of the *civitas* in Hobbes's *Leviathan*, so "natured" Others are dealt with by the authority of sovereign civil power today. Within the Anglo-American spheres of civil powers, in both the British and American Leviathans, Native and African Americans historically have borne the burden of representing nature's Others. With the global circulation of Leviathan empires from the West, the burden of representing the state of nature—the abstraction of historical human conditions in the scientization of the Other—extends well into our present historical horizon on a global scale. There it marks off people of color around the world by stereotypes and fetishisms, and by brute, irrational, and unmitigated natures. They fall beyond the pale of civil society, which renders them ready subjects of Leviathan's coercive sovereign power. Hobbes's scientific practices remind us that abstractions are essential to the productions of knowledge, whether of human beings as a species or as groups. They are also important for the manner in which they circulate throughout signifying systems, including sociopolitical regimes. However, Hobbes's *Leviathan* also discloses the ways in which abstractions can be dangerously oriented toward totality, replicating themselves into culturally debilitating stereotypes, which having become "natural," overdetermine people of color by the permanent fixture of an unmediated natural condition.

Notes

1. Thomas Hobbes, *Leviathan*, ed. Richard Tuck (New York: Cambridge University Press, 2006), 3.
2. Ibid., 9.
3. Ibid.
4. Ibid., 91–92; cf. Ps. 34:14.
5. Ibid., 91.
6. Ibid., 89.
7. Ibid., 91.
8. Ibid., 89.
9. Ibid., 120.

6

John Locke on Property

TINK TINKER (WAZHAZHE NATION)

Thus in the beginning all the world was America, *and more so than that is now; for no such thing as* money *was any where known. Find out something that hath the* use and value of money *amongst his neighbours, you shall see the same man will begin presently to enlarge his possessions.*

—John Locke[1]

John Locke (1632–1704) was an english* businessman and politician, a slave owner and international slave trader, who is perhaps best remembered as an ethicist for his brilliant justification of international land theft—stealing other people's property with a facade of utmost legal and moral propriety—and for his philosophical support for the unbridled accumulation of wealth. Locke is highly regarded by both eurowestern liberals and neoconservative pundits, as he seems to offer something for both ends of the contemporary dominant society's political spectrum. Most important for Indian peoples of north America, however, he has come to be regarded as the foundation for eurowestern notions of the private

---

*My use of the lower case for such adjectives as "english," "christian," "biblical," etc., is intentional. While nouns naming religious groups might be capitalized out of respect for each Christian—as for each Muslim or Buddhist—using the lower case "christian" or "biblical" for adjectives allows readers to avoid unnecessary normativizing or universalizing of the principal institutional religious quotient of the eurowest. Likewise, I avoid capitalizing such national or regional adjectives as american, amer-european, european, eurowestern, etc. I also refer to north America. It is important to my argumentation that people recognize the historical artificiality of modern regional and nation-state social constructions. Quite paradoxically, I know, I insist on capitalizing White (adjective or noun) to indicate a clear cultural pattern invested in Whiteness that is all too often overlooked or even denied by american Whites. Moreover, this brings parity to the insistence of African Americans on the capitalization of the word Black in reference to their own community (in contra-distinction to the *New York Times* usage). Likewise, I always capitalize Indian and American Indian.

ownership of property. Moving beyond Descartes' codification of the european cultural notion of radical individualism, Locke's theory of private ownership of property has come to be known as *possessive individualism*. This put Locke's colonial interests in a historical conflict with the indigenous cultures of those who were the target of english colonialism, a conflict that continues into the present. American Indians, for instance, continue to live a cultural system rooted firmly in community and a communitarian value system. Following Locke's Puritan instincts and the earlier european church reformation, colonial missionaries are still attempting to replace this communitarian value system with a theology of individualism. This chapter will briefly summarize Locke's philosophy from an ethics perspective, but it will focus more generally on what White interpreters (fans of Locke) call the "contradiction" inherent in Locke's position on slavery and then more particularly on the anti–American Indian racism that is blatantly inherent in his theories on property and the accumulation of wealth.

LOCKE AND LAND THEFT

According to Locke, God wanted english folk to take over the vacant "waste" lands of north America. Yet they were not vacant at all. They were actually widely inhabited, but by Locke's judgment they were inhabited by peoples who had failed to develop their lands adequately. So God wanted english agriculturalists, who were invested in a money economy that allowed for a much greater accumulation of wealth, and who could use their God-given superior culture to generate new wealth by stealing aboriginal Indian land (that is, for legitimate, legally justifiable, and under some divine command based on moral rationale, to take someone else's land by conquest), remove those people from the land, and repopulate the land with englishmen. Locke was one of the key euro-White philosophers and thinkers of the european seventeenth century. An obviously brilliant man, Locke was broadly educated. He served as a physician and medical researcher; as a highly placed political activist as well as a political theorist; as the business manager for a colonial landholding corporation with interests in north America; and as a scientist who became a friend of Isaac Newton and with Newton, the chemist Robert Boyle, and other early scientists founded the English Royal Society. Yet he is most remembered and still widely taught today as a philosopher and political theorist who continues to deeply influence the development of ethics and political theory and practice. At the same time, Locke was an early european exemplar of the racist White supremacism that was only then in the midst of emerging. Although he would not yet have called himself White, his philosophical argumentation and socioeconomic practice clearly place him in the context of burgeoning White european supremacist thinking.

His philosophical writings helped to rationalize (and ultimately to legalize) the theft of lands from aboriginal landowners by White english invaders based on his own understanding of the superiority of english culture and english ways.

Particularly important to this process was his essay "On Property," chapter 5 in his *Second Treatise of Government*. It is in this essay that Locke so carefully builds a fictional narrative about Native Peoples in order to justify grand larceny in the minds of good christian folk in Europe. Ultimately, it is this essay that so heavily shapes the legal and philosophical basis for all property ownership and property laws in the United States today, and it does so by creating a legal logic for engaging in colonial occupation and coercive control of Native peoples.[2] Indeed, it is Locke's notion of the social contract that creates the modern notion of the "rule of law," and the control of another people's property is the first order of business for Locke's rule of law. He begins by very creatively inventing a way for moral christian (White) folk to decide that the other folk in question (American Indians) never really owned the property in the first place—even though they may have lived on the land from time immemorial.

In the *Two Treatises* Locke argues vehemently against slavery. Already in his opening words to the *First Treatise of Government*, Locke voices his abhorrence of slavery in general with the condemnation that slavery "is so vile and miserable an Estate of Man, and so distinctly opposite of the generous Temper and Courage of our Nation; that 'tis hardly to be conceived, that an Englishman, much less a Gentleman, should plead for't." Locke then returns to his refutation of slavery in chapter 4 of the *Second Treatise*. Yet if we read the *Two Treatises* carefully, it is clear that Locke never intended to include african peoples in his tirade against slavery. Indeed, his condemnation of slavery has nothing at all to do with the slave trade in which he was himself so deeply invested. Rather, it had more to do with the nature of civil government in England and his political dispute with an ardent royalist political writer. As attested by his personal financial investments in two companies, the Bahamian Adventurers and the Royal Africa Company, Locke must have all too easily differentiated (ethically and morally) between the enslavement of White people and the enslavement of African Blacks. The Bahamian Adventurers ran plantations in the Bahamas on the basis of the coerced and nonremunerated labor of some four to five thousand African slaves. The Royal Africa Company was a business venture trading in kidnapped Blacks off the atlantic coast of Africa, supplying among others the very plantation enterprises in the Bahamas of which Locke was an owner. Through the advice of his patron Ashley Cooper, Locke invested rather heavily in both of these companies in 1672, becoming a part owner of each.

A close and contextual reading of the *Two Treatises* underscores that the slavery Locke opposed so vehemently in the *Two Treatises* was a slavery of the english people themselves: White people, in a political system of absolute monarchy. His antislavery rhetoric is precisely intended to counter Robert Filmer's defense of absolute monarchy, characterizing it as an enslavement of the people. Locke's vociferous outburst against slavery, then, is about english people and explicitly about the english political system of governance. Locke never even considered and certainly never intended extending his principle on slavery to non-White (meaning nonenglish) peoples.

INTERPRETATION OF LOCKE

To understand who John Locke was and his continuing importance, we need to briefly characterize his theoretical and methodological position. Locke was first of all an empiricist, building his political theory on experience and sense perceptions of reality. It is this empiricism that derives from Locke's early and long involvement in the physical sciences as a student and close associate of Robert Boyle and others. He was engaged in medical research at the time he was hired by a wealthy english politician and businessman as the gentleman's personal physician. This commitment to the physical sciences made empiricism a natural methodological choice.

Second, Locke was a proponent of a social contract theory. According to this view, human civilization emerged as a result of some conscious communal decision to build a form of community governance in which people would give up what he describes as the absolute and unencumbered freedom experienced by every individual in an original state of nature, where no one was constrained by anyone else. In return, people would have a community-contracted rule of law that would allow for the (legally protected) ownership of property and the accumulation of personal wealth, as well as a greater degree of personal safety. This contractarian modality was certainly not new with Locke, but Locke pushes beyond Thomas Hobbes and in a quite different direction.

Third, to pursue his social contract idea, Locke argues a natural law theory. What he calls the "State of nature" was not merely for Locke an edenic fantasy of some human past—even if we might today accuse him of creating a fictive narrative of that past. Rather, it served Locke's purpose of justifying the need for a social contract leading to civil government—and ultimately allows for social choices in creating governing structures. If the governing structure is socially contracted, then it is not itself a natural (or divinely constituted) event. Here Locke is again countering the divine right of monarchy as a naturally occurring structure for ruling a people. We can add one more important piece of the puzzle. In his development of early modern notions of property, Locke builds on the foundational idea of individualism already rampant in european praxis since the european renaissance and ecclesial reformation periods. The radical eurowestern notion of individualism has become entrenched in eurowestern cultures. Locke's expansion of the idea, however, which has become a simplistic favorite of neo-classical (so-called neoliberal) economics (especially those associated with the excesses of the Milton Friedman / free market school of capitalism), is the notion of "possessive individualism," already mentioned above.

Locke's move toward the private ownership of property is authorized under this notion of natural law. Thus the origin of private property is part of the natural law for Locke and not just a condition that begins under the social contract of what he calls political life. The latter (commonly called today the "rule of law") is invoked in Lockean doctrine as part of the set of needs that results in the social contract as an agreement among people to help regulate the ownership of property.

Locke can be seen to articulate two paradoxically different perspectives with regard to wealth: an egalitarian position that seems to be supportive of the poorest members of society; and a clear defense of individual wealth and the disproportionate distribution of wealth.[3] At the same time he is widely regarded as perhaps the key founder of modern notions of democracy and liberal republican state government that captivated political processes in Europe and north America and have been increasingly imposed on the rest of the human population of the world (Iraq and Afghanistan being just the most acute examples of the moment). Notions of liberty and freedom that became so important to the french revolution a century after Locke and especially for the rebellion of the english colonies in north America find their initial modern formulation in Locke. Locke did not begin the process that led to ending the european notion of the divine right of monarchy and absolute rule.[4] Rather, Locke's social thought was the next step in pressing the antifeudalism that had generated the (puritan) english civil war of the 1640s, the generation before Locke's adulthood. It should be added here that in the context of his natural law argumentation, Locke also formulated a conception of natural rights, the beginnings of what has become contemporary eurowestern human rights theory, a discourse wholly founded on the emergent notion of european individualism. Indeed, Locke's pervasive individualism continues at its deepest theoretical essence to stain the whole of modern human rights discourse, a discourse that regularly disallows the voice of indigenous communal wholes.

Thus it has become a commonplace to report that as a theorist and as a political agitator, Locke was a staunch opponent of tyranny, especially the tyranny he saw inherent in the absolute power exercised in monarchy. Locke was the favorite theorist of the radical Whig party in their movement and became a key player in the english "Glorious Revolution" of 1688, which deposed Charles II from the throne of England and installed a new monarch who was much more subordinate to the rule of the english Parliament.[5] It was this revolution, rather than the french revolution more than a century later, that shaped the beginning of european democracy as we see it today. His *Two Treatises of Government*, written in the ferment that led to this revolution, was a theoretical attempt first of all to establish a basis for civil government. Yet it was equally focused on legitimizing the english colonial projects in the Americas (including the Caribbean) and Africa, projects in which Locke was himself heavily invested, financially as well as politically.

Locke's more-romantic liberal defenders want to claim the egalitarian Locke as the modern liberal hero of egalitarian democracy and personal freedom. At the same time, they prefer to dismiss the upper-class slave-owner unbridled-accumulation-of-wealth Locke as an aberration of his basic principles. In promoting an alternative interpretation of the *Treatises*, for example, legal scholar Jeremy Waldron argues that Locke would allow the poorest to share in the "surplusage" of the production of those who are wealthier and even to take surplus goods. Indeed, Waldron goes on to propose, "Lockean government may have to be continually interfering to redistribute surplus goods from the rich to the most needy."[6] But this is not the Locke who was so deeply invested, politically and financially, in the beginnings of english colonialism.

Waldron argues that Locke surreptitiously sneaked a Lockean idea into the Carolina Constitution, allowing slaves in the carolina territory to have freedom of religion (paragraph 107). In other words, as long as you remember you are a slave and have to obey your master, you can have freedom of religion; believe what you will: just do exactly as you are told otherwise. Waldron then wrongly connects this passage in the Carolina Constitution to Locke's condemnation of slavery in general in the *First Treatise*.[7] Yet it becomes painfully clear that in condemning slavery, Locke had no intention whatsoever of including the african slaves of his own investments. Here is the quote from Carolina Constitution:

> Since charity obliges us to wish well to the souls of all men, and religion ought to alter nothing in any man's civil estate or right, it shall be lawful for slaves, as well as others, to enter themselves, and be of what church or profession any of them shall think best, and, therefore, be as fully members as any freeman. But yet no slave shall hereby be exempted from that civil dominion his master hath over him, but be in all things in the same state and condition he was in before. . . . [From par. 107 we skip down to par. 110.] Every freeman of Carolina shall have absolute power and authority over his negro slaves, of what opinion or religion soever.

THE HISTORICAL CONTEXT

In 1666 Locke became acquainted with politician Anthony Ashley Cooper (aka "lord" Ashley or "lord" Shaftesbury in the now antiquated english caste system). Cooper, one of the wealthiest persons in England, first sought out Locke for medical advice. Early the next year Locke moved into Cooper's mansion to serve as his personal physician, live-in scholar, business manager, and political consultant. Among the important duties Cooper gave over to Locke was the secretariat of two important aspects of Cooper's financial empire. He was very early made secretary to the Lords Proprietors of the Carolina Corporation (1669–75) and then secretary of the Board of Trade and Plantations (1673–74).[8] The latter was a colonial institution, a government agency designed to manage England's growing colonial enterprises in the Americas and Africa and to oversee local colonial governments. By 1660, when Cooper was a member of the king's privy council, he had resurrected this privy council subcommittee. One Lockean scholar describes the Board of Trade and Plantations as "the body which administered the United States before the American revolution."[9] So it was natural that Cooper, as a key power politician on the privy council, would elevate his young protégé John Locke to provide oversight of the Board in 1673.

The other secretariat to which Cooper advanced Locke was a business venture, Cooper's principal economic venture in the colonial enterprise. The business was a corporation chartered by the english king (Charles II) in 1663 for holding (and retailing) a huge chunk of American Indian lands in north America (the future North and South Carolinas).[10] Cooper was one of the eight "lords proprietors" of the corporation, all of whom were high-ranking and very influential english politicians. It was Locke, then, who was called upon to draft the Fundamental Constitutions of Carolina for the corporation in 1669, and he was again involved in the thorough revision completed in August 1682.[11]

In these two capacities in particular (as secretary of these two boards), Locke was "one of just half a dozen men who created and supervised both the colonies and their iniquitous systems of servitude."[12] Indeed, Locke's political activism, his political influence, and his economic participation in the english colonial project continued to the end of his career. Years after his first secretariat of the Board of Trade, the new king, William of Orange, appointed Locke to the newly restructured Board, a position that he held from 1696 to 1700, at the end of his public career. He is reported to have been its most influential member. In all of these capacities, Locke became the genius behind the legitimizing of White theft of (legally, speaking in colonizer language, "ownership of and immigration into") Indian properties.

As one of the principal authors of the Carolina Constitution, Locke developed a political structure far different from the one he helped install in his own England as a result of the so-called Glorious Revolution. The carolina territories, or plantations, were to be ruled by a feudal aristocracy in order to generate the greatest wealth for the investors in England. The context in colonial north America (and thus in Carolina) was one in which the racial shift to distinguish White indentured servants from african servants had just begun to be institutionalized in colonial law. From 1654 onward, beginning in Virginia,[13] african servants were no longer to be treated like White indentured servants; rather, their (short-term) servanthood was suddenly interpreted in the (White-cum-racially-based) social contract of the colonies as a perpetual slavery. More important, the numbers of african persons imported as slaves then began to multiply; Carolina, like Virginia, had quickly become dependent on slave labor, so that the Carolina Company functioned in a context where profit (the accumulation of wealth) was largely generated by slave labor. In this context, then, Locke created a constitution for managing the carolina territory in which a master was to be granted absolute legal "authority and power over his negro slaves."

It becomes all the more apparent that this is colonial hegemonic discourse when we become aware that in 1671 the "lords proprietors" of the Carolina Corporation elevated Locke himself to the status of nobility in the Carolina territory with the title of landgrave. This position of colonial nobility, by regulation in the Carolina Constitutions, which were drafted by Locke a couple of years earlier, was accompanied with a grant of 48,000 acres of Indian land. Thus Locke became an actual owner rather than a merely a bright colonialist bureaucrat on the payroll. With a minority share in the Carolina Province also came a seat in the colonial legislature of the carolina territory. Like many of the english elites who were appointed to the title, Locke never actually came to Carolina to take up his office of authority and power there, although he frequently enough fantasized about it in personal correspondence during the years before the 1688 revolution, which saw his political fortunes shift considerably upward in England.

Here is what we have thus far: Locke was an economic elite heavily invested in both slave-owning plantations (Bahamas Adventurers) and in the slave trade itself (the Royal African Company—and part owner of a slave ship). He was heavily invested both in north American land thievery (the Carolina Corporation) and in the philosophical justification of land thievery. And he was a highly placed political elite involved in establishing and managing the english colonial machinery of the first english empire. In the midst of this busy life, he was also a philosopher and political theorist. Needless to say, he has been very important in the world of eurowestern ethics and the development of ethical discourse.

LAND AS PRIVATE PROPERTY

To understand the complexity of Locke's chapter "On Property," we need to begin by understanding the fiction that Locke creates to describe Indians as non-owners of their own land. This mythic fiction is rooted in Locke's imagination of the beginnings of human existence, something he calls the "state of nature." Indians belong to this "state of nature." In this state the whole world belonged to all people as a commons, and all were free to use whatever they could in order to sustain their lives. No one owned any part of it (as a private property), but all have equal access to the whole of it as a "commons" and are free to hunt or gather as they please. This only changes when someone "improves" a piece of land (agriculturally) through the use of one's own labor. In Locke's argument, then, what sets any property aside as an individual's private property is labor. The labor of one's own hands takes a piece of property out of the realm of the common by marking the property.[14] However, we know that english property owners in north America included, as Locke would also insist, the labor of one's owned human slaves. The evidence of this labor is english-style agriculture. It is by working the land, and working it agriculturally, that one marks it as one's own and establishes the right to claim a piece of land as private property. The basics of his argument are readily apparent in an oft-quoted text:

> God and his reason commanded him to subdue the earth, i.e., improve it for the benefit of life, and therein lay out something upon it that was his own, his labour. He that in obedience to this command of God, subdued, tilled and sowed any part of it, thereby annexed to it something that was his property, which another had no title to, nor could without injury take from him.[15]

Locke had never been to America but had financially invested himself in the Carolina Company, was highly placed politically in the english government, and was involved in establishing colonial policy. He continued the development of an english narrative that depreciated the value of indigenous peoples in north

America and invalidated their own ownership of property in their own land on a legal technicality that he devised himself. Conveniently for Locke (who was by now the fictitious—but entirely legal—landowner in the Carolinas), Indians failed to actually own land as property. By his definition they were merely hunters and gatherers on the land, nomads and not agriculturalists. Living off the wild produce of the earth, Indians failed to figure out how to enclose property for agricultural purposes, he claimed. As long as Indians were hunting in a forest, the only property marked by an Indian person's labor would be a deer killed for food or fruits gathered from unplanted trees.[16] Only when the land is tilled agriculturally and planted does the earth itself (meaning a particular cleared plot) become marked by labor and thus some person's private land.

The lie is an ethnographic (and ethnocidal) fabrication. To sustain this lie, Locke and others had to ignore the intense farming of corn in north America even though these agricultural sites were the first places claimed by the colonial invaders.[17] With this notion Locke not only builds the foundation for the private ownership of property in England, but also canonizes the legal fiction to justify stealing indigenous lands from aboriginal owners throughout the various empires of Europe in succeeding centuries.[18] That legal fiction continues to function in U.S. courts to this day and in courts around the world. For this empirical scientist and brilliant philosopher to engage in the mere creation of a fiction about Native Peoples is curious enough. But that fiction first of all about American Indians becomes ultimately about other indigenous folk in Africa, Asia, the Pacific Islands, Australia, Aotearoa/ New Zealand, and even the north of Europe (e.g., Samiland).

CONCLUSION

To identify Locke as a White supremacist can be seen as a bit of a curiosity in one regard. First of all, european peoples had only begun to differentiate themselves in racialized terms as different from other peoples in the world. Locke tends to identify himself, for instance, as an englishman and not as a White person. Yet it is clear that by Locke's time, color *did* matter and distinctions were beginning to be made more and more clearly. Locke is writing in England at precisely that moment in north American colonial history when the enslavement of african peoples was being separated from the indentured-servant status of europeans, exactly at that moment when slavery on the basis of black skin color was being transitioned into "perpetual" slavery. As England's colonial magistrate, as secretary for the Board of Trade, in charge of colonial administration in north America, Locke would have been fully informed on this transition in the state of Black slaves.

While one might argue lamely for some ambiguity in Locke's understanding of slavery, there is certainly no ambiguity when we turn to his exploitative writing about America and its Native Peoples. Locke's language, however, of anti-Indian racism and White supremacy is not new to Locke himself. Locke was merely continuing a discourse that had been long developed in Europe in order to justify european colonialism, the conquest of Native Peoples, and the theft of their lands. This insight is not intended to excuse Locke's crass and self-serving abjection of Native Peoples but merely to explain how such destructive thinking and acting could find easy expression in Locke's writing. Because of his influence, Locke's reinforcement of White supremacism became a vital contribution not only to the developing racism of his day but also for the centuries of european and amer-european empires that were to follow.

While Locke, the great defender of freedom, ironically found the state of perfect freedom in the state of nature to be onerous, American Indians continue to think back on our traditional life on the land as an ideal way of being. Indeed, we might like to find our way back to that state. Turning Locke against himself, my Shawnee colleague and political science scholar Glenn Morris often refers to October 11, 1492, as "the last day of perfect freedom!"[19]

Notes

1. John Locke, *The Two Treatises of Government*, ed. Peter Laslett, 2nd ed. (New York: Cambridge University Press, 1970), 49; original ed., 1689.

2. See, e.g., Barbara Arneil, *John Locke and America: The Defense of English Colonialism* (Broadridge, UK: Clarendon Press, 1996), 2. By analyzing Locke's repeated references to America in the *Second Treatise*, Arneil argues that the document as a whole (*Two Treatises of Government*) was written as a defense of England's colonial policies in north America. "In particular . . . the famous chapter on property . . . was written to justify the seventeenth-century dispossession of the aboriginal peoples of their land, through a vigorous defence of England's 'superior' claims to proprietorship."

3. See the discussion of John F. Henry, "John Locke, Property Rights and Economic Theory," *Journal of Economic Issues* 33, no. 3 (1999): 609, cited from Questia, www.questia.com. Henry cites Neal Wood in this regard (among others): "The 'pro-bourgeois' camp is quite right in finding historically new and distinctive elements in Locke's approach, and the 'anti-bourgeois' critics are equally correct in stressing Locke's antipathy to merchants, monied men, and commerce." Neal Wood, *John Locke and Agrarian Capitalism* (Berkeley: University of California Press, 1984), 16.

4. For american thinkers in 1776 like Thomas Jefferson, Locke was the canonical source for their revolution against their rightful ruler, the english king. See Arneil, *John Locke and America*, chap. 7, "Locke, Jefferson, and the Amerindian," 168–200.

5. Locke, a noncombatant intellectual, was actually in exile in France at the moment of the revolution's denouement, but he accompanied the wife of the new monarch (William of Orange) across the Channel back to England after victory was secure.

6. Jeremy Waldron, *God, Locke, and Equality: Christian Foundations in Locke's Political Thought* (New York: Cambridge University Press, 2002), 178–85.

7. Ibid., 199, 205.

8. The formal title of the Board of Trade was and is "The Lords of the Committee of Privy Council appointed for the consideration of all matters relating to Trade and Foreign Plantations." It was first established by the english king called James I in 1621. By the mid-nineteenth century the board's control of colonial matters passed into the hands of the "Colonial Office," a new and powerful bureaucracy of the british government, but the Board of Trade continued in one fashion or

another. In 1966 civil aviation came under its purview; by 1974 it was reshaped as the Board of Trade and Industry. Colonial institutions have a way of enduring, but their spirit continues long after the institution itself is gone. See the british government's description of the history of the Board: http://www.berr.gov.uk/aboutus/corporate/history/outlines/DT-1970-1974/page13920.html. Accessed 03-08-2011.

9. Jean Yolton, *A Locke Miscellany: Locke Biography and Criticism For All* (Bristol, UK: Thommes Antiquarian Books, 1990), 127.

10. Cooper made his first movement into the colonial venture as early as 1646 when he invested financially in a Barbados plantation. By 1660 he was a member of the english king Charles II's Privy Council. It was in this capacity that he helped to reorganize the Privy Council's Committee on Trade and Plantations. And it was as an important politician and businessman that he was made one of the "lords proprietors" of the Carolina Company in 1663, appointed so by the king, Charles II. See Tim Harris, "Cooper, Anthony Ashley, First Earl of Shaftesbury (1621–1683)," in *Oxford Dictionary of National Biography* (Oxford University Press, September 2004); online edition, subscription required, http://www.oxforddnb.com.bianca.penlib.du.edu/view/article/6208.

11. David Armitage, "John Locke, Carolina, and the Two Treatises on Government," *Political Theory* 32, no. 5 (2004): 602–27.

12. Martin Cohen, *Philosophical Tales* (Boston: Blackwell Publishing, 2008), 101.

13. In 1654 a Virginia court declared John Casor, an african Black, to be a "slave for life." Frank W. Sweet, *Legal History of the Color Line: The Rise and Triumph of the One-Drop Rule* (Palm Coast, FL: Backintyme Publishing, 2005), 117.

14. Locke, *Two Treatises*, II: v. 27.

15. Ibid., v. 32.

16. Thus a later american Lockean, Andrew Jackson, in his annual message to congress in December 1835, could easily dismiss any Indian claims to ownership of their own land as mere "usufructuary rights," which they ceded to the whites. Luther Hill, *A History of the State of Oklahoma*, vol. 1 (1908), 77, http://www.usgennet.org/usa/topic/historical/ok_10.htm. The speech was in part a rationale for Indian Removal.

17. The stunning estimate is that some two-thirds of the world's good resources today are American Indian in origin, from corn and potatoes to tomatoes, hot peppers, and chocolate. Not too bad for "nonagriculturalists." Emory Dean Keoke and Kay Marie Porterfield, *Food, Farming, and Hunting: American Indian Contributions to the World* (New York: Facts on File, 2005); Jack Weatherford, *Indian Givers: How the Indians of the Americas Changed the World* (New York: Three Rivers Press, 2010), chaps. 4–5; Barbara Alice Mann, *George Washington's War on Native America,* Native America: Yesterday and Today (Lincoln: University of Nebraska Press, 2008), unearths long-hidden U.S. government archives that report the huge agricultural wealth of Indian communities in the Ohio River Valley areas attacked so viciously by U.S. military forces in a straightforward war of territorial conquest during the Washington presidency.

18. The fiction was already an established part of the colonial rationale, going back at least to John Cotton and his celebrated sermon to the puritan group in London as they were set to leave on the *Arbella* to establish the Boston colony in 1630.

19. Morris is at the University of Colorado Denver. He has been the key organizer for the Colorado chapter of the American Indian Movement. His comment has been made at more than one event protesting the celebration of this thing called columbus day.

7

Jean-Jacques Rousseau
on Order

VICTOR ANDERSON

I conceive of two sorts of inequality in the human species; one, which I call natural or physical, because it is established by nature and consists in the difference of ages, health, bodily strengths, and qualities of mind or soul; the other, which may be called moral or political inequality, because it depends upon a sort of convention and is established, or at least authorized, by consent of men.

—Jean-Jacques Rousseau[1]

EUTAXIA AND ROUSSEAU'S "DISCOURSE ON INEQUALITY"

In Western political liberalism, sometimes referred to as civic republicanism, the language of order, *eutaxia*, is derived from a complex history of Greek and Latin metaphysics and politics. To be sure, it has been the controlling rhetoric for not only maintaining the unity of the West's political self-understanding but also its intellectual culture, whether in philosophy, theology, morality, or politics. *Eutaxia* enjoyed a long and secure history of effects, protected well metaphysically by early modernity's retrieval of late Stoic natural law philosophy, ethics, and politics. As a controlling logic of political liberalism, *eutaxia* would give way to an onslaught of philosophical challenges from natural history, Darwinian evolution, positive philosophy, radical empiricism, behaviorism, logical positivism, historicism, existentialism, and every antifoundationalist move circulating throughout so-called postmodern discourse.

Once taken for granted in modern political thought, the rhetoric of order has few adherents today. Still, the rhetoric of order, *eutaxia*, meaning good order, survives in our hermeneutical appropriations of Plato's *Republic*, Aristotle's

Politics, Cicero's *De civitas*, Augustine's *City of God*, and Thomas Aquinas's *Political Treatises*—and early modern theorists of civic republicanism from Spinoza's *Tractatus*, Locke's *Social Contract*, Montesquieu's *Spirit of the Laws*, and Rousseau's *Discourses*.

Jean-Jacques Rousseau was born in 1712 in Geneva but lived most of his life in France. In 1750 he published his (first) *Discourse on Science and Arts*, in 1754 the (second) *Discourse on the Origin of Inequality*, and in 1762 the work for which he is most renowned, the (third) *Discourse on Political Economy or the Social Contract*. He died in 1778 at the age of sixty-six. His was an enlightened mind that brought throughout his life not only philosophical notoriety but also disdain for his views on arts, music, science, education, and government. He was a true libertine and perhaps, with the exception of *Émile*, no text articulates his libertarian views so pointedly as the second *Discourse*, notwithstanding the work of which he is most exclaimed, *Of the Social Contract*. This short essay focuses on *eutaxia*, or the rhetoric of good order in Rousseau's *Discourse on the Origin of Inequality*. To maximize space, I draw heavily on Maurizio Viroli's book *Rousseau and the "Well-Ordered Society"* (1988).

To appreciate *eutaxia*, it is best to approach it from the side of its antithesis: nature. Here, from the start, we are met with a basic metaphysical frame, the nature/order dialectics. Nature is best understood as the privation of rationally ordered social meaning, understanding, and value, or worth. It is best understood in relation to Rousseau's account of the *natural man* and his *natural goodness*. Rousseau differs from Hobbes exactly in his understanding of the state-of-nature doctrine. Rather than a state of warring interests, the state of nature is completely opposite; there are no wars because wars imply rational interests. The natural man is presocial. This does not mean that he is without fellows, but that the *natural man* is lacking interests. Rather, he is a student of nature and lives by nature. He conducts his life by nature, living in relation to nature as an animal among other animals.

According to Rousseau, natural man was never more free than as a creature "dispersed among the animals," observing and imitating their work, developing instincts of "beasts." Like every beast, he is amoral and apolitical. As in Rousseau's *Émile*, natural man is a child of nature, surviving, taking no regard for what dignity or worth he may receive from others, which is the seed of rank and degree. He cooperates with others out of no higher motive or interest than necessity. With a Spartan disposition, he kills and leaves behind the weak only because they cannot contribute to his and his fellow's survival, not being the fittest. "The savage man's body being the only implement he knows," says Rousseau, "he employs it for various uses of which, through lack of training, our bodies are incapable; our industry deprives us of the strength and agility that necessity obliges him to acquire."[2] Natural man lives by a natural goodness that is contrary to the civilized, and is characterized by

> the extreme inequality in our way of life: excess of idleness in some, excess
> of labor in other; the ease of stimulating and satisfying our appetites

and our sensuality; the overly refined foods of the rich, which nourish them with binding juices and overwhelm them with indigestion; the bad food of the poor, which they do not even have most of the time, so that their wants incline them to overburden their stomachs greedily when the occasion permits; late nights, excesses of all kinds, immoderate ecstasies of all the passions, fatigues and exhaustion of mind, numberless sorrows and affliction which are felt in all conditions and by which souls are perpetually tormented; these are the fatal proofs that most of our ills are our own work, and that we would have avoided almost all of them by preserving the simple, uniform, and solitary way of life prescribed to us by nature.[3]

For Rousseau, good ordering, *eutaxia*, lifts natural man from his natural goodness and constructs ordered social relations characterized by hierarchies, power relations between castes and classes, free and indentured, masters and slaves that give concrete form to a well-ordered state. On Rousseau's account, this is the irony—no, the tragedy—of *eutaxia* for civilized society.

Behind the rhetoric of order in modern liberal politics is a recovery of late Stoic ethics among sixteenth- and seventeenth-century British and continental political theorists. However, this suggests that the early modern appropriations of *eutaxia*, right or good ordering, belong to an antecedent history in the rational formation of the social life-world envisioned by Plato and Cicero, the primary figures retrieved in this early modern humanism. Viroli explains that "ordering and correct placing" were thought of as "two terms identical in meaning; for the Stoics also define due ordering *eutaxia* as a setting out of things in the positions most suited and fitted for them."[4] Such is Augustine's appropriation of *eutaxia* in his conception of "peace," where in his *City of God*, Augustine argues for the intricate connection of peace and order.

This is a conceptual linkage that appears to have been previously transmitted within the Christian community and expressed in the writings of the apostle Paul, particularly in his doctrines of the gifts of the Spirit to the churches and their necessity for the *eutaxia* of the Church (1 Cor. 14:40). Augustine of Hippo writes: "The peace of men is orderly harmony. The peace of the home is the orderly harmony of command and obedience on the part of those who live together. The peace of the city is the orderly harmony of command and obedience on the part of the citizens." Here, at least for Augustine, the good order, which guarantees the peace of the city, depends on the allocation of "things to their proper place, taking into account those respects in which they are equal or unequal."[5] Augustine's rhetoric of order directly points us to the political discourse on inequality.

In Rousseau's *Discourse on the Origin of Inequality*, order is defined as "the allocation of each part of the whole to its proper rank and place. Seen in this way, order implies a series of ranks and stations, some more elevated than others. It is not that each part has a different role to play, but that there are also different degrees of merit and worth."[6] Elsewhere Rousseau invokes the language of order to suggest that "everything happens for the best in the system of the universe.

Everyone has his proper place in the ideal order of things; the important thing is to find that place and avoid upsetting that order."[7]

ROUSSEAU, *EUTAXIA*, AND THE BODY POLITIC

For purposes of this short essay, our philosophical problem arises when the metaphysics of order—which marks out the natural way of life, being, or the universe—extends to the cultural spheres of morals and political relations, where the allocation of degree and rank constituting a harmonious universe is pressed from a metaphysics of nature into political and moral relations. Rousseau puts the problem this way: "Each man[8] is forced to accept his place in society since social order requires—and in this it is an exact parallel of what happens in the universe—that differences of rank should be respected and preserved just as they are. If it were not so the body politic, like the universe, would fall into chaos."[9]

Here chaos does not refer to nature, which is premoral and prepolitical; instead, chaos is the opposite of *eutaxia,* the well-ordered state, civilization. How does the Stoic metaphysics of order, a vision of cosmic harmony, extend to civilization to determine moral and political inequalities that result in slavocracy and the social death of the body politic? *Eutaxia* produces a species logic, so that to properly belong to a species (X), an individual (any instance of $X_1, X_2, X_n \ldots$) would possess the necessary and essential properties that define (X). Now the distinctively human is defined metaphysically from the nonhuman; the worth and dignity of the individual, as an instance of (X), is nonmorally established; and the value and dignity of the individual are intrinsic as a member of (X). The individual's worth and dignity are rationally established by one's participation in the human species. If, to properly be a member of the human species, a human must possess (1) a rational soul and (2) meet the necessary bio-genetic conditions particular to the human species, then (3) every instance of a human being will necessarily possess conditions (1) and (2). Hence, all are equally human if they possess a rational soul and are mortal.

Now by admitting that there is no inequality in worth or dignity pertaining to the natural excellence of the human, insofar as all are equal in natural justice (Hobbes) or natural goodness (Rousseau), it does not follow that there are no inequalities accidental to individuals or groups. Indeed, it was the view of early modern liberalism that moral and political inequalities were artificial and not intrinsically human. They are not "according to nature." Moral and political inequalities, on Rousseau's account, are rooted in the accidents and contingencies that are associated with the processes of socialization from nature or the primitive to the political body (civilization).

For Rousseau, the body politics is architectonic of civilization, whose roots lie in the social contract. The body politic is derived from an aggregate consensus of citizens. The key word, *aggregate*, is highly significant. It signifies a realm of pure rationality, statistical reason, and already points to an exclusionary politics of inequality within and outside the body politic. An aggregate does not consider individuals as distinct instances of being-as-such. Rather, they are accounted for as an instance within a class and/or group of things. Indeed, Rousseau's talk of an aggregate consensus, therefore, points toward totality over the particular. And for Rousseau, society is the rationalized ordering of an aggregate consensus of citizen into a rationalized political body.

To be sure, the political body has its antecedent uses in both pagan and Christian sources. However, for our purposes, it is to be explicated in relation to *eutaxia*. The order/body configuration aims at legitimating the advancement of liberal democracy over and against political anarchy and tyranny (order/chaos). Under the well-ordered body, the state or political community is constituted a political person, a corporate entity "formed by the union of all the individual members."[10] This union is made possible through a social contract—an agreement by which the many negotiate the power and right they humanly possess in order to preserve their individual right in relation to the right of other members.

The problem that Rousseau's body politic or political body answers is how "to find a form of association which defends and protects with the whole force of the community, the person and goods of every associate, and by means of which each, uniting with all, nevertheless obeys himself, and remains as free as before."[11] Rousseau argues that the moral/political meaning of the body politic is an answer to the problem of how the natural right of the individual might be preserved within an organic unity of needs and goods that sustain the natural right of each individual, while legitimating a system of moral and political inequality. And the right by which each is preserved as an individual—yet obligated to the will of the whole, or what he calls the general will—is the right of free association, freedom itself. Freedom, without compulsion, constitutes the political body, rendering it a voluntary union of wills that is rationalized around the common good—not the natural goodness, which is Rousseau's natural man. In its demands for a common good, the political body is the free association of rational wills, forming a social contract. This association is voluntary and thus free, an assertion of moral wills, which by enlargement becomes the general will. "Each of us," Rousseau says, "puts in common his person and his whole power under the supreme direction of the general will; and in return we receive in a body every member as an indivisible part of the whole."[12]

Just as the physical body cannot preserve itself in freedom without the moral will, so the political body cannot preserve itself in freedom without the general will. As the individual human body can enter into a state of crisis, disequilibrium, and die, so the political body can also enter into crisis and disequilibrium, and its life of freedom will die. The ill ordering of the social-life world brings the state into slavery, putting to an end the natural goodness of the natural man with his natural justice, which lies in his natural freedom as a creature of nature. The death of the body politic lies in its deprivation of good order. Here is Rousseau:

> The body politic, just as the human body, begins to die at its moment of birth and carries within itself the causes of its destruction. But each can have a constitution more or less robust and suited to preserve it for a longer or shorter time. The constitution of man is the work of nature; that of the State is the work of art. It does not rest with men to prolong their lives; it is the responsibility of men to prolong that of the State as far as possible, by giving it the best constitution that it can give. The best constituted will come to an end, but later than another, if no unforeseen accident brings about its premature destruction.[13]

For Rousseau, the life of the political body will depend on how well ordered, *eutaxia*, the power, right, and interest of each member are related the one to the other, so that the right of each may be guaranteed by the whole, and the legitimacy of the whole is preserved by the good ordering, *eutaxia*, of its members, which establishes rank, merit, degree, and worth within the well-ordered state. Rousseau writes:

> The principle of political life is in the Sovereign authority. The legislative power is the heart of the State; the executive power is its brain, which gives movement to all the parts. The brain can fall into paralysis and the individual still lives. A man remains an imbecile and lives; but as soon as the heart has ceased its functions, the animal is dead.[14]

Rousseau did not have a more-advanced theory of physical death available to him; nevertheless, his analogy is suggestive. The political community, the body politic, whose moral will is dead or ill constituted, dies when lacking the *eutaxia* of justice, goodwill, the right ordering of human relations by *natural justice*, which orders human worth and dignity in freedom. That political community enters into slavery and dies as a genuinely *human* community. What remains, says Rousseau, is a political beast.

Rousseau's discourse presents an interpretation of human life that reflects the North Atlantic European anxiety of genius. Civil society is advancement not from chaos but from nature. It is nature's outgrowth and a work of human art, of which the voluntary construction of the state, society, and civilization mark its genius. As advancement from nature, civil society, the body politic, mutates from the "noble savage" (although as Nicholas Dent reminds us, the term never appears in Rousseau's writings).[15] It signifies a transmutation from the natural man and his natural goodness toward civilization. This transmutation signs, seals, and delivers into the discourse of modernity the primitive/civilized dialectics that even today marks off our dialectics of the Other.

In the West, the dialectics of the Other is civilized humanity in civil society feeling itself sovereign in reason and power, yet existing in perpetual anxiety that is driven by its ironic forgetfulness of its primordial goodness. Natural goodness and natural justice are foreclosed by the degenerative forces of power and interests. Civil society produces a body politic without either a well-ordered soul or a well-ordered general will.

Civil society is the ironic burden of European genius and its greatest contribution to universal world history. It represents the advancement of humanity into civilization from nature to the well-ordered state. On Rousseau's account, however, civil society ushered the West into the persistent anxieties of social chaos, class divisions, anarchy, and rationalized barbarism of each over the whole and the whole over each. Its effects are well displayed in fascist regimes and genocide, extending from the transatlantic slave trade and the Trail of Tears to the Holocaust and genocidal brutalities throughout colonized worlds. Each move represents the extermination of Rousseau's natural man, primitive humanity. Rousseau's discourse on the origin of inequality is anything but a complement to the advancement of absolute reason over the natural man. This theorist of the social contract, the association of rational wills, united by a rationally determined common good, which is typified by "The Rights of Man," says:

> The first person who, having fenced off a plot of ground, took it into his head to say *This is mine* and found people simple enough to believe him, was the true founder of civil society. What comes, wars, murders, what miseries and horrors would the human race have been spared by someone who, uprooting the stakes or filling in the ditch, had shouted to his fellow men; Beware of listening to this imposter; you are lost if you forget that the fruits belong to all and the earth to no one! But it is very likely that by then things had already come to the point where they could no longer remain where they were. For this idea of property . . . was not conceived all at once in the human mind. It was necessary to make much progress, to acquire much industry and enlightenment, and to transmit and augment them from age to age, before arriving at this last stage of the state of nature.[16]

Eutaxia, as the architectonic concept of civil society, has done its work in the production of Hobbes's artificial man and Rousseau's the body politic. *Eutaxia* marks off the civilized from the primitive, the simple from the advanced, leaving behind in its wake the noble savage, with Rousseau's natural man and his natural goodness falling prey to the demonic moral and political forces of civil society.

> Let us therefore take care not to confuse savage man with the men we have before our eyes. Nature treats all the animals abandoned to its care with a partiality that seems to show how jealous it is of this right. The horse, the cat, the bull, even the ass, are mostly taller, and all have a more robust constitution, more vigor, more strength and courage in the forest than in our houses.[17]

Under *eutaxia*'s domesticating force, what results are sterility, alienation, slavery, and social death not only of the Other but also the rationally ordered body politic. Rousseau's dialectics of the Other and *eutaxia* is a tragic genealogy: "In becoming sociable and a slave," natural man "becomes weak, fearful, servile; and his soft and effeminate way of life completes the enervation of both his strength and his courage."[18]

Rousseau's language is fateful. Civil society, the rationally ordered body politic, is the work of the calculating and strategic reason. Here, legislative reason governs the conduct, actions, and responsibilities of the citizen. In civil society, the "natural goodness" and "natural justice" of prepolitical humanity are vacated; law fills the void. Having constituted itself by political and legislative reason, civil society cannot return to these premoral conditions of "natural humanity." To do so would mean the slow dying of the body politic. Rousseau's discourse is a critical reminder of what Montesquieu says of slavery:

> Slavery, properly so called, is the establishment of a right which gives to one man such a power over another as renders him absolute master of his life and fortune. The state of slavery is in its nature bad. It is neither useful to the master nor to the slave; not to the slave, because he can do nothing through a motive of virtue; nor to the master, because by having an unlimited authority over his slave, he increasingly accustoms himself to the want of all moral virtue, and thence becomes fierce, hasty, severe, choleric, voluptuous, and cruel.[19]

Rousseau's *Discourse on the Origin of Inequality* maintains that *eutaxia* fulfills itself in the enduring cultural significance of power and domesticity that circulates between natural humanity and civil society, and between the primitive and civilized.

Notes

1. Jean-Jacques Rousseau, *The First and Second Discourses*, ed. Roger D. Masters, trans. Roger D. and Judith R. Masters (New York: St. Martin's Press, 1964).
2. Ibid., 106.
3. Ibid., 109–10.
4. Maurizio Viroli, *Jean-Jacques Rousseau and the "Well-Ordered Society,"* trans. Derek Hanson (New York: Cambridge University Press, 1988), 54.
5. Ibid., 55.
6. Rousseau, *First and Second Discourses*, 54.
7. Viroli, *Jean-Jacques Rousseau*, 53, quoting Jean-Jacques Rousseau, *Julie, ou, La Nouvelle Héloïse*, in *Oeuvres completes* [*OC*], ed. Marcel Raymond et al., 5 vols. (Paris: Gallimard, Bibliothèque de la Pléiade, 1959–95), 2:563.
8. Where directly quoting or referring to Rousseau's talk of "natural man," I will use his terms; my own interpretations will use "natural humanity."
9. Rousseau, *First and Second Discourses*, 56.
10. Jean-Jacques Rousseau, *Of the Social Contract, or, Principles of Political Right; and Discourse on Political Economy*, trans. Charles M. Sherover (New York: Harper & Row, 1984), *The Social Contract*, Book One, VI, §46 (p. 15).
11. Ibid., VI, §40 (p. 14).
12. Ibid., VI, §45 (p. 15).
13. Book Three, XI, §260 (pp. 84–85).
14. Ibid., XI, §261 (p. 85).
15. Nicholas Dent, *Rousseau* (New York: Routledge, 2005), 41.
16. Rousseau, *First and Second Discourses*, 141–42.
17. Ibid., 111.
18. Ibid.
19. Baron de Montesquieu, *The Spirit of the Laws*, trans. Thomas Nugent (New York: Hafner Press, 1949), 235.

8

Immanuel Kant
on Categorical Imperative

JAMES SAMUEL LOGAN

Ever since the Enlightenment, race theory and its inevitable partner, racism, have followed a crooked road, constructed by dominant peoples to justify their domination of others.

—Nell Irvin Painter[1]

The great force of history comes from the fact that we carry it within us, are unconsciously controlled by it in many ways, and history is literally present in all that we do. It could scarcely be otherwise, since it is to history that we owe our frames of reference, our identities, and our aspirations.

—James Baldwin[2]

KANT'S BIOGRAPHICAL NARRATIVE: A BRIEF SKETCH

There is little doubt that if one were to make an inquiry into which modern philosopher most clearly articulates the Enlightenment project that reason is the vehicle for humanity's progress toward liberation from unjust authorities, it is the Prussian-born Immanuel Kant (1724–1804). Kant was born the sixth of nine children to Johann Georg Kant and Anna Regina Reuter, in the Baltic city of Königsberg, East Prussia, on April 22, 1724. At this time Königsberg was a rather isolated outpost of German culture. Kant's parents belonged to a Protestant Pietist sect that "rejected the emphasis on theological dogma, formal ceremonies, and ritual observances that were salient attributes of orthodox Lutheranism of the eighteenth century." Within this formative religious setting, Kant developed a personality described by the poet Heinrich Heine (1797–1856), a great admirer of Kant, as "obsessive-compulsive."[3] Heine notes, moreover, that Kant had a "pretty boring" life and "history" of rigid regimentation:

> The history of his life would be hard to write, since Kant had neither life nor history. Rising from bed, coffee-drinking,[4] writing, lecturing, eating, walking, everything had its fixed time; and the neighbors knew that it must be half past four when they saw professor Kant in his gray coat with his cane in his hand step out of his house door. . . . [There was a] strange contrast between the outer life of the man and his world-destroying thoughts.[5]

The social context that shaped Kant's personality and character, and that would service the "world-destroying thoughts" he would later produce, included the significant influence of his father, Johann Georg Kant. Johann was a harness maker of Scottish descent; he was rigidly honest and hardworking. He was also "deeply intolerant of lies." Kant evidently internalized this intolerance to the point of later developing and maintaining an unyielding argument (in his 1797 essay "On a Supposed Right to Lie out of Altruistic Motives") denying the existence of such a right even to save the life of a friend.

Although Kant's aversion to the Protestant Pietism of his parents and school-teachers was internalized in his maturity, substantial expressions of doctrinal Christian Pietism are, nonetheless, apparent in his personal life, moral philosophy, and philosophy of religion.[6] With regard to Kant's personal life as the oldest son of five surviving children, his adherence to obligations set forth by the footprints of Pietism was evident:

> His relation to his siblings was not especially close—they had little in common, and Kant rarely communicated with them. But Kant, not surprisingly, had a keen sense of family obligation. He did not fail to assist them and their children financially when it became possible for him, "as our parents have taught us," he wrote to his brother. Three sisters, evidently illiterate (they signed their names with an X), supported themselves as servants until their marriage to craftsmen: Maria Elisabeth to a shoemaker, Anna Luise to a toolmaker, and Katharina Barbara to a wigmaker. Kant's brother Johann Heinrich attended the university and became a school-master and country pastor. Though not educated—in later years, he adorned his letters to his famous older brother with fragments of Latin proverbs—Johann Heinrich must have disappointed Kant when he referred to the latter's great work [*Critique of Pure Reason*] as, "your Critique of Purified Reason" (*gereinigten Vernunft*). Kant left substantial legacies to Johann Heinrich's children as well as to his other nephews and nieces.[7]

This abbreviated biographical sketch of Kant's life cannot do justice to the complex factors that gave the modern Western world (arguably) the chief luminary of the German Enlightenment. Yet this writer suggests that any consideration of Kant's "Categorical Imperative" cannot simply ignore the life influences that gave us the mature Kant and his "world-destroying" philosophy.

It matters that Kant was a small man in stature who, according to John T. Goldthwait, was "stooped and stunted by deformity from birth." It matters that Kant remained a lifelong bachelor, with no discernable record of having had a love affair. Goldthwait goes on to observe in summary regarding Kant's personal and professional narrative:

> He shuns any intimacy with women, he does not see even his own sister from year's end to year's end. He lives in a house purchased with the savings scrimped together through many years of austere living. He is unemotional; he indulges in no vices nor luxuries. Having been brought up in strict piety, he has not the capacity for the trivial pleasures of the fancy or the imagination. He is known for punctuality in his regimen, serving neighboring housewives as a timepiece with his regular departures for his lecture hall or his constitutional walk. He is the most eminent figure in the University of Königsberg. He has achieved renown throughout Germany. . . . He is a great intellect, the first man to elucidate a Categorical Imperative from the dictates of reason; and he is a stern moralist who can achieve the rare self-discipline necessary to live up to its unrelenting obligation. In a word, we have the picture of what the Germans call *Verstandesmensch*, a man who lives rigidly according to reason.[8]

Indeed, a rendering of Kant's biographic history offers critical context for understanding his idea that reason is the foundation and guarantor of the Categorical Imperative, "the very apex of Critical Philosophy, which commands the individual to act only according to a policy that could be the basis for action by every human being."[9] There is, in fact, an internalized ticking narrative that shapes every human being's presence in the world—for better, for worse, and all points in between. To be sure, the great Black American writer James Baldwin was right when he said, "You drag your past around with you everywhere, or it drags you."[10]

KANT'S CATEGORICAL IMPERATIVE

In 1785 Kant published his first contribution to moral philosophy, *Groundwork of the Metaphysic of Morals*. The text is primarily a work of metaethics, focused on an articulation of an a priori supreme principle of morality: the Categorical Imperative. Undergirding the Categorical Imperative is the proposition that standards for moral action cannot be derived from any experience-dependent (or a posteriori) investigation of human behavior. Indeed, Kant contends that a morality based on assessments of human experiences or a consideration of consequences is really descriptive anthropology or psychology. In social contexts that compel us to think and act according to a supreme and universal moral standard, a limitation of the social sciences is that they can only tell us how humans *do* behave but not how they *ought* to conduct their lives. Moreover, Kant contends that a standard for a supreme principle of morality cannot be derived from an analysis of human nature, for people are capable of morality not because they are human, but because they are rational beings. In order for a principle of morality to be supreme, it must be applicable to all rational beings and therefore must rest on the one thing that these beings have in common: reason. So, for example, maxims like one should never lie, steal, break a promise, or fail to extend charity are based in reason: such maxims function as universal laws, governing not only my individual actions, but the actions of all rational others.

In Kant's view, it is human goodwill that provides the power motivating humans to act, not by impulse or feelings or emotions, but by reason. The essence of reason for Kant is consistency, and the test of consistency is universal validity. For a moral action to be rational, it must be motivated by an a priori principle of conduct (a principle prior to experience). The principal (or law) of universal validity is a standard that rational beings impose on themselves. And the proper function of reason is to produce a will that is good in itself, and free of anything external to itself. Citing his own language with regard to the critical "autonomy of the will" tied to his concept of freedom, Kant defines the will "as a kind of causality belonging to living beings so far as they are rational. Freedom would then be the property this causality has of being able to work independently of determination by alien causes." Indeed, freedom of will can be nothing other than autonomous, that is, free: "the property which will has of being a law to itself." Driving this point home in the construction of the Categorical Imperative, Kant argues that

> the proposition "Will is in all its actions a law to itself" expresses, however, only the principle of acting on no maxim other than one which can have for its object itself as at the same time universal law. This is precisely the formula of the categorical imperative and the principle of morality. Thus a free will and a will under moral laws are one and the same.[11]

On Kant's account, the only thing in the world, or outside of it, that can be taken as "good without qualification," or as a self-contained good in itself, is *a good will*. All moral concepts, then, correspond to an autonomous/free good will, which has its "seat and origin" in reason completely a priori. In Kant's point of view, the most ordinary human reason as well as the most speculative "cannot be abstracted from any empirical, and therefore merely contingent, knowledge."[12]

In light of the above-mentioned considerations of the Categorical Imperative, three significant propositional summaries arise: (1) For an action to have moral worth, it must be done from duty; (2) An action done from duty does not find its moral worth in the consequences to be achieved through it, but by the maxim by which it is determined (the test of universal applicability); and (3) Duty is the necessity of an action done from respect for the (practical) law. With these basic propositions in mind, rational beings have an obligation to treat themselves and others with dignity and respect, as ends rather than as means to an end.

THE CATEGORICAL IMPERATIVE WITH RESPECT TO KANT'S "SCIENTIFIC" THEORY OF RACE

This fellow was quite black, . . . a clear proof that what he said was stupid.

—Immanuel Kant[13]

I now turn to an evaluation of the liberative usefulness, the *freedom-inspired utility*, if you will, of Kant's formulation of the Categorical Imperative for darker-hued peoples of the world, who from ancient times to the contemporary present have needed to consider their routinely blood-soaked freedom from the subaltern,[14] "underside of history." If one were to examine the universality claim of the Categorical Imperative in relation to Kant's "scientific" development of human racial hierarchies, serious difficulties emerge, especially if you happen to be a member of the social-cultural invention called the Black race. First, one must wonder about the degree to which, if at all, persons of Black (African or Negro) stock (or others Kant identifies as the "savage" peoples of the world) are capable of functioning rationally, as required by the Categorical Imperative. Second and perhaps equally as important, one ought to wonder if any human being should embrace the Categorical Imperative for moral insight and direction.

In 1788 Kant published an essay titled "On the Use of Teleological Principles in Philosophy." This essay claims that Negroes and Indian peoples (dispersed northward out of Africa and Asia, respectively) are naturally predisposed to lack "an immediate drive for activity." Put another way, they were deficient in "the drive for persevering, which we call industry," and therefore lacked the mental capacities to be usefully settled peoples in northern climates.[15]

By the time Kant was expressing such views, he had already given more than a decade to a disciplined and systematic construction of racial theory. The philosopher Emmanuel Chukwudi Eze has correctly noted that Kant "sought to establish an inherent human rational capacity responsible for historical progress from the 'primitive' to the 'civilized,' partly by classifying mankind [*sic*] into various races on the basis of skin color."[16] Kant distinguishes among four fundamental races: Whites, Blacks (Negroes), Hun (Mongol or Kalmuck), and Hindu or Hindustani.[17] He proceeds to divide humans according to specific "natural dispositions," which fit members of each race to their (geo-physical) location in the world. For example, "blackness"; "a thick, turned up nose and thick, fatty lips"; "the evaporation of the phosphoric acid (which explains why all Negroes stink)"; "oily skin, which weakens the nourishing mucus necessary for the growth of hair"; physical strength, fleshiness, and agility; and a propensity for being "lazy, indolent, and dawdling"; all stem from "well-suited" climate adjustments toward the environment in which the Negro originated: a climate of humid heat and warmth, foul humid air, and a "so amply supplied" motherland.[18]

Although natural dispositions vary among races, they all derived from an original and ideal "stem genus," according to Kant. Moreover, Kant contends that the original stem genus was a race of "white brunette" people, who must have evolved "between the 31st and 52nd parallels in the Old World." As it "happens," this race of White brunette people were best approximated by the "'white' inhabitants of Europe ('very blond, soft white-skinned, red-haired, pale blue eyes'), particularly in 'the northern regions of Germany.'"[19] In contrast to privileged groups of White European peoples (Italians, Germans, English, and Spanish), the racial inhabitants of Africa (even when geographically dispersed), North America, and the Orient were counted among the world's savages with respect to a capacity to comprehend the morally beautiful. For example, with reference to certain

> "Canadian savages" of the "New World," Kant contends that all these have little feeling for the beautiful in moral understanding, and the generous forgiveness of an injury, which is at once noble and beautiful, is completely unknown as a virtue among the savages, but rather is disdained as miserable cowardice. Valor is the greatest merit of the savage and revenge his sweetest bliss. The remaining natives of this part of the world show few traces of a mental character disposed to the finer feelings, and an extraordinary apathy constitutes the mark of this type of race.[20]

With regard to the capacities of "the Negroes of Africa" to comprehend the morally beautiful, Kant insists that, by nature, they have "no feeling that rises above the trifling." Citing and drawing favorably upon the philosopher David Hume (1711–76), Kant "challenges anyone to cite a single example in which a Negro has shown talents." In the context of "New World" slavery, he goes on to cite Hume's sentiment "that among the hundreds of thousands of blacks who are transported elsewhere from their countries, although many of them have been set free, still not a single one was ever found who presented anything great in art or science or any other praiseworthy quality, even though among the Whites some continually rise aloft from the lowest rabble, and through superior gifts earn respect in the world."[21] Kant also finds "the blacks" to be "very vain" and "so talkative that they must be driven apart from each other with thrashings."[22] Of the treatment of women "in the land of blacks," Kant finds it a prevailing reality that the feminine sex lives in the "deepest slavery."[23]

Today large numbers of historians, postcolonial scholars, critical race theorists, and others have identified and corrected many of the unfortunate and powerful inaccuracies forwarded as racial Truth by Kant. His construction of a (geonatural) scientific theory of race has been particularly unfortunate in the service of undergirding the long history of European military, missionary, and cultural conquest expressed in imperialism and colonialism. Kant was largely unconcerned with such realities during the formation of his Categorical Imperative and race theory. And he lived as a privileged beneficiary of his European geocultural location and racial stock.

While most scholars and students today focus on Kant's Critical Philosophy, attention to natural science (physical geography and biology) and social science (anthropology) were not tangential to his life's work. Eze reminds us that already in 1756 Kant was the first to introduce geography into the curriculum of study at the University of Königsberg. Later, in the winter of 1772–73, Kant began teaching anthropology at Königsberg. According to Eze, "it was the first such program of study in any German university."[24] Eze points out that

> quite often, teachers and students of the history of modern science and the history of modern philosophy pay little or no attention to the enormous amount of research and writing undertaken and accomplished by the philosophical luminaries of the eighteenth century, the Age of Reason. For example, in nearly all standard programs of study of Immanuel Kant, rarely is it noted that Kant devoted the largest period of his career to research in, and teaching of, anthropology and geography.[25]

In his career Kant offered more courses in anthropology and geography (72) than in subjects for which he is more noted: logic (54), metaphysics (28), moral philosophy (20), and theoretical physics (20). Eze goes on to argue that since "questions of race and of the biological, geographical, and cultural distribution of humans on earth occupied a central place in both Kant's science of geography and anthropology, it can hardly be said that his interest in the 'race problem' was marginal to other aspects of his career."[26] So it cannot be taken lightly when Kant insists that "humanity is at its greatest perfection in the race of whites. The yellow Indians do have a meager talent. The Negroes are far below them and at the lowest point are a part of the American peoples."[27] So too we should take seriously Kant's profoundly misguided and deleterious judgment that "the inhabitant of the temperate parts of the world, above all the central part, has a more beautiful body, works harder, is more jocular, more controlled in his passions, more intelligent than any other race of people in the world. That is why at all points in time these peoples have educated the others and controlled them with weapons."[28]

We should be appalled by Kant's presumption that nature's wisdom not only discourages racial migrations across the globe by rendering races ill equipped to exchange one climate for another, "especially the exchange of a warm climate for a cold one,"[29] but also his serious questioning of the natural capacities of non-White races for moral agency and reasoned intellect. One also cringes at Kant's support of Black enslavement and his related view that Black people will never be good laborers unless they are coerced into activity.[30] With regard to Native Americans, who vie with Black people for the lowest rungs of humanity, the philosopher Pauline Kleingeld has correctly summarized Kant's 1788 view that "native Americans . . . are a race (or rather, a semirace) stunted in its development because their ancestors migrated to a different climate before they had fully adapted to their earlier environments. As a result, they are weak, inert, 'incapable of any culture'; and they occupy the lowest level of racial hierarchy that Kant claims to have determined."[31]

In her provocative essay "Kant's Second Thoughts on Race," Kleingeld has been one of too few commentators willing to acknowledge and shed light upon the terrible inconsistencies between Kant's formulations of the Categorical Imperative and his hierarchical race theory:

> The racial hierarchy, defended with biased reading of travel reports and teleological race theory, goes against the presumption of human equality which one would expect from someone with a universalistic moral theory. After all, the basic moral principle which Kant formulates during the 1780s, the Categorical Imperative in its several versions, is, at least in its wording, addressed to all humans (or, even more broadly, to all rational finite beings). Although Kant's own *definition* of race as such is formulated merely in terms of heritable differences in physical appearance, he nevertheless connects his understanding of race with a hierarchical account according to which the races *also* vary greatly in their capacity for agency and their powers of intellect. This was despite the fact that there were well-known and esteemed authors who provided much evidence to the contrary in works that Kant himself had reviewed and commented on. Moreover, Kant's race theory and its implications for global migration cast his cosmopolitanism in a disconcerting light—at least his cosmopolitanism of the 1780s.[32]

Indeed, the great philosopher who believed that Negroes could be "disciplined and cultivated but never genuinely civilized" and who could hardly believe that women (the "fairer sex") were capable of principles, expressed prejudices that seriously undermined the alleged egalitarian and universal impulses of the Categorical Imperative.[33]

While acknowledging the very serious contradictions between Kant's Categorical Imperative and his construction and defense of racial hierarchy, some scholars today contend, as does Kleingeld, that "Kant radically revised his views on race during the 1790s." Defending the post-1780s Kant in her provocative "Second Thoughts" essay, Kleingeld argues that

> he makes no mention of a racial hierarchy anywhere in his published writing of the 1790s, however, and what he does say about related issues contradicts his earlier views on a racial hierarchy and a plan of Nature designed to restrict human migration (after an initial dispersal across the globe). . . . In *Toward Perpetual Peace* [1795] and the *Metaphysics of Morals* [1797], Kant clearly departs from his earlier position in a number of ways. First of all, he becomes more egalitarian with regard to race. He now grants a full juridical status to non-whites, a status irreconcilable with his earlier defence of slavery. For example, his concept of cosmopolitan right, as introduced in *Toward Perpetual Peace* (8:358), explicitly prohibits the colonial conquest of foreign lands.[34]

Kleingeld goes on defending Kant, arguing that

> in his notes for *Toward Perpetual Peace* (1794–5), Kant repeatedly and explicitly criticizes slavery of non-Europeans in the strongest terms, as grave violations of cosmopolitan right (23:173–4). He formulates a scath-

ing critique of the conduct of European powers elsewhere in the world. He sharply criticizes "the civilized countries bordering the seas," whom he accuses of recognizing no normative constraints in their behavior towards people on other continents and of regarding the "possessions and even the person of the stranger as a loot given to them by Nature." Kant censures the slave trade (the "trade in Negroes"), not as an excessive form of an otherwise acceptable institution, but as in itself a "violation" of the cosmopolitan right of blacks (23:174). Similarly, he criticizes the fact that the inhabitants of the Americas were treated as objects belonging to no one, and "were displaced or enslaved" soon after Europeans reached the continent (23:173–4).[35]

Kleingeld wants today's readers to know that in Kant's 1790s exposition of cosmopolitan right, which is inspired by the social-contractual envisioning of the French Revolution (1789–99), Africans, Native Americans, and Asians can now govern themselves and sign contracts with foreign powers for access to their lands and resources. This is a sure sign, on Kleingeld's view, of Kant's newfound egalitarianism. But one must wonder if this newfound egalitarianism would have extended to the idea of Europeans signing contracts with Africans, Native Americans, and Asians for access to the lands of Europe. In any case, as the decade of the 1790s was winding to a close, perhaps it is important to note that Kant's *Anthropology from a Pragmatic Point of View* (1798) offered no significant discussion of the allegedly different characteristics of the races, except for very brief comments related to the assimilation of people of the same race ("for example, the white race").[36]

In all this, Kleingeld hopes that today's readers of Kant will come to the view that "Kant gave up the hierarchical view of races in the context of his elaboration of his political theory and theory of right."[37] The Kant whose Categorical Imperative was troubled by an *inconsistent universalism*, in Kleingeld's view, had during the 1790s transformed into a *consistent universalism* with regard to race, although not on the problem of sex/gender. My own reading of Kant's work in the decade before his death in 1804 leaves me wondering if he was simply calling for a revision of how the "civilized" powers of the world ought to more humanely treat the *still* lesser races of the world—the still (relative to Whites) ignorant and uncivilized peoples. But even assuming (for the sake of argument) that Kleingeld (and those who agree with her concerning Kant's conversion) are right, I nonetheless suggest that oppressed peoples ought to still seriously question the validity and soundness of the Categorical Imperative for subaltern survival, justice seeking, and flourishing. Can subaltern peoples really submit to a moral philosophy that dogmatically and absolutely refuses continuous reconfiguration in view of the severity of systemic brutality? All subaltern peoples of the world might do well to refuse the intellectual and moral dictates of the Categorical Imperative as formulated by Kant.

Any notion of moral reason that believes humans can ultimately consider and practice morality outside of (conscious or unconscious) teleological, consequence-based considerations fails to understand the inescapable influences of every human being's bone-deep historicity. In this regard Kant was no different from any other human who has ever walked the earth. His social location, his family, his physical limitations, his faith, his community and nation, his language and customs, and yes his race—all contributed to his construction of the Categorical Imperative. Moreover, at the level of thought or ideas, Kant's moral philosophy must be critiqued and disenchanted. This is because any claim about the existence, in rational beings, of a *pure and good will* capable, a priori, of complete separation from considerations that calculate effects, consequences, aims, purposes, or goals is a highly dubious proposition. Indeed, it must be recognized that Kant, who in his humanity profoundly understood the limits of reason, came to the a priori-ness of the Categorical Imperative a posteriori—subsequent to, and in the context of, inescapable empirical experience in the world. Even a pure and good will cannot escape this fact, for even to conceive of the a priori, one must dwell in the world of experience. These realities compel me to confirm that Kant's fervent claim is false that "a categorical imperative excludes interest" and that (on account of reason) it is possible for humans to simply say "I ought to do this" without necessary ties to anything humans happen to want.[38]

So, unless today's advocates of the Categorical Imperative understand their moral viewpoint as but one of many varied and conditioned social constructions in the service of better human associations in time and space, all current subaltern peoples of the world—west, east, south, north—would do well to refuse its dictates. If, on the other hand, today's followers of the Categorical Imperative understand it as one narrative of morality among many, then that is acceptable. If commitment to the Categorical Imperative expresses itself in "unconditioned" principles of justice and truth that denounce corruption, defend the weak, and defy oppressive authorities—wonderful. Maybe then it would not matter so much if people give their faith and fidelity over to a Categorical Imperative theology that worships freedom as a capacity of a causality called *the pure and good will*. After all, such a claim may not be all that different from the proposition "There is a God." Both are postulates of practical reason; both are beliefs that are accepted; but neither can be considered items of "knowledge" under a strict (empirical) sense of the term.

Freedom of the will on *Kant's* terms, like the Hebrew and Christian meaning of Kant's first name, Immanuel ("God [is] with us"), is ultimately a matter of faith and not rational certainty. This is so because reason cannot secure the complete end(s) it desires with regard to either knowledge of God or metaphysics.[39] Given this reality, the ultimate moral question for subaltern peoples of the world *ought* to be one of "moral philosophy of faith—indeed, the Categorical Imperative—*in the service of what?*" Sometimes otherwise normative moral rules and conduct that hold human associations together in unity, trust, and peace will need to be selectively and carefully circumvented in order to resist and confront hegemonic orthodoxies, dogmas, and actions. To be sure, sometimes "cheating," "stealing," and "lying" in the name of freedom from the most horrific and grotesque episodes of individual and collective human history will be a categorical imperative for subaltern peoples (and their allies)—and this in the service of what is right, good, and fitting.

Notes

1. Nell Irvin Painter, *The History of White People* (New York: W. W. Norton, 2010).
2. James Baldwin, "The White Man's Guilt," in *Ebony* 20, no. 29 (August 1965); repr. in his *The Price of the Ticket: Collected Nonfiction, 1948–1985* (New York: St. Martins Press, 1985), 409–14.
3. Immanuel Kant, *Groundwork of the Metaphysics of Morals*, trans. Thomas E. Hill and Arnulf Zweig (New York: Oxford University Press, 2002), 8.
4. Thomas E. Hill Jr. and Arnulf Zweig, translators of this edition of *Groundwork*, find Henie to have been inaccurate on this point and contend, "Kant was a tea drinker."
5. Ibid., 8.
6. Ibid., 9.
7. Ibid.
8. Immanuel Kant, *Observations of the Feeling of the Beautiful and Sublime* (Berkeley: University of California Press, 2003), 2–3.
9. Ibid., 4.
10. Baldwin, *Price of the Ticket*, 641.
11. Immanuel Kant, *Groundwork of the Metaphysic of Morals*, trans. H. J. Paton (New York: Harper & Row, 1964), 114, 70.
12. Ibid., 79.
13. Kant, *Observations*, 113.
14. In contemporary postcolonial and various other "critical" disciplines, the term "subaltern" is vigorously debated and contested. The term is grounded in the work of the Italian Marxist Antonio Gramsci (1881–1937). "Subaltern" has come to denote any person or group of inferior rank and station, whether because of race, ethnicity, sex/gender, sexual orientation, class, national origin, physical and/or mental difficulties, religion, or combinations of these. Subaltern persons routinely find themselves outside hegemonic social, political, economic, cultural, and geographic power structures, yet the "subaltern position" is one from which to subvert the authorities holding hegemonic power. Subaltern peoples are quite heterogeneous and diverse in the midst of their (often) overlapping struggles for survival, justice, and well-being against the hegemonies of ruling authorities and classes.
15. Immanuel Kant, *Toward Perpetual Peace and Other Writings on Politics, Race, and History* (New Haven: Yale University Press, 2006), 47, 54–55; Pauline Kleingeld, "Kant's Second Thoughts on Race," *Philosophical Quarterly* 57, no. 229 (October 2007): 573.
16. Immanuel Kant, "On the Different Races of Man," in *Race and the Enlightenment: A Reader*, ed. Emmanuel Chukwudi Eze (Cambridge, MA: Blackwell Publishing, 1997), 65.
17. Ibid., 15. This delineation of the races from the first rendering in English of the 1777 version of Immanuel's "Of the Different Human Races" signals the importance of race to Immanuel's overall Enlightenment project. As the philosophers Robert Bernasconi and Tommy Lott have correctly observed in their text *The Idea of Race*, "'Of the Different Human Races' is widely recognized as the first attempt to give a scientific definition of race based on a clear distinction between race and species." Robert Bernasconi and Tommy Lott, *The Idea of Race* (Indianapolis: Hackett Publishing Co., 2000), 8.

18. Kant, "Different Human Races," 17.
19. Translated from Kant's original 1775 version of "Different Races of Man," in Eze, *Race and the Enlightenment*, 38, 43, and 47–48.
20. Kant, *Observations*, 111–12.
21. Ibid., 110–11.
22. Ibid., 111.
23. Ibid., 113.
24. Emmanuel Chukwudi Eze, ed., "Introduction," in *Race and the Enlightenment*, 2.
25. Ibid.
26. Ibid.
27. Immanuel Kant, "Physical Geography," in Eze, *Race and the Enlightenment*, 63.
28. Ibid., 64.
29. Kant, *Toward Perpetual Peace*, 47.
30. Ibid., 54–55.
31. Kleingeld, "Kant's Second Thoughts," 574; cf. Kant, *Toward Perpetual Peace*, 48.
32. Kleingeld, "Kant's Second Thoughts," 574–75.
33. Ibid., 582.
34. Ibid., 586.
35. Ibid., 587.
36. Immanuel Kant, *Anthropology from a Pragmatic Point of View*, ed. by Günter Zöller and Robert B. Louden, trans. by Mary Gregor et al. (New York: Cambridge University Press, 2007), 23–24.
37. Kleingeld, "Kant's Second Thoughts," 592.
38. Kant, *Groundwork*, ed. by H. J. Patton, 35.
39. Cf. Kant, *Toward Perpetual Peace*, 57.

9

John Stuart Mill
on Utilitarianism

ILSUP AHN

John Stuart Mill was one of the most outstanding British intellectuals of the nineteenth century. He was born in London on May 20, 1806, as the eldest son of a Scotsman, James Mill, and an English woman, Harriet Burrow. From his early years, Mill was deeply influenced by utilitarian philosophy. His father was a disciple of Jeremy Bentham (1748–1832), founder of the modern utilitarian tradition, and James Mill educated his son according to Benthamite principles. By the time of his death in 1873, John Stuart Mill had made significant contributions to economic, political, and philosophical thought. Mill's public life was deeply interconnected with the high tide of British imperialism. From the age of seventeen, and following his father, he worked for thirty-five years for the East India Company, which was then a symbol of British imperialism. He eventually reached one of the highest positions in the company's London office, where he remained until 1858, when the East India Company was taken over by the British government, following the Indian Mutiny.[1]

Although Mill was a lifelong supporter of women's rights (*The Subjection of Women* [1869]) as well as of liberal ideals (*On Liberty* [1859]), he also defended British imperialism.[2] The controversy around his views on and involvement in

81

British imperialism is one of the most contentious in recent years among scholars studying Mill. In this essay, I will focus on the possible connection between his utilitarian philosophy and his defense of British imperialism. Even though a significant amount of research has been conducted with regard to Mill's attitudes toward imperialism, a critical examination of the possible link between his utilitarianism and his liberal imperialism has not been sufficiently done. As a result of this investigation, I argue that although his utilitarianism was not a driving force of the Eurocentric (particularly British) imperialism of the nineteenth century, it played an important role in morally justifying not only British imperialism but also the contemporary global order dominated by Western colonialism. Liberal as he was, the only thing Mill could do with his liberalism was to argue against the abusive administration of imperialistic governance, but not against imperialism as such. In this sense, following Stephen Holmes, I label his stance on imperialism as "liberal imperialism" or "benign colonialism."[3]

MILL'S UTILITARIANISM

In his book *Utilitarianism*, Mill epitomizes the essence of his utilitarian perspective as follows: "The creed which accepts as the foundation of morals, Utility, or the Greatest Happiness Principle, holds that actions are right in proportion as they tend to promote happiness, wrong as they tend to produce the reverse of happiness."[4] How does he, then, define happiness? In short, happiness, according to Mill, is "intended pleasure, and the absence of pain."[5] Mill also adds that this "theory of morality" is grounded in the "theory of life": "that pleasure, and freedom from pain, are the only things desirable as ends; and that all desirable things (which are as numerous in the utilitarian as in any other scheme) are desirable either for the pleasure inherent in themselves, or as means to the promotion of pleasure and the prevention of pain."[6] If we follow Mill's dictum, a happy life is not only desirable but also morally right.

Does Mill, therefore, imagine a possible situation in which what is desired and what is morally right are at odds? He seems to be aware of this potential issue, although he does not specifically address it as such. Referring to the potential issue indirectly, Mill suggests first that desire should be distinguished from will. He wants to distinguish the naked desire from the habituated desire shaped in the form of will. Mill begins his deliberation by raising a question: "How can the will to be virtuous, where it does not exist in sufficient force, be implanted or awakened?"[7] Mill answers the question by saying that we can implant the will by habituating desire in the form of will in accordance with the principle of utility. He writes, "Only by making the person desire virtue—by making him think of it in a pleasurable light, or of its absence in a painful one. It is by associating the doing right with pleasure, or the doing wrong with pain."[8] For Mill, then, "will is the child of desire, and passes out of the dominion of its parent only to come under that of habit."[9] Therefore, if we successfully habituate the desire in the form of will according to the principle of utility, what is desired becomes what is morally right.

Mill's conception of the good, which resides in the states of pleasure or happiness, needs to be further analyzed because he differentiates his conception from Bentham's narrow and misconceived notion of the quantitative good. Unlike Bentham, Mill recognizes two basic types in characterizing pleasure: "quantity" and "quality." Pleasures and pains, then, have qualitative differences as well as quantitative differences. Mill holds that the principle of utility is compatible with the fact "that some *kinds* of pleasure are more desirable and more valuable than others."[10] By introducing the concept of qualitative differences among pleasures and pains, Mill effectively responds to the objection that utilitarianism is a doctrine worthy only of swine. Mill's utilitarianism thus presupposes that there is a superiority of the mental aspect over the corporal aspect. "It must be admitted, however, that utilitarian writers in general have placed the superiority of mental over bodily pleasures chiefly in the greater permanency, safety, uncostliness."[11] Between the higher and lower pleasures, Mill holds, the higher pleasure always has an intrinsic superiority.[12]

Although Mill's complex mapping of pleasures according to their quantitative and qualitative differences overcomes Bentham's narrow quantitative hedonism, Mill's utilitarianism becomes vulnerable to more complex and intricate criticism. Since this essay focuses on the critical link between Mill's utilitarianism and his attitudes toward imperialism, I directly address the critical problem embedded in Mill's utilitarianism. Emphasizing his qualitative hedonism as a way to differentiate from Bentham's quantitative hedonism, Mill epitomizes the moral implication of his utilitarian principle: "It is better to be a human being dissatisfied than a pig satisfied; better to be Socrates dissatisfied than a fool satisfied."[13] Simple as it may seem, this statement, in fact, is not simplistic at all. In interpreting Mill's statement, most readers, including many critics, recognize that it merely points out the key thesis that when it comes to the comparison between quantitative and qualitative pleasures, the latter always prevail. Jonathan Riley thus writes, "The higher pleasure's infinite superiority means that it is more valuable in terms of pleasure than any finite amount of the lower pleasure. Its superiority over the lower pleasure is unlimited, in other words, because it continues to be more valuable no matter how large the finite mass of lower pleasure is assumed to become."[14] In my perspective, however, Mill's statement reflects much more serious moral implications, providing us with a crucial clue as to how his utilitarianism is linked to his liberal imperialism.

First, we ought to see that Mill's seemingly simple statement, in fact, manifests two different sets of moral evaluation. In order to see this distinction, we must decode the encoded meaning of the word "better," which Mill seems to employ so innocently, apparently unaware of its potentially explosive signification. The word "better" primarily appears to be used to assess the moral superiority of qualitative pleasure over quantitative pleasure, which he believes to be objective and universal. Mill, however, goes one step further by dovetailing this theoretical-objective evaluation with that of a practical-subjective evaluation in specifically comparing "Socrates" and a "fool." Since Socrates apparently enjoys qualitative pleasure, unlike a fool, who would just indulge in quantitative pleasure, Mill judges that Socrates is morally superior to a fool. The theoretical-objective moral superiority of qualitative good to quantitative good is diverted to the practical-subjective moral judgment in assessing the moral superiority of one individual (Socrates) over another (a fool). This moral reasoning, however, is highly questionable because in dovetailing the theoretical-objective moral valuation with the practical-subjective moral judgment, Mill commits a reductionist fallacy. The complex moral worth of an individual is largely reduced to the kind of pleasures that person enjoys. If we follow Mill's argument further, then, we would have to affirm that Socrates, a Greek philosopher and educator, is morally superior to Spartacus, a Roman slave and gladiator. Would Mill agree with this proposition that Socrates is morally superior to Spartacus?

If Mill were to disagree with this proposition, then he would have to face an even more serious problem because his disagreement would ultimately imply that Mill's utilitarianism lacks any moral criterion to judge the slave system as such. If a slave enjoys a quality of pleasure equal to that of a master, how could we judge that slavery is morally problematic? The slave system as such, therefore, would become a morally irrelevant issue in Mill's utilitarianism. Yet this is not what Mill argues. Mill's utilitarianism can only endorse the proposition that Socrates is morally superior to Spartacus. According to Mill, then, it is better for us to create a society in which Spartacus would live as a free citizen. For Mill, however, Socrates is still morally superior to Spartacus in that Socrates is believed to enjoy a higher level of qualitative pleasure than Spartacus ever could.

In the following section, I examine how Mill's moral evaluation of "better," which originates in the moral superiority of qualitative pleasure over quantitative pleasure, is applied on the societal plane in comparing one society with another, going beyond the individual level. For Mill, just as Socrates is "better" than a fool, a civilized society is "better" than a noncivilized society, which he calls a "backward" society. The civilized life of the advanced society, according to Mill, is morally superior to the noncivilized life of the society perceived to be backward.

MILL'S ATTITUDE TOWARD IMPERIALISM

What does Mill's utilitarianism have to do with his attitude toward European colonialism? In a nutshell, Mill's utilitarian value system provides a moral justification for his defense of European colonialism in international relations. Mill also supports the moral justification of European colonialism with his philosophy of history. According to Mill, world history is essentially a history of civilization's development.[15]

Capturing Mill's philosophy of history, Beate Jahn writes, "International or world history, the history of humankind, is basically a history of cultural—or, in

[Mill's] words, civilizational—development."[16] According to Jahn, Mill's philosophy of history contains the four broad stages of civilizational development:
"savagism, slavery, barbarism and civilization."[17] These four stages, however, can
be reduced to two stages: noncivilized and civilized nations. Among the civilized
nations, Mill places England at the top of the highest stage.[18] His philosophy of
history is grounded in an important perception that civilization is superior to all
lower stages of development, morally as well as politically. On this basis, therefore, "Mill provides a moral justification for the general ordering of international
affairs based on the rule of civilized over barbarian peoples."[19]

According to Mill, it is a truism that the civilized are morally superior to the
noncivilized in the same way that Socrates is morally superior to Spartacus. At the
bottom of his moral evaluation lies his fundamental utilitarian principle that the
moral worth of qualitative pleasures is superior to that of quantitative pleasures.
From Mill's perspective, then, the civilized are not only culturally "refined" but
also historically "advanced" and morally and politically "superior." The moral
hierarchism originating in the superiority of quality to quantity in pleasure can
be logically viewed on a global scale in the form of European colonialism above
those perceived to be noncivilized "savages" and "barbarians." It is thus crucial
for us to see that Mill's utilitarian value system is the moral backbone of his
benign colonialism. In this regard, Don Habibi writes:

> The driving force behind Mill's colonialism was his utilitarian value sys-
> tem. . . . He subscribed to a form of hedonism that distinguished higher
> forms of pleasure from inferior, lower, or simple pleasure on the basis of
> quality. Thus, for Mill, the ultimate good calls for maximizing the higher
> pleasures. For individuals, this involves self-improvement, development
> of potential, and the refinement of character. For groups, societies, and
> nations, this requires creating an environment conducive to development
> and progress.[20]

Regarding Mill's attitude toward European colonialism, we should not mis-
interpret that Mill uncritically endorsed any forms of colonialism. Although he
acknowledged the need for enforcement and restraint of the noncivilized people
by the civilized government, he opposed brutal and exploitative imperialism.
Mill clearly differentiates between a severe form of despotism and a benign form,
even though he argues that despotism can be legitimately incorporated as a mode
of government in dealing with "barbarians." In this context, Mill's enlightened
view of imperialism is best exemplified by the role he played as the chairman of
the Jamaica Committee, formed in 1866 to prosecute Governor Edward Eyre of
Jamaica for mass murder in suppressing the Morant Bay Rebellion of 1865. At
that time Jamaica was a British colony, and the mass killing was regarded as the
murder of British subjects. As J. Joseph Miller points out, Mill prosecuted Eyre
not simply because Eyre threatened a colonial system. To Mill, Eyre represented
a particular vision of colonialism, which was fundamentally at odds with Mill's
benign colonialism.[21]

Mill's benign colonialism is distinguished from the brutal and exploitative kind: he emphasized that colonial governance should aim at the "improvement" of the colonized. In *Considerations on Representative Government*, Mill elucidates the role and goal of his benign colonialism: "The step which they have to take, and their only path to improvement, is to be raised from a government of will to one of law. They have to be taught self-government, and this, in its initial stage, means the capacity to act on general instructions. What they require is not a government of force, but one of guidance."[22] Therefore we can see that Mill was highly critical of a government that only cares about its national interest. He thus writes, "But of all attitudes which a nation can take up on the subject of intervention, the meanest and worst is to profess that it interferes only when it can serve its own objects by it."[23] Indeed, Mill perceives that a brutal and exploitative form of despotism cannot fit with the higher moral standard of civilized nations. Ultimately for Mill, benign imperialism for the sake of collective civilization and the progress of colonial people was regarded as morally justifiable. He then applied this perspective to the British colonial relation with other colonies such as India.[24]

Even though Mill's view on European colonialism sounds paradoxically humane, his benign colonialism was actually nothing but a paternalistic proposal for European colonialists that allowed them to mistreat those they regarded as inferior to them. Without doubt, this paternalistic proposal was deeply problematic because it is fundamentally discriminatory in nature. Mill clearly divides the rules of the game according to the domains where "civilized" people "belong." "There is a great difference (for example) between the case in which the nations concerned are of the same, or something like the same, degree of civilization, and that in which one of the parties to the situation is of a high, and the other of a very low, grade of social improvement."[25] For Mill, then, the discrimination of people by the perceived degree of civilization is not only legitimate but also called for. Critical of Mill's discriminatory view, Jahn summarizes it as follows: "This denunciator of despotism in the domestic context considered despotism the ideal rule of a free people over a barbarous or semi-barbarous one."[26]

CONCLUSION

It is true that Mill's attitude toward European imperialism is discomforting and even offensive; nevertheless, we should not fail to give him due credit for his work on the issues of women's rights and the rights of the poor and minorities.[27] As mentioned above, Mill's support of imperialism was morally justified by his utilitarianism. In his book *Utilitarianism*, Mill specifically outlines his case: "Utilitarianism, therefore, could only attain its end by the general cultivation of nobleness of character, even if each individual were only benefited by the nobleness of others, and his own, so far as happiness is concerned, were a sheer deduction from the benefit."[28] For Mill, his benign type of colonialism is morally legitimate because it would ultimately enhance the total happiness of noncivilized people by way of cultivating the nobility in their character. From a perspective of an ethicist of minority groups, the most significant weakness of Mill's utilitarian moral theory lies in the poor condition of his concept of "quality." Mill was surprisingly uncritical of his own concept of quality, which he conceived solely in contrast to the concept of quantity. This lack of self-criticism is reiterated in the same way in his uncritical conception of civilization. Although he substantiates the concept of civilization with such elements as the "diffusion of property and intelligence, and the power of co-operation,"[29] he established his conception of civilization on a reductionist logic that fails to incorporate the rich, diverse, and deep characteristics of other cultures. As a result, although Mill's utilitarianism aims to arrive at the state of "happier, nobler, and wiser," he does not even bother to define what it means to be a part of such a state. He just takes it for granted that his understanding of civilization is, at base, objective.

Mill's reductionist tendency is also deeply embedded in his justification of the benign kind of British colonialism. It is ironic that even though he is arguing for the "good of others," it is hard to verify the meaningful presence of others in his writings on British colonialism. In promoting his benign colonialism, he largely ignores the perspective of those who are directly affected by the policies he endorses. In Mill's philosophy of utilitarianism as well as in his thought of benign imperialism, therefore, we only discover "Otherless others." The concept of others in Mill's utilitarian project is merely a reduced concept that is designed only to fit into his Eurocentric category. If Mill had developed a deep and significant friendship with someone from a "noncivilized" world, he might have changed his attitude toward Eurocentric imperialism, just as his wife, Harriet Taylor, critically influenced and changed his view on women and their rights. In sum, although Mill's utilitarian moral philosophy cannot be held accountable for the Eurocentric imperialism of the nineteenth century, it at least played an important role in justifying the contemporary global order dominated by Western colonialism in the name of the "greater good."

Notes

1. The Indian Mutiny (1857–58) was a widespread but unsuccessful rebellion against British rule in India, which began with Indian soldiers (Sepoy) in the Bengal army of the British East India Company.
2. Uday Singh Mehta, *Liberalism and Empire: A Study in Nineteenth-Century British Liberal Thought* (London: University of Chicago Press, 1999), 2; Bhikhu Parekh, "Liberalism and Colonialism: A Critique of Locke and Mill," in *The Decolonization of Imagination: Culture, Knowledge and Power*, ed. Jan Nederveen (London: Zed Books, 1995), 94. Parekh, for instance, summarizes Mill's defense of British imperialism as follows: "Mill maintained that just as a civilized society had a right to rule over a primitive or semi-civilized society, a more civilized group or nationality within a civilized society had a right to 'absorb' and dominate inferior groups."
3. Stephen Holmes, "Making Sense of Liberal Imperialism," in *J. S. Mill's Political*

Thought: A Bicentennial Reassessment, ed. Nadia Urbinati and Alex Zakaras (Cambridge: Cambridge University Press, 2007).

4. John Stuart Mill, *Utilitarianism* (1861; New York: Library of Liberal Arts, 1957), 10.
5. Ibid.
6. Ibid.
7. Ibid., 50.
8. Ibid., 51.
9. Ibid.
10. Ibid., 12.
11. Ibid.
12. Ibid., 14.
13. Ibid.
14. Jonathan Riley, "Millian Qualitative Superiorities and Utilitarianism, Part II," *Utilitas* 21, no. 2 (June 2008): 128.
15. Although Mill's philosophy of history is not systematically developed, we can trace his thought in several of his books. Chapter 4 of his *Considerations on Representative Government* ([1861] in *On Liberty and Other Essays*, ed. John Gray [Oxford: Oxford University Press, 1991]), is a particularly valuable resource.
16. Beate Jahn, "Barbarian Thoughts: Imperialism in the Philosophy of John Stuart Mill," *Review of International Studies* 31 (2005): 601.
17. Ibid., 604.
18. John Stuart Mill, "A Few Words on Non-Intervention," in *The Collected Works of John Stuart Mill*, Vol. XXI, ed. John M. Robson (1859; Toronto: University of Toronto Press, 1991), 113, 115.
19. Jahn, "Barbarian Thoughts," 613.
20. Don Habibi, "The Moral Dimensions of J. S. Mill's Colonialism," *Journal of Social Philosophy* 30, no. 1 (Spring 1999): 132.
21. Joseph J. Miller, "Chairing the Jamaica Committee: J. S. Mill and the Limits of Colonial Authority," in *Utilitarianism and Empire*, ed. Bart Schultz and Georgios Varouxakis (New York: Rowman & Littlefield, 2005), 172.
22. Mill, *Considerations on Representative Government*, in *On Liberty and Other Essays*, 233.
23. Mill, "A Few Words on Non-Intervention," 114.
24. Mill writes in his 1858 essay "A Constitutional View of the India Question" in *The Collected Works of John Stuart Mill*, Vol. XXX: "India has hitherto been administered, under the general control of Parliament, by a body, who holding aloof from the party conflicts of English politics, devoted their whole time and energies to Indian affairs. The great Corporation, which gained India for this country, has hitherto been considered the best qualified to conduct its administration, under the authority of the Crown, subject, when necessary, to the veto of the Board of Control" (176).
25. Mill, "A Few Words on Non-Intervention," 118.
26. Jahn, "Barbarian Thoughts," 617.
27. There is currently a debate regarding Mill's attitude toward the race issue, which I cannot cover in this essay due to the limited space. However, Mill's view on race is well reflected in his 1850 article "The Negro Question." It was noble for him to argue against Thomas Carlyle's outright racism, as published in an 1849 issue of *Fraser's Magazine* under the title "Occasional Discourse on the Negro Question." Although Mill would not be characterized as a racist, scholars such as Bart Schultz, "Mill and Sidgwick, Imperialism and Racism," *Utilitas* 19.1 (2007), and Anthony Bogues, "John Stuart Mill and 'The Negro Question': Race, Colonialism, and the Ladder of Civilization" in *Race and Racism in Modern Philosophy*,

ed. Andrew Valls (Ithaca: Cornell University Press, 2005), are critical of Mill's racist tendency in conjunction with his attitude toward imperialism. See also Falguni A. Sheth, "John Stuart Mill on Race, Liberty, and Markets," in *Race, Liberalism, and Economics*, ed. David Colander, Robert E. Prasch, and Faguni A. Sheth (Ann Arbor: University of Michigan Press, 2007), and Georgios Varouxakis, "Empire, Race, Euro-centrism: John Stuart Mill and His Critics," in *Utilitarianism and Empire,* ed. Bart Schultz and Georgios Varouxakis (New York: Rowman & Littlefield, 2005). Both scholars are sympathetic with Mill on the issue of race.
28. Mill, *Utilitarianism*, 16.
29. John Stuart Mill, "Civilization," in *Collected Works*, 124.

10

Friedrich Nietzsche on Will to Power

EDWARD P. ANTONIO

From now on there will be more favorable preconditions for more compre-hensive forms of dominion, whose like has never yet existed. And even this is not the most important thing; the possibility has been established for the production of international racial unions whose task will be to rear a master race, the future "masters of the earth"; a new, tremendous aristocracy, based on the severest self-legislation, in which the will of philosophical men of power and artist-tyrants will be made to endure for millennia—a higher kind of man who, thanks to their superiority in will, knowledge, riches, and influence, employ democratic Europe as their most pliant and supple instrument for getting hold of the destinies of the earth, so as to work as artists upon "man" himself.

—Friedrich Nietzsche[1]

Friedrich Wilhelm Nietzsche (1844–1900) was born in Röcken in Saxony. His father was a Lutheran pastor. Although he trained as a philologist and held no formal qualifications in philosophy, he is known as one of the most prolific philo-sophical thinkers of the nineteenth century. He became a professor of philology at the University of Basel at the age of twenty-four. His major works include *Thus Spoke Zarathustra* (1883–85), *The Birth of Tragedy* (1872), *Beyond Good and Evil* (1886), *On the Genealogy of Morals* (1887), *The Antichrist* (1888), *Ecce Homo* (1889), and *The Will to Power* (1901). He was not only an accomplished philolo-gist but also a brilliant social critic. However, his brilliance was tarnished by his views on women and the way in which he applied his famous notion of "will to power" to marginalized communities. He succumbed to madness in 1889.

My goal is this short study is to show that, for all its empirical, psychological, epistemological, and ultimately metaphysical complexity, Nietzsche's doctrine of will to power is, at least from a postcolonial perspective, immensely troubling because it is ethically and politically dangerous. It is troubling because it embodies an unapologetic metaphysics or ontology of domination, an account of reality as force that justifies domination and destruction of the weak by the strong and powerful. We should not be misled by the fact that because much of what Nietzsche says about the will to power is historically framed by a self-referential Eurocentrism (Nietzsche is writing mostly about Europeans for Europeans), it has no deadly historical ramifications for non-Europeans or non-Whites.[2]

In this chapter I read Nietzsche's doctrine of will to power in a postcolonial register. This means more than simply interrogating its metaphysics (the raison d'être for which it may be said to exist or its social and economic deployments). By postcolonial reading, I mean a reading that is situated in a certain epistemic space more or less unrecognized by the doctrine of will to power yet inaugurated by the historical force of the many practices of colonialism—itself the articulation of the will to power—that provides the background against which Nietzsche thought and wrote. What marks out the postcolonial is not necessarily the official demise of the colonial or the declarative carving out of some territorial space of political autonomy, but the possibility of instituting a critique of the desirability of colonialism as both a historical project and as a set of political practices.

WILL TO POWER

If we follow Nietzsche's own lead, it is clear that the concept "will to power" is not easy to define. Nietzsche accuses philosophers like Arthur Schopenhauer of proceeding as if the notion of "will" is "the best-known thing in the world." Schopenhauer had claimed that "will" is the unoriginated thing-in-itself and that it was known to us on the basis of immediate intuition, without any assistance from reason. In contrast, Nietzsche declares that "willing," far from being so indubitably given, "seems to me to be above all something *complicated*, something that is a unity only in name." It is the complexity of the doctrine hinted at here that any adequate attempt to explicate Nietzsche's understanding of it must take seriously. First of all, this means disabusing ourselves of the prevailing misunderstanding that in our time simply assimilates it to political domination. One encounters this sort of misunderstanding whenever the phrase "will to power" is invoked in popular discourse. Many otherwise philosophically literate people take the phrase to mean "power hungry," "love of power," "autocratic," or "megalomania." Although it is possible to show that some of these meanings are directly implicated in the idea of will to power, none of these phrases, taken alone, sufficiently grounds Nietzsche's philosophical understanding of this doctrine. Second, taking the complexity of the doctrine of will to power seriously means attending to the many and various ways Nietzsche himself uses the concept.

I shall isolate at least four aspects of this doctrine before I subject it to postcolonial critique. Nietzsche has a fourfold understanding of the doctrine of will to power. The first is metaphysical, the second epistemological, the third psychological, and the fourth political. In his book *Beyond Good and Evil*, in the same passage in which he is critical of Schopenhauer's problematic notion of will, Nietzsche says that all willing involves a plurality of sensations. There is the sensation that constitutes the conditions "*away from which* we go," and one that constitutes the condition "*toward which* we go." In addition, there is what is called "muscular sensation." Furthermore, the activity of willing is connected with thought or thinking (Nietzsche calls it "ruling thought") such that if we were to separate the two, willing itself would disintegrate. Along the thinking side of willing Nietzsche places affect, what he calls the "affect of the command."[3]

This raises several interesting points. Notice that the activity of willing is manifold or is dispersed across a plurality of identities; in one turn it is connected with the condition of possibility (origination), and in another turn with the teleology (goal) of human activity; it is associated with the muscular. This reference to the muscular is significant because it connects with the many points at which Nietzsche invokes physiology.[4] The use of sensation in this passage establishes will to power as primarily an empirical doctrine rooted in Nietzsche's prioritization of sensory experience. This is the traditional meaning of sensation in the history of philosophy, as in Descartes, Locke, Hume, Kant, Hegel, and other thinkers. It is thus more than just a psychological doctrine.

Nietzsche argues that the second property of will is thought, or what he calls "ruling thought," which is inseparable from it. The reference to thought here grounds will philosophically or epistemologically. This is important because Nietzsche's perspectivism, which defines his epistemology, is an integral part of his thought and, I maintain, of his metaphysics of domination and thus of the political aspect of the will to power. Nietzsche characterizes the third property of will as emotion. This is the psychological dimension of will or willing. When Nietzsche mentions emotion, however, he is speaking of it in essentially political terms. His way of stating this aspect of will constitutes the fourth aspect of the will to power, which is political. He makes a double move in which (1) emotion is linked to "freedom of the will," or the emotion to command; (2) he also takes the goal of command to be obedience.

According to Nietzsche:

> freedom of the will is essentially the emotion of supremacy in respect to him who must obey: "I am free; 'he' must obey"—this consciousness is inherent in every will; and equally so is the straining of the attention, the straight look that fixes itself exclusively on one thing, the unconditional judgment that "this and nothing else is necessary now" the inward certainty that obedience will be rendered—and whatever pertains to the position of the commander. A man who *wills* commands something within himself that renders obedience, or which he believes renders obedience.[5]

This statement already points to the politics and the ethics that undergird Nietzsche's idea of will to power. I shall come back to this shortly.

THE METAPHYSICAL DIMENSION

I have already suggested that will to power has a metaphysical dimension. This can be seen in how Nietzsche, at various places in his writings, identifies will to power with the totality of reality. For example, in *Beyond Good and Evil* he thinks that "our entire instinctual life"—which necessarily includes thought and all organic functions, including procreation and nutrition—can be explained as one characteristic expression of will: as will to power. Thus he not only defines *all* active force unequivocally as will to power; he also asserts that "the world seen from within, the world defined and designated according to its 'intelligible character'—it would simply be 'Will to Power,' and nothing else."[6] In addition to identifying the will to power with the makeup of the world, Nietzsche also identifies it with causality. In the passage I have just been discussing, he is clear that the causality of the will is causality tout court. This, among other things, can be taken to mean that power is not neutral but is productive of certain effects.[7] Elsewhere in the notes published after his death under the title *The Will to Power*, Nietzsche once again declares that the world, understood as an eternal "monster of energy," is nothing but the will to power, and that humans are themselves nothing but this will to power.[8] What we have here is a totalizing and naturalistic vision of the world in which everything is reduced to power relationships. However, the totalization of will to power does not mean that power is distributed equally in all domains of reality. For Nietzsche, it is the inequalities (not equalities) in the operations of will to power that actually are most constitutive of its structure. What totalization entails is the idea that Nietzsche intends to advance an all-encompassing account of all of reality. He repeatedly asserts that all of life and not just some part of it is the will to power.

Here I stress the metaphysical structure that underlies Nietzsche's notion of will to power because it is in terms of this structure that the world and, within it, nature, humans, and power itself are defined. I am using the term "metaphysics," partly following Tsarina Doyle, to describe a comprehensive, self-grounding explanatory framework claiming the will to power, or force and causality, as ultimate reality.[9] According to Nietzsche, power is a natural, causal, self-organizing force endowed with an inner intelligibility that deploys itself empirically in both nature and in social relationships. Power is the necessary or ontological principle of all causality, social and natural. What follows from this is that the metaphysical grounding of the will to power makes the hierarchical structures, processes, and relationships it promotes and sustains to be inevitable and necessary.

NIETZSCHE AND RACE

The naturalistic account of will to power ought not to mislead anyone into thinking that Nietzsche's interest is simply or primarily in organic, physical, or natural processes: it is also deeply social and political. For example, in a remarkable passage in *Beyond Good and Evil*, Nietzsche writes: "'Exploitation does not belong to a depraved or imperfect and primitive society: it belongs to the *nature* of the living being as a primary organic function; it is a consequence of the intrinsic Will to Power, which precisely is the Will to Life. Granting that as a theory this is a novelty—as a reality it is a *fundamental fact* of all history: let us be so far honest towards ourselves!'"[10] This is why in book 4 of *The Will to Power*, and in a manner consistent with his notion of will to power as essentially defined by the hierarchy of command and obedience, he is able to propose several ideas that merit serious attention. Among these ideas Nietzsche taught (1) the need to reinscribe hierarchy, or what he calls the "order of rank" and interprets directly as a matter of power: "What determines your rank is the quantum of power you are: the rest is cowardice";[11] (2) the idea of two types of life: the distinction between ascending life (the strong) and decaying life (the weak).[12] This is not a matter of freedom struggling against power. It is rather a matter of power and strength conquering freedom.[13] It is a question of being prepared to sacrifice freedom or (which is the same thing) of instigating slavery as the price for supremacy and dominance. (3) The distinction between strong and weak types of people is not a vague or abstract distinction but one with definite social content, articulated in terms of a racial anthropology of the superior or higher type. These higher types are represented by "the noble," "the aristocratic," "the masters," "the rich," "the brave," the blond or the Aryan, and so forth.[14]

By contrast, weak types are represented by "the common man," "the plebeian," "dark-colored," "black-haired," the man who, unlike the higher type's truthful nature, is a liar.[15] It must be added here that Nietzsche's weak type includes women and slaves. He says that women have a congenital tendency for subordination.[16] Regarding slaves, it is well known that Nietzsche advocated master morality over slave morality.[17] According to Nietzsche, it is necessary to enunciate a compelling doctrine that will serve as a *breeding agent* for "strengthening the strong, [but] paralyzing and destructive for the worldly-weary."[18] Nietzsche calls these worldly-weary "the decaying races" and has no hesitation in proclaiming the need for their destruction. The decaying races are the bearers of decadence, a condition that Nietzsche saw as permeating the whole of Europe. Decadence resulted from the spread of democratic and egalitarian tendencies, the rise of the herd, the mob, the masses, and so forth.[19] In *The Antichrist*, as elsewhere, Nietzsche extols inequality as natural and posits a hierarchy of three classes: those with intellectual power, those with muscular strength, and the mediocre.[20]

What is one to make of all of this? I am aware of the debates about the ambiguities surrounding Nietzsche's use of the idea of race. I am also aware that it is difficult to characterize Nietzsche as a racist in any straightforward sense since his theory of race is largely implicit. Indeed, he does not always use terms such as "blond" or "black" consistently. Black is not always a sign of that which is bad or evil, nor is white or blond a sign of intrinsic goodness. Moreover, Nietzsche was not the obvious anti-Semite that his appropriation by the Nazis turned him into. He had a complex relationship to Jews and to Judaism.[21] He believed that Jews were necessary to the survival of Europe and fantasized about their assimilation into European culture as part of the solution to the racial decadence that he thought he saw all around him. He fell out with his friend Richard Wagner over the problem of anti-Semitism and was critical of Schopenhauer's treatment of Jews. To complicate the picture even further, when Nietzsche speaks of the noble or the higher types, his examples are drawn from various groups, such as the Arabs, the Romans, the Japanese, the Germans, and the Scandinavian Vikings. Indeed, Nietzsche believed in the careful mixing of races (he was, in this sense, a forerunner of at least some sort of hybridity). Saying all of this has the potential effect of encouraging us to let him off the hook lightly on the pretext that his thought is complex or that he did not think about race in rigid terms.

I propose several lines of critiquing Nietzsche's anthropology of will to power. The first is to observe that Nietzsche wrote at a time when slavery and racism in Europe and the Americas continued unabated. Yet he repeatedly and unqualifiedly denigrated slave morality (as if slave morality was nothing but the sorry celebration of victimhood) and identified the weak and the powerless as excellent candidates for enslavement. Moreover, he also wrote at a time when European colonial powers were vying with each other for control and domination of the earth and its peoples, a time when colonialism was being justified in theory and practice by appealing to nature, religion, race, and power. The Berlin conference of 1884–85, which "officially" divided Africa into European colonial territories, happened while Nietzsche was at the height of his writing career.

This is why the quote with which I open this essay is so significant. Nietzsche had right in front of him the empirical, *sensory* manifestation of the devastating effects of the will to power. Why did he not qualify his arguments in light of prevailing sensory reality? One response is simply to say he did not care or was blind to what was actually happening around him. Both responses would be correct, for as he envisages it, will to power does not care and is a blind force. Or was he simply being consistent with his stated view that the price of power is the sacrifice of the many for the sake of aristocratic domination? This too is correct. Did he not realize that it is possible to distinguish between good and bad forms of will to power? In that case he was simply a bad philosopher.

However one defines "race," weakness, gender, and so forth, it is morally wrong and evil to advocate for the annihilation of the weak, the powerless, and the sick (Nietzsche habitually equates weakness with sickness). After Auschwitz, the genocide of Native Americans, and widespread slavery, there ought to be no argument about this unless we think nihilistic fascism is acceptable, and then under what conditions exactly? Colonial history and other histories of Othering are littered with examples of the work of such nihilism.

Nietzsche's ambiguous use of race was not simply a matter of personal style but a strategy of ethical, if not metaphysical, reticence that was widely shared in the nineteenth century. In turn, this reticence is nothing but the willful indifference of the will to power to its own depredations. This reticence is important because it simultaneously suppresses and reveals the different ways in which racism could sometimes function as pure description or positive difference, sometimes as racial indifference, and sometimes as opposition to itself. In Nietzsche we see how, bestriding all these functional categories, race in the nineteenth century is situated between ideology and explanation. His thought participates in this structure by enunciating and circulating a terrifying anthropology of power that, these ambiguities aside, is not just indifferent to human suffering but instead actively promotes that suffering. For this reason Nietzsche's philosophical legacy is deeply troubling.

Notes

1. Friedrich Nietzsche, *The Will to Power*, trans. Anthony M. Ludovici (New York: Barnes & Noble, 2006), 960.
2. I do not deal here with Nietzsche's contribution to the vocabularies of freedom, social location, and perspectivism, which those of us peddling liberation take so much for granted these days. I do not see how Nietzsche the advocate of freedom can be rescued from his politically destructive nihilism by invoking his critique of traditional authoritarianism.
3. Friedrich Nietzsche, *Beyond Good and Evil: Prelude to a Philosophy of the Future*, trans. Helen Zimmern (New York: Barnes & Noble, 2007), 19.
4. Nietzsche regularly makes reference to physiology and uses biological metaphors to articulate his philosophy. References in *Beyond Good and Evil* and in *The Anti-Christ: A Criticism of Christianity*, trans. Anthony M. Ludovici (New York: Barnes & Noble, 2006), bear this out. See also Gregory Moore, *Nietzsche, Biology and Metaphor* (Cambridge: Cambridge University Press, 2002); and Christopher Upham Murray Smith, "Friedrich Nietzsche's Biological Epistemics," *Journal of Social and Biological Structures* 9 (1986): 375–88.
5. Nietzsche, *Beyond Good and Evil*, 19.
6. Ibid., 34–36.
7. Nietzsche's notion of will to power cannot be adequately grasped without some understanding of his notion of causality, which involves a detailed reworking of Kant's idea of force. Indeed, the three ideas of force, causality, and will to power go together and can be defined one in terms of the other.
8. Nietzsche, *Will to Power*, 549–50.
9. For an argument that Nietzsche's doctrine of will to power is metaphysical, see Tsarina Doyle, *Nietzsche on Epistemology and Metaphysics: The World in View* (Edinburgh: Edinburgh University Press, 2009). The last three chapters of the book are especially relevant.
10. Nietzsche, *Beyond Good and Evil*, 154–55.
11. Nietzsche, *Will to Power*, 858.
12. Ibid., 857.
13. Ibid., 859.
14. Friedrich Nietzsche, *On the Genealogy of Morality*, trans. Maudemarie Clark and Alan J. Swensen (Indianapolis: Hackett Publishing Co., 1998), 28–31.
15. Ibid.
16. Nietzsche's misogyny is astounding. See Friedrich Nietzsche, "On Little Old and Young Women," from *Thus Spoke Zarathustra* and thereby in *The Portable Nietzsche*, trans. Walter Kaufmann (New York: Penguin, 1954), 178–79; idem, *Will to Power*, 460; idem, *Human, All Too Human*, trans. Helen Zimmern and Paul V. Cohn (New York: Barnes & Noble, 2008), 182–96.

17. Nietzsche, *Genealogy of Morality*, 19–28. Briefly, master morality evaluates things in terms of good and bad (moral judgment is expressed in degrees) while slave morality does so in terms of good and evil (moral judgment is expressed in terms of radical opposites). The former is a morality of natural, creative self-affirmation, and the latter of *ressentiment*. Ressentiment involves both the characterization of nobility as evil and the celebration of suffering at the hands of nobility as a virtue. On the one hand, it is parasitic on condemning the external; it valorizes altruism and selflessness; it is a morality of the weak. On the other hand, noble morality is the morality of the strong and valorizes egoism and selfishness.

18. Nietzsche, *Will to Power*, 862.

19. On decadence as a central theme in Nietzsche's diagnosis of the social ills of European society, see Jacqueline Scott, "On the Use and Abuse of Race in Philosophy: Nietzsche, Jews and Race," in *Race and Racism in Continental Philosophy*, ed. Robert Bernasconi and Sybil Cook (Bloomington: Indiana University Press, 2003).

20. He says: "In all this, I repeat, there is nothing arbitrary, nothing 'artificial,' that which is *otherwise* is artificial, by that which is otherwise nature is put to shame. . . . The order of castes and the order of rank merely formulate the supreme law of life itself; the differentiation of the three types is necessary for the maintenance of society and for enabling higher and highest types to be reared; the *inequality* of rights is the only condition of there being rights at all. A right is a privilege." Friedrich Nietzsche, *The Antichrist*, 64–68.

21. See James Winchester, "Nietzsche's Racial Profiling," in *Race and Racism in Modern Philosophy*, ed. Andrew Valls (Ithaca and London: Cornell University Press, 2005), 255–76. Also, on decadence as a central theme for Nietzsche, see Scott, "Use and Abuse of Race."

11

Michel Foucault on Power

ANDREA SMITH

Michel Foucault was born on October 15, 1926, in Poitiers, France. He was a French philosopher strongly influenced by Kant and Nietzsche. His thinking was also deeply rooted in Marxism, even as he was critical of Marxist politics and theory. Although Foucault's work is often cited as disenabling activism, as will be discussed later in this chapter, Foucault was involved in leftist political and intellectual projects. He was a member of the French Communist Party in 1950–53, before he became disillusioned and left. In 1968 the French government created a new experimental university, Paris VIII, and appointed Foucault the first head of its philosophy department. Foucault appointed mostly young leftist academics. The Ministry of Education, which objected to the fact that many of the course titles contained the phrase "Marxist-Leninist," decreed that students from Paris VIII would be ineligible to become secondary school teachers. Foucault joined the resulting student protest by occupying administration buildings and fighting with police. He also helped found the Prison Information Group to provide a way for prisoners to voice their concerns. He eventually died of AIDS-related illness in 1984. Though he did not himself embrace the term "postmodern" or "poststructuralist," his work is often seen as foundational to this intellectual tradition.

Foucault was the author of several volumes, including *The Order of Things*, *The Archaeology of Knowledge*, *Madness and Civilization*, *The Birth of a Clinic*, *The History of Sexuality*, and *Discipline and Punish*. His work is too vast to summarize in the space of a short chapter, but I will address some key contributions that are of particular relevance to those interested in the intersections of racial justice and Christian social ethics.

POWER

Why is that when revolutionary groups do seize the state or capital, they seem to generally replicate the same uses of power employed by those they fought against? Foucault seeks to address this question with his articulation of "power." Within the context of Native organizing, for instance, most Native activists who fight against U.S. policies know that if the United States were to disappear tomorrow, life would not significantly improve for most Native peoples. Foucault contends that this contradiction emerges because of an inadequate conceptualization of power whereby one group of peoples is understood to have all the power and then to repress other groups of peoples. The political project that emerges from this inadequate conceptualization is that subordinate groups simply need to seize the power held by dominant groups.

According to Foucault, power is not something owned by one group and then exercised over another group; rather, it is dispersed through microcircuits that affect everything we do. Essentially, there is no "outside" power. At the same time, power never acts unilaterally or monolithically: where there is power, there is always resistance. Power is not simply repressive; it is also creative. It creates the world we come to see as "normal." Structures of domination operate not only by one group of people's repressing Others through state or economic power, but also through circuits of power that shape the way we even understand the world. Consequently, it is not a surprise that society does not necessarily radically change when another group of people seizes formal power because logics of domination are continuing to operate through a microphysics of power that shape what we even consider political possibilities to be.

A popular critique of Foucault's analysis of power and its implications for political practice is that because Foucault locates power everywhere, it is essentially nowhere. Hence his analyses make it impossible to theorize strategies of resistance against hegemonic uses of power, such as multinational capitalism or government repression, because power analyses become focused on the individual rather than on social structures.

According to postcolonial theorist Edward Said,

> Foucault has also turned his attention away from the oppositional forces
> in society which he had studied for their undeterred resistance to exclusion
> and confinement . . . and decided that since power was everywhere it was
> probably better to concentrate on the local micro-physics of power that sur-

round the individual. The self was therefore to be studied, cultivated, and, if necessary, refashioned and reconstituted.[1]

Marxist feminist scholar Nancy Hartsock further argues that Foucault's analysis of power is not equipped to deal with social structures. Foucault "loses track of social structure and instead focuses on how individuals experience and exercise power."[2] Foucault, she claims, is also pessimistic about social change and is content merely to describe power relations rather than to engage in political action. Hartsock invokes the eleventh Feuerbach Thesis: "To paraphrase Marx, the point is to change the world, not simply to redescribe ourselves or reinterpret the world yet again."[3]

A closer reading of *Power/Knowledge* and *History of Sexuality* suggests that these critiques may be based on misreadings of Foucault, at least in some stages of his writings. Though Foucault argues that power does not *issue* from the state or other structures of domination, he does note that these structures do *possess* a disproportionate amount of power. It is true that Foucault does not often focus on "juridico-discursive" uses of power, such as those found in the state; still, he does believe these uses of power exist. Thus Foucault explains:

> When I say that power establishes a network through which it freely circulates, this is true only up to a certain point. . . . I do not believe that one should conclude from that that power is the best distributed thing in the world. . . . We are not dealing with a sort of democratic or anarchic distribution of power through bodies.[4]

Consequently, it seems incorrect to assert, as does Said, that Foucault is primarily concerned with refashioning the individual and is unconcerned with transforming larger global structures. In fact, Foucault argues the opposite: "The individual . . . is not the vis-à-vis of power; it is, I believe, one of its prime effects."[5] It would be difficult to argue that Foucault is only concerned with refashioning the individual since Foucault questions the necessity and prior existence of the individual itself and also argues that our society's focus on individual refashioning is itself part of the discourse of power that he is questioning. Instead, his primary focus seems to be on how a confluence of global and local uses of power transforms and creates individuals on the local level. "Let us not, therefore, ask why certain people want to dominate, what they seek, what is their overall strategy. Let us ask, instead, how things work at the level of on-going subjugation, at the level of those continuous and uninterrupted processes which subject our bodies."[6] In his interview "Body/Power," Foucault clearly addresses the relationship between state power and the local microphysics of power. The interviewer asks Foucault if he is neglecting the importance of the state apparatus in focusing on the uses of power in everyday life. Foucault replies:

> I don't claim at all that the State apparatus is unimportant, but it seems to me that among all the conditions for avoiding a repetition of the Soviet experience and preventing the revolutionary process from running into the

ground, one of the first things that has to be understood is that power isn't
localized in the State apparatus and that nothing in society will be changed
if the mechanisms of power that function outside, below and alongside
the State apparatuses, on a much more minute and everyday level, are not
also changed.[7]

Thus Foucault does not preclude us from addressing hegemonic forms of power;
rather, he encourages us to address the fact that struggles for state or economic
power are not sufficient to shift prevailing power practices if we do not address how
power relations are simultaneously enacted on the microlevel of everyday life.

I thus maintain that Foucault's analysis does not actually preclude us from
talking about liberation or emancipation. Foucault seems to clearly argue that
addressing local uses of power should be done *in conjunction with* changing state
apparatuses. Foucault locates himself within the Marxist tradition, which is concerned with the macrostate and economic institutions: "I quote Marx without
saying so. . . . It is impossible at the present time to write history without using a
whole range of concepts directly or indirectly linked to Marx's thought and situating oneself within a horizon of thought which has been defined and described
by Marx."[8] Using Marxist social analysis as a base, Foucault's work focuses on
the uses of power that Marxist thought neglects. Foucault's power analysis, I
argue, cannot be understood outside of a context that comprehends the need for
large-scale political change.

Probably many followers of Foucault, who do not share his commitments to
changing larger social structures, have appropriated his work to delegitimize any
analysis of power on the macrolevel. And certainly his focus on the "care of the
self" in his later career can give fuel to critics who say that he is turning away from
large-scale social transformation. However, Foucault, at least in many stages of
his career, argues that while power is multiple, it can be organized into a more-
or-less coherent form of domination. "Dispersed, heteromorphous, localized
procedures of power are adapted, reinforced and transformed by these global
strategies." Similarly, while resistance is also multiple, "it can be integrated in
global strategies."[9]

It is true that Foucault does not offer the hope of a once-for-all revolution.
However, he does not preclude radical transformation. He explicitly asks and
then answers: "Are there no great radical ruptures, massive binary divisions,
then? Occasionally, yes. . . . Resistances [are not] . . . a promise that is of necessity betrayed." These "plurality of resistances" suggest not that "revolution" is
impossible, but that the revolution is permanent and ongoing.[10]

TRUTH

Imbedded in Foucault's analysis of power is "truth" itself. In his analysis of various centers of "power/knowledge," from sexuality to prisons, Foucault sought
to demonstrate that the very things we assume to be true are themselves the

consequences of power. For instance, he observes that while psychologists tried to determine the "truth" about homosexuality, their quests created the truths they were purportedly just describing. Ironically, Foucault argues, we mistakenly believe our liberation comes from finding the truth about ourselves when the very mode of truth-telling is itself part of capitalist ideology. That is, during the rise of capitalism, the body becomes the site of regulation such that power relations no longer seem to be that. Rather, we become normalized to believe that there is a certain way a "normal" person should want to live. Those who challenge social norms become marked, not so much as outlaws, but rather as sick or deviant. This deviance is managed through a technology of the soul, where the soul seeks liberation from the things that repress it by confessing its truth. Ironically, the confessing self seeks liberation within a set of power relations that entraps the confessing self into thinking its inability to tell the truth is the source of its oppression.

Rey Chow takes up Foucault's analysis to explain how this mode of truth-telling is racialized. The bourgeoisie are normal and healthy: all those then become classified in relationship to their deviance from their norm. This classification is racialized. The modern state is fundamentally stratified in terms of those who get to be the norm, and those who desire to become the norm. Within this system, people of color in particular fall into the Foucauldian trap of thinking that the liberation is not structural, but requires our confessing our truths and demonstrating the worth of our cultures. As Chow contends, we believe that if we properly perform our ethnicity, we will be granted humanity.[11]

This critique of "truth" creates some anxiety among liberation activists who contend that this antifoundationalist approach renders the projects of identifying truth and adjudicating moral claims impossible. In addition, they worry that if we understand identity to be socially constructed, it therefore does not exist. Therefore racial or gender groups have no basis by which to articulate political claims based on identity.

In actuality, Foucault's critique of truth does not preclude us from taking stands, making arguments, or forming opinions. Foucault's analysis cannot be equated with intellectual or moral relativism. Relativism is really the flip side of universalist notions of truth. That is, claims to universalism and objectivity rest on the notion that individuals can transcend their historicity to decide what is eternally and cross-culturally true. Similarly, relativism rests on the notion that individuals can escape their grid of intelligibility with its particular regime of truth and see multiple truths. Foucault contends that all individuals live within regimes of truth that have their own logic and standards of truth, standards that allow individuals within that regime to adjudicate between truth claims. If a person's regime were to become destabilized, it would mean that the person is in the grip of another (partially competing) regime, not living without a regime altogether. Because we know our regime of truth is historically conditioned, we know that it is flexible and given to change, but we are not capable of disbelieving its "truths" as long as we are living under it. The fact that truth is historically conditioned, therefore, does not make it less true for us.

While Foucault did not address identity politics directly, Judith Butler provides a helpful reminder about the importance of not using a Foucauldian analysis to fall into a vulgar constructionism. Certainly there are many followers of Foucault who do lapse into vulgar constructionism and argue that because, for instance, race is socially constructed, it does not exist. Consequently, there is no need for racial justice organizing. But this kind of approach would be inconsistent with Foucault's actual analysis. As Butler states:

> If the notion of the subject [or identity], for instance, is no longer given, no longer presumed, that does not mean that it has no meaning for us, that it ought no longer to be uttered. On the contrary, it means only that the term is not simply a building block on which to rely, an uninterrogated premise for political argument. On the contrary, the term has become an object of theoretical attention, something of which we are compelled to give an account.[12]

GOVERNMENTALITY/CARCERAL SYSTEM/ NORMALIZATION

As previously mentioned, Foucault argues, particularly in *Discipline and Punish*, that with the advent of capitalism, punishment changed its focus from a technology of the body to a technology of the soul. While physical penalties—such as confinement, forced labor, and so forth—affect the body, their effects are an intermediary step for reaching the soul. Modes of punishment have shifted from public displays of torture to institutions of surveillance and regulation, which serve to normalize the prisoner into the social order. Essentially, governance shifts from rule through sovereign power exercised by the king to governmentality whereby power operates through modes of normalization in which power relationships themselves become rendered invisible.

This system of punishment is predicated on the existence of an individual with rights. As Foucault argues in *The Order of Things*, the existence of "man" (or the individual) as the primary site of philosophical investigation is a recent phenomenon. According to Foucault, the advent of a person is related to a shift in ethical forms. The old form is predicated on an external moral code, whereas the new form of ethics is internally lodged within the individual's self.[13] Thus the purpose of punishment as "spectacle" is to coerce people to recognize and respect the power of the sovereign, whereas punishment as "surveillance" entails producing subjects with internally derived ethics that conform to the social order. Foucault also argues that it is important to analyze the prison within a larger context of societal surveillance that is situated in other institutions, such as schools and hospitals, which have the cumulative effect of regulating and normalizing subjects. Foucault asks,

> Is it surprising that the cellular prison, with its regular chronologies, forced labour, its authorities of surveillance and regulation, its experts in morality,

who continue and multiply the functions of the judge, should have become the modern instrument of penalty? Is it surprising that prisons resemble factories, schools, barracks, hospitals, which all resemble prisons?[14]

This larger context Foucault terms "the carceral system."

To concretize this analysis, Timothy Kaufman-Osborn, in his analysis of the connections between lynching and the death penalty, explores how the death penalty supersedes lynching in that it allows the state to reproduce White supremacy while disavowing this reproduction by allowing racism to be perpetrated under the cover of law and bureaucracy:

> The practices constitutive of due process . . . are a "pretense" not in the sense that they render capital punishment and lynching identical, but rather in the more-subtle sense that they mask the continued articulation of the racial contract within a polity that no longer openly espouses the rhetoric of White supremacy.[15]

Kaufman-Osborn mirrors Philip Deloria's analysis of institutionalization of anti-Indian racism within U.S. policy in the 1900s, as the state began to condemn extralegal massacres of Indian peoples. Instead, colonization was maintained through government bureaucracy rather than vigilante violence.[16] Indians essentially became transformed from enemies of the state who must be killed to social deviants, misfits who must be regulated. Thus in both cases we see that, as Foucault observes, genocide and White supremacy become routinized through the law. White supremacy is so well maintained through processes of regulation that it seems to disappear.

Joy James has argued that Foucault's economy of punishment would not seem to apply to peoples who are not considered individuals with rights. While Foucault argues that punishment as public spectacle was ending in the eighteenth century, the lynching of African Americans and the torture of "enemies of the state" in prison continued.[17] Hence, this notion that power through governmentality has superseded power through sovereign exercises of torture and spectacle excludes the histories of racial terror that continue today. Instead, we must look at these modes of rule as operating in conjunction with each other rather than in historical sequence. And, unlike *Discipline and Punish*, Foucault appears to more clearly state in *Security, Territory, Population*, that these modes of rule—sovereignty, discipline, and biopower—do continue to operate concurrently, even as one mode may be more predominant at any particular time in history or place.[18]

RACE AND BIOPOWER

Foucault has been widely critiqued for not addressing race and colonialism both in terms of content and method. Foucault's prominent methodological approach of genealogy in which he tries to tell the history of things that claim to have no history (such as "sexuality, "prisons," "the soul," and so on) often relies on investigating how capitalism reshapes European society. However, as Ann Stoler contends in *Race and the Education of Desire*, Foucault neglects how the rise of capitalism is coterminous with the rise of colonialism. As previously mentioned, Foucault analyzes how the focus on the self reflects the shaping of bourgeois identity in relationship to poor peoples and working classes. Stoler recognizes, however, that the preoccupation with the bourgeois self is not simply concerned with distinguishing that self from the poor or working class within a European context, but also from the racialized Others that are being colonized by Europe.[19] In *A Critique of Postcolonial Reason*, Gayatri Spivak further observes that Foucault's methodology often relies on an unquestioned Orientalism. That is, to explain various facets of bourgeois society, he juxtaposes it to an undifferentiated Orient. An example would be his discussion of "scientia sexualis" in the West, which he explicates in a binary, oppositional relationship to the traditions of "ars erotica"—truth derived from sexual pleasure—that supposedly marks the practices of the Orient.[20] Spivak explains how this kind of analysis is predicated on a simple Native informant who serves as a foil for the more-complex European subject.[21]

But as Ann Stoler and Rey Chow state, despite Foucault's ethnocentricism and general lack of engagement on issues of race and colonialism, it is important not to overlook an important contribution he does make to our understanding of race and genocide in his articulation of biopower. This articulation is discussed in the last chapter of *History of Sexuality* as well as in a lecture series published as *Society Must Be Defended*. He questions why in this period of so-called liberal democracy so many wars of genocide are committed, and yet these wars are *not* seen as contradictions to democracy. Though we often articulate racism as an aberration to democracy or as a result of scapegoating in times of social crisis, Foucault argues that racism is endemic and permanent to the modern state. As mentioned previously, the rise of the carceral system entails a shift from punishment to normalization. This shift is effected through a policing of the body through the technology of the soul. That is, the person who fails to follow the norms of society becomes less a criminal and more of a "deviant," who must undergo processes of normalization.

However, society simultaneously polices collective bodies and manages them as populations. In the service of life, others are allowed to die. "One might say that the ancient right to take life or let live was replaced by a power to foster life or disallow it to the point of death. . . . One had the right to kill those who represent a kind of biological danger to others."[22] Consequently, entire populations become marked as expendable because they are viewed as threats to the colonial world order.

> Wars are no longer waged in the name of a sovereign who must be defended; they are waged on behalf of the existence of everyone; entire populations are mobilized for the purpose of wholesale slaughter in the name of life neces- sity; massacres have become vital. It is as managers of life and survival, of

bodies and the race, that so many regimes have been able to wage so many wars, causing so many men to be killed.[23]

Racism is the necessary precondition that marks certain people for death in a society based on normalization. Modes of death may not be direct physical extermination but can include creating social conditions that mark communities of color suitable for death. If we refer back to Philip Deloria's previously described Foucauldian analysis of how Indian genocide becomes normalized through governmentality, we can see a shift in Indian policy from one in which Native peoples are directly killed in various Indian massacres, to one in which they become managed and policed as populations through the Bureau of Indian Affairs. Yet these policies may create as many deaths through toxic waste siting, inadequate health-care funding, and so forth. Thus a Foucauldian analysis of the biopower of racism seriously calls into question the idea of "racial progress." From Foucault's perspective, racism is not any less severe now than in previous times. Racial logics are manifest through population politics in which racism essentially becomes normalized. The "life" of society simply requires the deaths of those populations that threaten it.

Foucault's analysis of biopower also demonstrates how any social justice movement that is structured on a logic of normalization, where it must eliminate "threats" (via violence or other such strategies) to maintain its "life," will also necessarily have racism structured into its very being. A classic example could be the extent to which many Christian activists, religious leaders, and thinkers who are based in communities of color will often speak against homosexuals in their own communities. Queer people of color become positioned as biologized threats to the well-being of communities of color. Foucault's analysis suggests that any social justice movement must always interrogate the manner in which it may operate through a politics of normalization and biopower—and hence by definition, a politics of genocide.

CONCLUSION

Foucault's analyses of power, truth, governmentality, and biopower are all critical to the development of liberatory ethics for communities of color. Foucault's analysis is certainly limited by his ethnocentrism. In addition, many followers of Foucault, who lack his commitment to justice and social change, often incorrectly deploy a Foucauldian analysis to disenable a politic of liberation or struggle, particularly for those engaged in racial justice struggles. Fortunately, however, many scholars and activists who do center race and colonialism in their work[24] are redeploying and expanding on Foucault's work to provide nuanced accounts for how we can further racial justice without inadvertently creating oppressive models for liberation that divide our communities in the name of justice.

Notes

1. Edward W. Said, *Culture and Imperialism* (New York: Vintage Books, 1994), 26.
2. Nancy Harstock, "Foucault on Power: A Theory for Women?" in *Feminism and Postmodernism*, ed. Linda Nicholson (New York: Routledge, 1990), 169.
3. Ibid., 174.
4. Michel Foucault, *Power/Knowledge* (New York: Pantheon Books, 1977), 99.
5. Ibid., 98.
6. Ibid., 97.
7. Ibid., 60.
8. Ibid., 53.
9. Ibid., 142.
10. Michel Foucault, *History of Sexuality*, vol. 1 (New York: Vintage Books, 1980), 96.
11. See Rey Chow, *The Protestant Ethnic and the Spirit of Capitalism* (New York: Columbia University Press, 2002).
12. Judith Butler, *Gender Trouble* (New York: Routledge, 1990), 179.
13. Michel Foucault, *The Order of Things* (New York: Vintage Books, 1980), 327–28.
14. Foucault, *Power/Knowledge*, 227–28.
15. Timothy Kaufman-Osborn, "Capital Punishment as Legal Lynching?" in *From Lynching Mobs to the Killing State*, ed. Charles Ogletree Jr. and Austin Sarat (New York: New York University Press, 2006), 48–49.
16. See Philip Deloria, *Indians in Unexpected Places* (Lawrence: University of Kansas Press, 2004).
17. See Joy James, *Resisting State Violence* (Minneapolis: University of Minnesota Press, 1996).
18. Michel Foucault, *Security, Territory, Population: Lectures at the College de France, 1977–1978* (New York: Palgrave, 2004), 107.
19. See Ann Laura Stoler, *Race and the Education of Desire* (Durham, NC: Duke University Press, 1995).
20. Foucault, *History of Sexuality*, 1:57.
21. See Gayatri Spivak, *A Critique of Postcolonial Reason* (Cambridge, MA: Harvard University Press, 1999).
22. Foucault, *History of Sexuality*, 1:138.
23. Ibid., 137.
24. For a few examples, see Chow, *The Protestant Ethnic and the Spirit of Capitalism*; Sora Y. Han, "Bonds of Representation: Vision, Race and Law in Post–Civil Rights America" (PhD diss., University of California–Santa Cruz, 2006); David Kazanjian, *The Colonizing Trick* (Minneapolis: University of Minnesota Press, 2003); Mark Rifkin, *When Did Indians Become Straight? Kinship, the History of Sexuality, and Native Sovereignty* (Oxford: Oxford University Press, 2010); Scott Lauria Morgensen, *Spaces between Us: Queer Settler Colonialism and Indigenous Decolonization* (Minneapolis: University of Minnesota Press, forthcoming in fall of 2011); Jasbir K. Puar, *Terrorist Assemblages* (Durham, NC: Duke University Press, 2007); Stoler, *Race and the Education of Desire*, 1997.

PART TWO
SOCIAL TRADITION

12

Walter Rauschenbusch
on Society

BEN SANDERS III

The purpose of this chapter is to examine the legacy of Walter Rauschenbusch (1861–1918) while remaining centrally concerned with the implications of White supremacy for doing ethics. I attempt to honor the legacy of Walter Rauschenbusch while also illuminating the shortcomings of his brand of the social gospel. As such, this study proceeds in three parts: a brief analysis of Rauschenbusch's social context; an analysis of the role of Manifest Destiny in the doctrine of the social gospel, and thus in Rauschenbusch's work; and a concluding word proposing how we ought to utilize the work of Rauschenbusch in light of its limitations.

THE SOCIAL CONTEXT OF WALTER RAUSCHENBUSCH

In the face of a developing industrial world, Walter Rauschenbusch was the outstanding champion of the social gospel movement: his *Christianity and the Social Crisis* (1907)[1] helped solidify the movement as the most resounding mode of progressive Christian thought in the twentieth century. As a movement for social change, the social gospel demanded that churches rethink the nature of their existence in light of social injustice, especially as this injustice was manifested in the lives of workers in an industrializing world. Ideally, industrialization represented the exaltation of capitalist competition, a competition that would propel modernity's humanity toward its final destiny as governor of a more-perfect social order. Socially, the economically driven competition of industrial capitalism produced a masochistic race for production, one in which the value of human life was trumped by the goods that humans and their machines could produce.

Rauschenbusch, at the insistent demand of his father, remained engulfed in his studies until he was twenty-four. He attended Gütersloh in Westphalia, Germany (mostly because his father, August, was concerned that he receive a proper German education), the University of Rochester in upstate New York, and Rochester Theological Seminary. Rauschenbusch's studies led him to reject the conservatism of his father, including the doctrine of biblical infallibility. Although his time as a student did not provide him with a conception of Christianity as a balm for societal anguish, or of salvation as best understood in social and not simply individual terms, it did provide space for deep spiritual questioning. It was during this time, to the consternation of many of his professors, that Rauschenbusch reinforced his stance as a theological liberal. As he was preparing to leave for the parish that would play a pivotal role in molding the man who would push the social gospel to new heights, Rauschenbusch, in an inquisitive and Protestant spirit, said to his parents, "I believe in the gospel of Jesus Christ with all my heart. What this gospel is, everyone has to decide for himself, in the face of God."[2]

After completing his seminary education, Rauschenbusch was called to the Second German Baptist Church of New York City, where he began his ministry on June 1, 1886. The church was located on the border of New York's Hell's Kitchen and exposed Rauschenbusch to social misery such as he had never seen before; this period introduced Rauschenbusch to the reality of social crisis. The newly assigned pastor wrestled long and hard with how to properly minister to the needs of his congregation and soon found that the individualistic evangelicalism that had permeated his upbringing was not gospel for these people. Indeed, Rauschenbusch soon came to realize that the church as he knew it did not have the ability to speak to the problems in Hell's Kitchen because it had no social conscience. The gospel that Rauschenbusch had known might convince individual members that they were saved from eternal damnation, but it could not speak to the systemic and systematic physical and psychological pain experienced every day by the members of his congregation. For this latter task, something else was needed.

It pained Rauschenbusch to discover that he would have to look outside of the church in order to infuse the gospel of Jesus with a social ethic, yet his conscience left him no choice. The decrepit living conditions of his congregants, and especially the untimely death of children in his community, made issues of social reform a necessity for Rauschenbusch's ministry. Despite the admonitions of his colleagues to focus on saving souls instead of reforming society, Rauschenbusch wrestled continuously with what it meant to receive salvation in a social order that cheapened the value of life itself. In order to shift his focus from otherworldly salvation to the kingdom of God, which is to come on earth as it is in heaven, Rauschenbusch needed to cultivate a social consciousness, which the church had repressed for so long.

His earliest political thinking was penned in *For the Right*, a Christian Socialist newspaper that he started with friend and fellow Baptist minister Leighton Williams. The short-lived excitement of *For the Right* (it lasted only eighteen months) combined with the persistent decline of his hearing led Rauschenbusch to consider resigning himself to a life of independent writing. Instead, his congregation convinced him to take a paid leave of absence. Thus, from March to December of 1891, Rauschenbusch returned to Europe, where he worked at a book that he intended to title *Christianity Revolutionary*.[3] His sabbatical work presented an opportunity to place his academic studies into dialogue with the deep existential questions he had begun to wrestle with as a New York pastor. While in Germany, his reflection and study reached an apex when he began to envision the kingdom of God as the governing concern of Jesus' historical ministry.

The kingdom of God, for Rauschenbusch, was not merely a history-shattering event to be waited upon, but a reality already among us. Indeed, it existed within the human heart and needed to be nurtured into fuller existence by addressing the ways that the industrial revolution had devalued human life. Rauschenbusch's spectacularly popular *Christianity and the Social Crisis* (1907) was an apologetic for understanding Christianity as vital to healing an unjust social order and thus revealing the kingdom. Christianity, owing to its prophetic Judaic roots, was a religion that sought to champion the poor, and Jesus was a Jewish prophet who had attained a deeper understanding of the kingdom of God by learning how to live a religious life that was unwavering in its drive for righteousness and social justice.

Yet Jesus' teaching had been diluted through the hellenizing of Christianity, which sought to separate spirit from matter and treated salvation as a gift of eternal afterlife attained by individuals within a hierarchical church. The church had thus become complicit with the dominant social order, trading prophetic existence and kingdom hope for a spirit of social and political complacency undergirded by theological escapism. Rauschenbusch's response was dangerous, and he thought it might lead to his being fired from his teaching post at Rochester Seminary (a position he had accepted in 1897). He advocated for Christian socialism while viewing the home (especially with a Victorian-styled mother caring for it), the school, and the church as socialistic in structure and vital to a happy, healthy social order. Here Rauschenbusch was trying to close the gap between the political and the personal order; he was also maintaining a connection between his pietistic upbringing and his development as a theological liberal.

Rauschenbusch's follow-up to *Christianity and the Social Crisis* was *Christianizing the Social Order* (1912).[4] This second book (which deepened certain ideas from the first while repeating others) came about, in large part, due to readers' desire for more of what Rauschenbusch had done in his initial treatise, but the title suggested a collapse of the church-state divide. Rauschenbusch tried to clarify that "Christianizing" the social order did not mean a theocracy, but was meant to drive home his central moral point: Jesus' concern for the poor had to be applied to the developing industrial social order if a humane, moral, and democratic society was to be maintained. Rauschenbusch used "Christianize," "moralize," "humanize," and "democratize" interchangeably in an effort to spur the spirits of those who clung to an unjust economic order in the face of social destitution, yet "Christianize" was afforded the highest place among these synonyms.[5] What is of vital importance to this piece is to understand how these synonyms, connected as they are to a larger Eurocentric tradition, functioned to perpetuate a social order in which White supremacy is history's alpha and omega.

MANIFESTING WHITE DESTINY: ANALYZING THE WHITE SOCIAL GOSPEL TRADITION

Undoubtedly Rauschenbusch's legacy is essential to remembering the tradition of progressive Christianity. Throughout his career, however, Rauschenbusch was painfully quiet when it came to addressing racism, and at other moments, outright racist. Though his own German heritage led him to speak out against racial and ethnic discrimination in his early years as a pastor, his pro-German sentiment turned into racist rhetoric later in his life, in the form of letters and public addresses. In writing to raise funds for the German department at Rochester, he sought to scare White Americans into agreeing that German immigration was a good thing by reminding potential donors of "the blacks of the south and the seething yellow flocks" that needed to be held at bay.[6] In a 1902 commencement address, Rauschenbusch advocated for a worldview in which Germans were remembered as a third of the Euroamerican trinity that had been vital in the construction of democracy (Anglo-Saxons, Germans, and Americans), while other "alien strains" had thrown a wrench into democratic plans.

Christianity and the Social Crisis rendered race and racism invisible; *Christianizing the Social Order* gave race only passing acknowledgment. And while *A Theology for the Social Gospel* (1917)[7] showed some disgust on the issue of lynching, Rauschenbusch's primary frustration was with the advent of World War I. Thus he is never centrally concerned with the issue of White supremacy, and his antiracist writing seems to amount to little more than thin rhetorical garb. What do race and racism mean within the context of Rauschenbusch's notion of Christian democracy as the kingdom of God? Is there space for the bodies of racial and ethnic minorities, their memories, and their ideas within a European democracy forged and delimited by White supremacy? Rauschenbusch, along with many of his contemporaries, saw evil as a spiritual force and sin as its socialized result. Thus racism, like many other social issues, was a problem of socialization and could be redressed by teaching Blacks to be good citizens within the existing social order. It is comprehensible that one could become so mesmerized by Rauschenbusch's "democratic" prose that his evasive (at best) and discriminatory (at worst) relationship with racial discourse goes unnoticed. Yet an examination of the context out of which the social gospel emerges reveals not just silence regarding issues of race, but also a collaborative relationship with the doctrine of White supremacy.

Gary Dorrien points out that the flaws of the social gospel were legion. Among these flaws were its "[baptism of] the Anglo-Saxon ideology of Manifest Destiny, and [rationalization of] American imperialism" and its failure to demand racial justice.[8] In order to go beyond surface engagements with the points at which Rauschenbusch's social gospel falls in line with the logic of White supremacy, one must gain a fuller grasp of the tradition (i.e., the White social gospel) that Rauschenbusch inherits. John Fiske (1842–1901), an American historian and philosopher, is a vital figure in this regard. Fiske was a leading advocate of Darwinism and sought to marry the doctrine of evolution to a theistic worldview. Fiske's theology-cum-evolutionary-theory was incredibly influential, especially among liberal Christians, who were trying to take science seriously without recanting faith. Yet history does not remember John Fiske primarily for his work as a Darwinist. This is because Fiske was also the leading theorist of Manifest Destiny.[9]

The role of Manifest Destiny is paramount in appraising the social gospel and race. Indeed, the belief in the divine right of Americans and Europeans (especially, for Fiske, those of English stock) to civilize the rest of the world saturated the foundations of the social gospel. It influenced Josiah Strong, whose *Our Country* was an apologetic for Anglo-Saxon imperialism on the grounds of racial superiority, and Washington Gladden, who, despite developing an appreciation for W. E. B. DuBois's *The Souls of Black Folk*, tried to imagine racial justice and integration as separate issues and defended the need for Christian civilization to continue its (imperial) global expansion.[10] Fiske adopted Charles Darwin's evolutionary racism, specifically the idea that the gradual extinction of inferior races would open the way for the proliferation of superior civilization, meaning the civilization of Europe and its bastard child the United States; Fiske gave this idea theological import by wedging his racist claims within God's plan for Anglo-Saxon humanity.[11] Whites were God's chosen people, not through the medium of covenantal promise, but through the medium of White supremacist culture, which crafted God in its own image.[12] Here science and religion befriend each other as Darwinism and Christianity are reconciled in the name of divine progress.

Rauschenbusch's thought *cannot* simply be equated with the thought of Fiske and others like him. The differences here are too outstanding and would render this conflation ahistorical. One of the individuals who influenced Rauschenbusch the most was Richard Ely (1854–1943), a political economist who opposed social Darwinism because he saw it as helping to prop up laissez-faire's individualistic political economy. Furthermore, it was Ely who helped Rauschenbusch to the belief that any gospel solely concerned with individual salvation abstracted from social reform was not the gospel in toto. The effect of Ely's social theory on Rauschenbusch contributed to the uniqueness of the latter's work.[13]

Though the fine distinctions between Rauschenbusch and his contemporaries are important, the vital point here is that in becoming an advocate of the social gospel (though Rauschenbusch found the term "social gospel" annoyingly redundant), Rauschenbusch *does* inherit much of the social theory of earlier social gospelers. It is within this larger tradition that the doctrine of Manifest Destiny, along with its inherent White supremacism, is allowed to survive and flourish. Framed within the doctrine of Manifest Destiny, the social, political, and existential anguish of racial minorities did not lead to an interrogation and indictment of imperial Whiteness as an internationally tragic yet culturally delimited phenomenon. Instead, the superiority of Whiteness in general and of Western European culture in particular was presupposed. Thus the problem of the color line, it was thought, would be ameliorated through one of two possible avenues: minorities would prove unfit for socialization and as a result, through improper social patterns, would have their problematic existence eliminated "naturally"; or through the process of socialization qua civilization, would learn to be good Christian (that is to say, White) citizens. Either way, race was rendered scientifically verifiable, racism socially justified, and the hierarchical valuing of human life necessary for social progress. Hence White supremacy, the bedrock of the United States' developing identity and the night side of its democratic experiment, remained not only unchallenged but embraced by early social gospelers, Rauschenbusch schizophrenically among them.

REVIVING THE LEGACY OF THE SOCIAL GOSPEL

The work of Walter Rauschenbusch espoused and developed extraordinarily helpful concepts (such as the notion of social salvation) and helped to streamline the idea that Christianity ought to be centrally concerned with constructing a just social order during a moment when capitalist greed and individualistic piety were running amok. For this work he must be remembered and honored as a positive contributor to both the world we inhabit and the tradition of social ethics. Yet his work must also be constructively criticized for its myopic diagnosis of society's ailments. In order to help Rauschenbusch's work continue to be salient while also simultaneously crafting a voice that can speak beyond Rauschenbusch's limitations, ethicists and theologians must look beyond the social gospel's Eurocentric roots in order to unearth a more complex and robust notion of what constitutes a just social order.

The development of the social gospel by African Americans reveals a more radically whole trajectory for progressive Christianity in the United States.

The relevance of the social gospel can be reappraised and expanded through an engagement with the fact that Blacks were resisting a social crisis of their own (suffering lynching at record rates along with popular notions of Black inferiority) while White men were advocating for workers' rights, often without mentioning the dehumanization of Black people. Black social gospelers, due in large part to their social locations, were able to nurture a tradition of Christianity that included White supremacy on its list of social ailments. Indeed, an examination of the social existences of African Americans during the period that gave birth to the social gospel quickly bursts the boundaries of traditional ethical analysis.

Indeed, much work is left to be done on the lineage of Black social gospelers who dedicated their lives to expanding the notion of social justice so that the issue of Black humanity was included in social analysis. These historical subjects rendered visible the hypocrisy of the U.S. social order by illuminating the fact that White supremacy was a governing factor in the construction of America.[14] The challenge left to contemporary ethicists and theologians is to reveal and undo the White supremacist boundaries that limit creative social possibilities by holding captive history, sociology, and theology, and thus circumscribing the possibility of creative epistemologies within the confines of Whiteness. Liberation beyond these confines has the potential to create nothing less than a radically different social order. Beyond the boundaries of White supremacy, the legacy of Walter Rauschenbusch (and of the social gospel in general) can be rendered not just memorable but also helpful in creating a more just society.

Notes

1. Walter Rauschenbusch, *Christianity and the Social Crisis* (New York: Macmillan, 1907).
2. Gary Dorrien, *Social Ethics in the Making: Interpreting an American Tradition* (Malden, MA: Blackwell Publishing, 2009), 90.
3. Christopher H. Evans, *The Kingdom Is Always but Coming* (Grand Rapids: Wm. B. Eerdmans Publishing Co., 2004), 93.
4. Walter Rauschenbusch, *Christianizing the Social Order* (New York: Macmillan, 1912).
5. Dorrien, *Social Ethics in the Making*, 100.
6. Ibid., 93.
7. Walter Rauschenbusch, *A Theology for the Social Gospel* (New York: Macmillan, 1917).
8. Dorrien, *Social Ethics in the Making*, 60.
9. See one of Fiske's most notable works: John Fiske, *American Political Ideas, Viewed from the Standpoint of Universal History* (New York: Harper & Brothers, 1885).
10. See Josiah Strong, *Our Country, Its Possible Future and Its Present Crisis* (New York: Baker & Taylor, 1891), and W. E. B. DuBois, *The Souls of Black Folk* (New York: Washington Square Press, 1970).
11. This type of rationale is certainly not unique to Fiske and the social gospel. Much work has been done on the development of such White supremacist reasoning and its relationship to and consequences for theological discourse. A classic in this regard is Cornel West, *Prophesy Deliverance! An Afro-American Revolutionary Christianity*, 20th anniversary ed. (Louisville, KY: Westminster John Knox Press, 2002).

12. J. Kameron Carter, *Race: A Theological Account* (New York: Oxford University Press, 2008). On this point I am indebted to the work of Carter, who explores the construction of Whiteness as a theological problem in a profoundly unique way.

13. Along with the impact of Richard Ely on Rauschenbusch's thought there is also the issue of what genre of historical progress Rauschenbusch espouses. It has been argued that Rauschenbusch's notion of progress was more Hegelian in nature than Darwinian; see Gary Dorrien, *The Making of American Liberal Theology*, vol. 2, *Idealism, Realism, and Modernity, 1900–1950* (Louisville, KY: Westminster John Knox Press, 2003).

14. This, however, opens up a large discourse of its own. What constitutes a Black social gospeler? How is such a person different from a social gospeler of European descent? Surely not all Blacks working for justice can be categorized as social gospel advocates. Furthermore, the issue of race does not merely produce a concern for the kingdom of God in Blackface; instead, it necessitates a reexamination of what justice, and therefore what the gospel, in and of itself is. One volume on Reverdy C. Ransom has taken steps toward beginning this important dialogue: Anthony Pinn, ed., *Making the Gospel Plain: The Writings of Bishop Reverdy C. Ransom* (Harrisburg, PA: Trinity Press International, 1999).

13

Reinhold Niebuhr on Realism

TRACI C. WEST

Christian realism is one of the most dominant themes in the vast canon of books and articles published by Reinhold Niebuhr (1892–1971) throughout much of the twentieth century. It epitomizes Niebuhr's profound religious engagement with major social issues and political struggles that captured public attention in the United States during his adult years. Christian realism, as embodied in Niebuhr's scholarship and activism, was an evolving, courageous effort to articulate a genuine commitment to just social conditions while taking into account the limitations imposed by specific, political situations. Niebuhr's Christian realism represents a pioneering effort in Christian social ethics. It stresses appreciation for the persistence of moral failure in human history without relinquishing the relevance of the transcendent goals of Christian faith and theology for the achievement of social good.

In this chapter I explore some of the racial implications of Niebuhr's Christian realist ideas. Because he consistently framed moral intentions and immoral outcomes as paradoxically bound together, it is fitting to examine some of the ways in which Niebuhr's Christian realist ideas simultaneously reinforced and countered White dominance in U.S. society. I begin with his formative German-American immigrant context of racial/ethnic identity, and then focus on his debunking of liberal illusions and his advocacy of proximate justice. I identify a few examples of religion scholars who have adopted and developed his ideas in their own ethical analyses.

Discussions of Niebuhr's Christian realism have taken place in multiple disciplines, including political science, history, philosophy, and religious studies. But most of those discussions have included minimal analysis of issues of race. My brief treatment below points out some of the racial implications in Niebuhr's realism that could be developed in the more extensive investigation that this subject deserves. Niebuhr's own writings often devoted attention to issues of race. Among other racial topics, his commentaries on the political plight of the Negro frequently punctuated his Christian realist arguments. When major interpreters of his realism within Christian theology and ethics largely ignore Niebuhr's views on race, they create a troubling legacy for Christian social ethics. Besides the misrepresentation of Niebuhr's ideas that this omission encourages, it perpetuates a distorting traditional model of academic inquiry. Studying Niebuhr becomes a rehearsal in tacit acceptance of supposedly racially neutral, universal moral themes arbitrated by a supposedly racially objective White expert. Perhaps most important, an opportunity is lost for refining a foundational tradition in Protestant Christian social ethics in a manner that might help us sort through some of the continuing racist social and political realities that restrict the pursuit of the common good in our societies.

GERMAN-AMERICAN "RACIAL" ROOTS

In an *Atlantic Monthly* article during World War I, Reinhold Niebuhr complained that the German-American immigrant was behaving in a manner "untrue to the virtues of his race."[1] Niebuhr criticized the quintessential German-American immigrant for failing to "to place the virtues and powers with which his race has endowed him" in the full service of the "ideals that animate the people with whom" the immigrants had allied themselves.[2] Niebuhr recognized a plight commonly experienced by new immigrants of having dual, competing national-cultural allegiances. This conflicted emotion was especially heightened for German-Americans during a time of U.S. war against Germany. But Niebuhr's public scolding of German-Americans additionally served the purpose of identifying what he considered to be their racial virtues and potential contributions to national life. He wrote: "No immigrant came to our shores more richly endowed with the characteristics of a unique civilization than the German immigrant."[3] Niebuhr also praised the industry and prosperity of German-American individualism while chiding them for manifesting "no great interest in a single one of the great moral, political, or religious questions that have agitated the minds of the American people."[4] He apparently defined German-Americans as an exclusively Christian group since he commented that even "the Jew" had made more significant social contributions "than the German-American."[5] Why did the Jewishness of Jewish German-American immigrants preclude their membership in the ranks of German-Americans? Did "the Jew" constitute a different racial category from that of Christian German-Americans?

This 1916 article represents one of the earliest articulations of his ideas about issues of race. Niebuhr identifies the superior virtues of his heritage: "the brilliancy, the ingenuity and sometimes licentious freedom" of the mind characterize "the German race."[6] It would be unfair to Niebuhr not to acknowledge the development and refinement of his realist understanding of race and racism in the subsequent decades of his scholarship. Yet evidence can be found here of what was to become a hallmark of Niebuhr's realism: attention to human moral failure. This *Atlantic Monthly* article stresses the moral failures of German-American Christians that unfortunately prevailed over the ideal capabilities with which they were endowed by virtue of being members of "the German race." Their lacking engagement with U.S. life and with other Christian Protestants was proof of their failure. Niebuhr's critique humanized his own German-American ethnic group during a time of significant anti-German sentiment in the United States.[7] It would be a mistake, however, to assume that his racially based claims about superior German qualities and concern about Christian German-American involvement in mainstream American life stemmed solely from a defensive reaction to wartime anti-German prejudice.

Niebuhr was raised in an extremely insular ethnic environment, typical of many Christian German-American communities in the Midwest. He was born to first-generation German immigrant parents in 1892 in Missouri. Ten years later, he and his family moved to Illinois. Between 1871 and 1880, over seven hundred thousand Germans immigrated to the United States, totaling more than one-quarter of all new U.S. immigrants during that period.[8] The Midwest became one of the major havens for German immigrants.[9] Reinhold Niebuhr was confirmed as a youth (and later ordained) in the German-speaking German Evangelical Synod of North America. His father was the pastor of Reinhold's local church and a leader in their denomination.[10]

Reinhold attended the denomination's preparatory school for boys, Elmhurst College in Illinois, where his classes and textbooks were all in German. After graduating, he enrolled at Eden Theological Seminary, on the outskirts of St. Louis. Eden was the German Evangelical denominational seminary from which his father had graduated in the 1880s.[11] At Eden, Reinhold was surrounded by a vast German-American community in St. Louis. During the early years of the twentieth century, over one-fourth of the half-million residents of the city of St. Louis were German-American.[12] In 1913, after completing his studies at Eden, Niebuhr went on to attend Yale's School of Religion (later Yale Divinity School).

In his biography of Reinhold Niebuhr, social historian Richard Fox titled his chapter about Niebuhr's years at Yale: "A Mongrel among Thoroughbreds."[13] The chapter emphasizes Niebuhr's embarrassment over the inadequacy of his education at the German-speaking Elmhurst and Eden when he compared himself to most of the other Yale students, who were from more-elite educational backgrounds. Relying on Fox's narrative, Cornel West, a philosophy and African American studies scholar, has described Niebuhr as "thoroughly intimidated and marginalized" at Yale and "ashamed of his Midwestern German accent."[14] But the young Niebuhr seems to have had another understanding of his racial/ethnic identity, besides viewing it as a "mongrel" source of shame and a reason to feel intimidated by his "thoroughbred" peers.

In a letter from Yale, written to Eden Seminary students via their school newspaper (edited that year by his younger brother Helmut Richard Niebuhr), Reinhold Niebuhr proudly cited the strong German intellectual influence at Yale.[15] He informed readers that "in the classes one hears nothing but German names referred to" and then listed seven examples of the (all male) German scholars who were studied at Yale. Furthermore, Niebuhr explained that although "somewhat ostracized" for their deficient academic preparation, the German Evangelical Synod students "have found this is somewhat compensated for by the fact that we speak and read German. We often find ourselves called upon to review German books not yet translated."[16]

Niebuhr also reported in his alumni missive that "the best known Yale theologian" holds degrees from five German universities. It is difficult to overstate the influence of German theology and philosophy at U.S. universities during the early twentieth century.[17] Harvard philosopher William James (who happened to be prominently featured in Niebuhr's 1914 BD thesis at Yale) encapsulated the influence of Germans in his 1903 statement about Harvard: "Our University, like most American universities, *is* Teutomaniac. Its ideals of scholarship and of the scholarly character have been inspired by German rather than French or English models."[18] In elite U.S. academic circles, German heritage seems to have enjoyed some degree of "thoroughbred" status. And Niebuhr apparently basked in the ways in which his ethnic connection to German intellectual traditions enhanced his own intellectual status at Yale. The ideals named as part of his German "racial" heritage in his 1916 *Atlantic Monthly* article were no doubt informed by this awareness, which was nurtured in his education.

At its core Reinhold Niebuhr's Christian realism requires concessions about the attainability of social ideals. When enfolding this widely regarded Niebuhrian premise into contemporary discussions of Christian social ethics, Niebuhr's base assumptions about ideal human traits demand reexamination. Possible linkages of ideal traits to racial hierarchies have to be ferreted out and discarded. Niebuhr's depictions of racial others, including claims about the weakness and lethargy of the Negro race in *Moral Man and Immoral Society*[19] and the Negro's cultural backwardness in *The Godly and the Ungodly*[20] demand scrutiny alongside of his attribution of superior virtues to members of his own "German race" in his early work.

In the twenty-first century, immigrant identity in the United States continues to be a site for racist hierarchical appraisals of the worth and virtues of particular racial/ethnic groups, as exemplified by the routine, unwelcoming treatment of immigrants who are Latinos/as or Muslim Americans. It is potentially too costly to the freedoms and human rights of these immigrant populations for contemporary Christian ethicists to risk even a conceptual contribution to essentialized racial categories that reinforce a Christian, White, European-American[21] citizen ideal by utilizing racially uninterrogated Niebuhrian themes.

LETTING GO OF FALSE ILLUSIONS, SETTLING FOR PROXIMATE JUSTICE

Reinhold Niebuhr's Christian realism relentlessly attacked liberal illusions. The deluding liberal notions he cautioned against included social gospel utopianism, Christian pacifism, philosophical overreliance on scientific reasoning and rationalism, and naïveté about communism's threat to democratic values. In the foreword to *The Children of Light and the Children of Darkness* (1944), he explained that the "Christian view of human nature is more adequate for the development of a democratic society than either the optimism with which democracy has become associated or the moral cynicism which inclines human communities to tyrannical political strategies."[22] Christianity, particularly in its recognition of human sinfulness, created a viable means for derailing the kind of cultural arrogance and hypocrisy that undermines democratic values.

For Niebuhr, the idea that all racial animosities could be dissolved was a central liberal illusion that helped to maintain racist hypocrisies in U.S. society. In *The Children of Light and the Children of Darkness*, he used immigration policies as an example of such hypocrisies. He pointed out that even as American liberalism anticipated a "frictionless harmony of ethnic groups" assimilating "into one racial unity, public pressure prompted legislation which gave preference to north-European groups in our policy of immigration."[23] He continued in this same section of *The Children of Light and the Children of Darkness* with an illustration of "the even more serious" problem entrenched in liberal social pretensions: justifications for racial prejudice against Black Americans. "The real crime of any minority group is that it diverges from the dominant type; most of the accusations leveled at these groups are rationalizations of the prejudice aroused by this divergence. The particular crime of the Negroes is that they diverge too obviously from type. They are black."[24]

Even though Niebuhr's arguments demonstrate how racial prejudice could be manifested in particular ways through the structural apparatus of state immigration policies or by targeting Black Americans as a stigmatized group, his realism always pointed back to basic human proclivities. The genesis of racial prejudice, he vigorously argued, lay in a prideful, willful human desire for power over another.

As womanist theologian Karen Baker-Fletcher points out, the Augustinian theological undergirding of Niebuhr's Christian realism requires human nature to be disciplined by humility. In her appropriation of Niebuhr's realism, Baker-Fletcher explains how one must recognize that "human nature, including my own, is basically flawed. I see the distortion of human nature in myself and the best of us."[25] Related to this necessity for humility, for Niebuhr, notions of justice must be tempered with love in order for justice to truly exist.[26] Within this realist emphasis of Niebuhr's, Christian ethicist Preston N. Williams found crucial building blocks for a Christian ethic that strives "to privilege the disinherited,"[27] offers guidance for addressing race issues, and provides the requirements for a just society.[28]

Niebuhr's realism has also been identified by scholars as having influenced the understandings of justice in Martin Luther King Jr.'s Christian theology and social ethics. The substance and degree of that influence are, however, a source of ongoing scholarly debate.[29] In a somewhat inflated claim, for example, U.S. social historian David L. Chappell explains: "What makes King a world-historical figure is his Niebuhrian pessimism about human institutions and his Niebuhrian insistence that coercion is tragically necessary to achieve justice."[30] I caution, however, that we may become trapped in the illusion of superior masculinist epistemologies if we focus for very long on assessing the ideas of a great male thinker (Niebuhr) in terms of his influence on a great male leader (Martin Luther King Jr.) according to arguments by (mostly male) contributors to King and Niebuhrian studies.

There are particular obstacles in Niebuhr's Christian realist analysis of liberal illusions and racial prejudice that significantly impede its antiracist potential. His emphasis on inevitability, for example, poses serious difficulties for envisioning antiracist political change. Niebuhr asserted the inevitability of both overt forms of racism as well as covert racial prejudice in the "benevolent condescension" of liberals.[31] Yet any suggestion of racial prejudice as ignorance that could be progressively dispelled through education or other rational means merely constituted another liberal illusion.[32] In Niebuhr's view, only proximate solutions were possible.

If one adopts a Christian realist approach of settling for proximate solutions to social problems, it may require accommodation to certain forms of racist inequalities that are considered to be by-products of unchangeable human dynamics. Concessions to the inevitability of racist resilience can diminish our ability to recognize the choices that individuals (and groups) make to perpetuate racism and undercut the impetus to develop a critique of those choices. A Christian realist perspective on racism can, therefore, discourage reflection on and innovation of social strategies to quell racist attitudes and inequalities.

GLOBAL RACIAL PROJECTIONS

Nowhere was Niebuhr more aggressive in his advocacy of proximate solutions than in his responses to global power struggles. He eschewed a messianic or God-ordained understanding of American exceptionalism, but simultaneously he seemed to cultivate another, secularized version of it. In *The Irony of American*

History, Niebuhr argued that a democratic political community in the United States "has had enough virtue and honesty to disprove the Marxist indictment that government is merely the instrument of the privileged classes."[33] The U.S. political culture, unlike "less healthy European nations," has successfully established "sufficient justice" mostly through "equilibrated power," that is, equilibrium or balance in economic power relationships in society.[34] These assertions communicate a troubling equivocation on the magnitude of White supremacist abuses in U.S. history, including such events as the genocidal attacks and rapes carried out against Native American nations in order to attain land wealth.

Niebuhr firmly acknowledged the validity of resentments harbored by formerly colonized peoples around the world due to Western imperialist exploitation of them. Nevertheless, he added, colonization's technical and educational benefits for their societies must be appreciated too.[35] One of the most negative consequences of imperialist exploitation, Niebuhr pointed out, was how "the arrogance of power reinforced ethnic prejudices; for the industrial world was 'white' and the non-industrial world was 'colored.'"[36] But then he qualified this view by problematically invoking his concept of political inevitabilities. Imperialist "White" exploitation of "colored" peoples on a global scale could be understood as an unavoidable consequence of how the powerful treat the weak.

A fundamental component of his arguments against communism in *The Irony of American History* incorporates a supremacist racial logic that also needs critique. Niebuhr suggests that the susceptibility of "the sleeping cultures of the Orient"[37] to the evils of communism is due, in part, to their particular cultural and spiritual deficiencies. Their spiritual traditions lack the "historical dynamism"[38] of Christian influences that have dominated the West. The dynamism of Christianity that supports democracy in the West has partly resulted from Christianity's "belief that man is to have dominion over nature, which is assumed in Biblical faith and which stands in contrast to a pious awe before nature in Oriental pantheism."[39] According to Niebuhr, Christianity's combined historical dynamism and highly developed individual self-consciousness have allowed democracy to be so successful in "our" Western world, unlike the pantheistic "Orient." He concluded that "a democratic society, in short, requires not only a spiritual and cultural basis which is lacking in the Orient but [also] a socioeconomic foundation which primitive and traditional civilizations cannot quickly acquire."[40]

A cryptoracist logic inhabits this aspect of Niebuhr's globally focused Christian realism. His sweeping historical caricatures of spirituality, culture, and democracy become indices of the inherent inferiority of non-Christian Asians in "the Orient" and of the superiority of the Western Christian Europeans and (White?) U.S. residents. When mentioned at all during this period of his anticommunist writings, the active historic role of Western Christianity in supporting the Atlantic slave trade, monarchies, dictators, colonization, and fascists are treated in a curious fashion. They are examples of historical dynamism: a Western capacity to evolve in ways for which "the Orient" is not spiritually and culturally equipped. Niebuhr fits literary and cultural theorist Edward W. Said's description of Orientalism and its racist cast. Said's typology features intellectuals who each understand themselves to be "the representative man of his Western culture" and steadfastly reassert "the technological, political, and cultural supremacy of the West,"[41] while identifying the difficulty of transforming the "unchanging 'Oriental' passivity" of "the Orient."[42]

These U.S. supremacy claims based on Niebuhr's realist writings captivated neoconservative U.S. intellectuals such as religion and public policy scholar Michael Novak. Novak adapted Niebuhr's Christian realist emphasis on U.S. economic and cultural achievements for his own political framework. Novak envisioned a realist, democratic capitalism where "liberty for individuals will flourish."[43] In *The Spirit of Democratic Capitalism*, published ten years after Niebuhr's death, Novak lamented the loss of Niebuhr's voice in U.S. political life. Among other reasons, Niebuhr was still needed to shatter liberal illusions that continue to "uncritically accept the oppressed of the Third World as a messianic force, [and] attribute Third World poverty to U.S. exploitation." Niebuhr's stalwart realist perspective was needed again because, in brief, "Niebuhr showed us a way to be faithful to the ideals [that] America helped to invent."[44] Novak's realist view of who invents the ideals that are crucial for economic success conform to cultural and racial hierarchies privileging U.S. residents over third-world peoples, and domestically, Whites over Blacks.[45]

Reinhold Niebuhr's Christian realism incorporates sufficient ambiguities and nuances to preclude simplistic, one-dimensional summaries of its racial and political biases. Yet there is a dangerous political malleability in its notions of tragic, inevitable, historical ironies. If one heedlessly adopts the racialized political assumptions in Niebuhr's Christian realism, it can require one to assume an apologist stance where it makes sense for realists to belittle the significance of past White supremacist injustices and accede to current ones because it seems like the prudent thing to do.

Notes

1. Reinhold Niebuhr, "The Failure of German-Americanism," *Atlantic Monthly* 118, no. 1 (July 1916): 14.
2. Ibid.
3. Ibid.
4. Ibid., 14–15.
5. Ibid., 16. Jewish immigrants constituted a significant minority of the German-American population in the late nineteenth and early twentieth centuries. Avraham Barkai, *Branching Out: German-Jewish Immigration to the United States, 1820–1914* (New York: Holmes & Meier, 1994), 8–9.
6. Niebuhr, "The Failure of German-Americanism," 17.
7. However, his criticisms in this article were so pointed that Niebuhr may have fueled anti-German-American sentiment. Richard Wightman Fox, *Reinhold Niebuhr: A Biography* (1985; Ithaca, NY: Cornell University Press, 1996), 44–46.
8. Lawrence H. Fuchs, *The American Kaleidoscope: Race, Ethnicity, and the Civic Culture* (Hanover, NH: University Press of New England, 1990), 55.

9. In Wisconsin in 1890, for example, 37 percent of the state's population consisted of first- or second-generation German-Americans, and they remained at 34 percent of the state population in 1910. Jürgen Eichhoff, "The German Language in America," in *America and the Germans: An Assessment of a Three-Hundred-Year History*, ed. Frank Trommler and Joseph McVeigh, vol. 1, *Immigration, Language, Ethnicity* (Philadelphia: University of Pennsylvania Press, 1985), 233.

10. William G. Chrystal, "'A Man of the Hour and the Time': The Legacy of Gustav Niebuhr," *Church History* 49, no. 4 (December 1980): 416–32.

11. Fox, *Reinhold Niebuhr*, 13.

12. Paul Michael Lützeler, "St. Louis World's Fair of 1904 as a Site of Cultural Transfer," in *German Culture in Nineteenth-Century America: Reception, Adaptation, Transformation*, ed. Lynne Tatlock and Matt Erlin (Rochester, NY: Camden House, 2005), 62.

13. Fox, *Reinhold Niebuhr*, 28. This title comes from a self-description by Niebuhr when he was a student at Yale, found in a letter to his mentor Samuel D. Press at Eden Seminary.

14. Cornel West, *American Evasion of Philosophy: A Genealogy of Pragmatism* (Madison: University of Wisconsin Press, 1989), 153.

15. Reinhold Niebuhr, "Yale-Eden," *Keryx* 4 (December 1914): 1–4; repr. in his *Young Reinhold Niebuhr, His Early Writings, 1911–1931*, ed. William G. Chrystal (1914; St. Louis: Eden Publishing House, 1977).

16. *Young Reinhold Niebuhr*, 57.

17. For a discussion of the influence of "German higher criticism" on Yale faculty during this period, see Roland H. Bainton, *Yale and the Ministry: A History of Education for the Christian Ministry at Yale from the Founding in 1701* (New York: Harper Press, 1957), 174.

18. William James, "Dedication of the Germanic Museum," in *William James: Essays, Comments, and Reviews, 1842–1910* (1903; Cambridge, MA: Harvard University Press, 1987), 79.

19. Reinhold Niebuhr, *Moral Man and Immoral Society* (1932; New York: Charles Scribner's Sons, 1960). Stephen G. Ray offers a helpful analysis of Niebuhr's references to the backwardness of Negro culture. Stephen G. Ray, *Do No Harm: Social Sin and Christian Responsibility* (Minneapolis: Fortress Press, 2003), 60–70.

20. Reinhold Niebuhr, *The Godly and the Ungodly: Essays on the Religious and Secular Dimensions of Modern Life* (London: Faber & Faber, 1958), 81.

21. I use the term "European-American" to call attention to the differing political locations of White European immigrants who become European-American U.S. citizens, and Black or Asian-European immigrants who become European-American U.S. citizens.

22. Reinhold Niebuhr, *The Children of Light and the Children of Darkness* (New York: Scribner Press, 1944), xv.

23. Ibid., 140.

24. Ibid., 141.

25. Karen Baker-Fletcher, "Providence, National Destiny, and the Knowledge of Good and Evil," *Quarterly Review* 23, no. 3 (Fall 2003): 233.

26. Reinhold Niebuhr, "Justice and Love," in *Christianity and Society* 15 (Fall 1950); repr. in *Love and Justice: Selected Writings of Reinhold Niebuhr*, ed. D. B. Robertson (Philadelphia: Westminster Press, 1957; repr., Louisville, KY: Westminster/John Knox Press, 1992), 28.

27. Preston N. Williams, "Christian Realism and the Ephesian Suggestion: Influences That Have Shaped My Work," *Journal of Religious Ethics* 25, no. 2 (Fall 1997): 234.

28. Ibid., 236.
29. Examples of this discussion can be found in discussions of Black theology and civil rights movement history. James H. Cone, "Martin Luther King Jr., Black Theology—Black Church." *Theology Today* 40, no. 4 (January 1984): 409–20; Keith D. Miller, *Voice of Deliverance: The Language of Martin Luther King, Jr. and Its Sources* (New York: Free Press, 1992), 58–59, 88–89, 104–5; George Shulman, *American Prophecy: Race and Redemption in American Political Culture* (Minneapolis: University of Minnesota Press, 2008), 102–4; Harold L. DeWolf, "Martin Luther King, Jr. as Theologian," *Journal of the Interdenominational Theological Center* 4, no. 2 (Spring 1977): 8.
30. David L. Chappell, *A Stone of Hope: Prophetic Religion and the Death of Jim Crow*, (Chapel Hill: University of North Carolina Press, 2004), 53.
31. Niebuhr, *Children of Light*, 144.
32. Ibid., 139.
33. Reinhold Niebuhr, *The Irony of American History* (1952; Chicago: University of Chicago Press, 2008), 100.
34. Ibid., 101.
35. Ibid., 112.
36. Ibid., 112–13.
37. Ibid., 123.
38. Ibid., 118.
39. Ibid., 119, 124.
40. Ibid., 126.
41. Edward Said, *Orientalism* (New York: Vintage Books, 1978), 246.
42. Ibid., 240.
43. Michael Novak, *The Spirit of Democratic Capitalism* (New York: American Enterprise / Simon & Schuster, 1982), 86.
44. Ibid., 332.
45. Novak also describes the emphasis on emotions in Black American religion as having a direct connection to their lower economic status compared to U.S. Whites, since, in his view, success under democratic capitalism requires the organization of the mind over emotions. Ibid., 219.

14

H. Richard Niebuhr on Responsibility

DARRYL TRIMIEW

In the field of Christian social ethics, many scholars owe a great debt to the scholarship and legacy of H. Richard Niebuhr (hereinafter referred to as Richard, to avoid confusion with his brother Reinhold) and the ethical tradition he helped establish known as "ethical responsibilism." As articulated in his influential text *The Responsible Self* (published posthumously in 1963), Richard's ethical approach details an ideal theological typology that has often been adapted to a variety of contexts.[1] In spite of Richard's sometimes limited perspective, responsibilism can be applicable to many Christian communities that utilize the notion of responsibility in their theological ethic. This is the genius of his text. Yet because of Richard's limited perspective, a corrective is often needed to broaden the scope of its applicability.[2]

The Responsible Self was written from a patriarchal, White-privileged perspective that if not heterosexist was probably still not knowledgeable of gay experience. It is not a text that conducts a diligent class analysis. Yet with all of its defects, Richard's social critical analysis was superior to most of the theological ethics of his contemporaries. Its limitations were not so much a limitation of Richard's intellect or spirituality. Rather, the limitations were those of his world, his church, and his academic community. That his responsible self was an empowered self and therefore a limited self with a skewed understanding of the world was the impetus for numerous correctives. Nevertheless, these are the problems of all moral reflections that come out of historical situations and are the products of flawed worldviews and limited ethicists.

Revisionists now acknowledge that Abraham Lincoln signed the Emancipation Proclamation while also being thoroughly racist. Yet Lincoln was merely an average American of his time. Looking back, we see that Lincoln was, in a sense, a victim of the racism of his era. Richard was similarly situated in terms of his time period. So are we all: victims of our era's moral blindnesses. For example, in his book *The Social Sources of Denominationalism* (1929), Richard totally misunderstood the emotional liturgy and liminality of much of African American Christianity. He wrote:

> Finally, the schism of the racial churches was and remains due to the difference in the culture levels of the two races. The Negroes, like the disinherited, required an emotional, empirical religion. The heart depressed by drudgery, hardship, forlornness craves not merely moral guidance but [also] exhilaration and ecstasy. Emotionalism in religion, however, was not only a reaction against the monotony and misery of laborious days on the plantation or in the factory; it was also the natural result of America's failure to provide the Negro with those educational opportunities which have brought about great changes in the religion of the disinherited and of the frontier. With the increasing, though still sadly deficient, education of Negro children and with the rise of a cultured Negro class[,] the colored churches have begun the transition from emotional naïveté to the doctrinal and ritual practices of the more sophisticated.[3]

Here Richard also confuses the word "cultured" with the term "formally educated" when making reference to his historic downtrodden Negro class. Negroes had "culture" and were "cultured" before and after Richard's era, although perhaps not an Emily Post sort of etiquette. Yet this is just one example of the moral blinders of his era that he was unable to remove. Equally important was his mistaken notion that theology is primarily a sophisticated system of ideas rather than a variety of ways of thinking about God, including simple confessions of faith expressed cognitively as well as through glossolalia and "emotionalism." If he had lived longer, Richard could not have accounted for modern White denominations such as the Assemblies of God (which did admittedly evolve out of a Black denomination) or for the phenomenal worldwide Pentecostal/charismatic movement. Accordingly, he devalued such lively worship and predicted the demise of the emotional glossolalia of the Black church, predicting that such practices would pass away as Negroes obtained more education and economic well-being. Such an assessment was certainly wrong, and therefore his evaluation of the religion was also wrong.

Yet the very parochialism of Richard is a human problem that besets us all. We are all born into an already-created world. We are all formed by a fallen society, and relatively few of us transcend the sinful worldviews, ethos, and covenants of our own group's social conditioning. Thus all of our theological ethical systems are both flawed and provisional. Having confessed that and acknowledging that there are defects in my own perspective and moral approaches, I can now turn to my continued critical evaluation of Richard.

THE PURPOSE OF THE CHURCH

H. Richard Niebuhr was partially correct when he asked, "Is not the result of all these debates and the content of the confessions or commandments of all these authorities this, that no substitute can be found for the definition of the goal of the Church as the increase among men of the love of God and neighbor?"[4]

On one level who can quarrel with this goal? It may be that the church has not fulfilled it that well in history, but the goal appears to be appropriate. Yes, perhaps, and perhaps not. This definition lacks specificity. It appears to focus too abstractly on a certain perception of God and of neighbor. Even Jesus of Nazareth had to be more specific in discussing what it means to love one's neighbor—hence the parable of the Good Samaritan. Perhaps the church has been less successful in fulfilling this goal precisely because it has not spelled out more fully what actions, inclinations, or attitudes it needs to actually effect such increases.

For example, slaveholding Christians frequently had such goals in mind (increase of love for God and neighbor), yet their failure to find the slave as their neighbor and brother allowed them to construe very truncated notions of the verb *love*. So many tried, perhaps under the influence of the church, to be loving slave masters, an impossibility, in the estimation of some. For most, a loving slave master makes as much moral sense as a loving rapist.

It is this lack of specificity as to just what constitutes increased love of God and neighbor that makes Richard so right, so often, without requiring from him the specificity of valuation and praxis determination that would demonstrate the very correctness of his ethical approaches. For instance, with reference to the "color line," he correctly analyzes the segregation of the churches to be due to White supremacy, or racism. But he overlooks the reality that Blacks and Whites in America also have different understandings of Christianity and the church. And the emotionalism and the African-oriented call-and-response of the Black churches expressed a religious/liturgical preference that made the White churches who had thought they had overcome racism still regard the Black churches as religiously inferior. As Albert Raboteau's seminal text *Slave Religion*[5] has established, in many respects African Americans remade Christianity into a religion of our own. Thus in the twenty-first century, with more formal education, many Blacks still prefer Black churches to White ones, primarily for cultural reasons and not merely because of racist boundaries and impediments. Similarly, White denominations such as Assemblies of God, which also concentrate on the ecstatic celebration of glossolalia, have not given up on this form of worship even though they have evolved in terms of their members' demographic profile: they are now more educated and also wealthier, with the accompanying higher social caste. Yet their liminality or celebration of the divine in ecstatic ways is not due just to a lack of education.

This may seem like a small mistake on the part of Richard that may easily be overlooked. However, this type of error in Richard's approach is quite important in the overall functioning of his approach to ethical responsibilism. Thus Richard's faulty social critical analysis is of significant import and is tied to theological-ethical error as well. Ethical responsibilism is, nevertheless, an attempt to be in covenant with God and neighbor in ways in which the other is taken seriously as one loved and cherished by God.

The misreading of the Other, as aforementioned, limits the effectiveness of ethical responsibilism and is a standard mistake in all forms of ethics. The failure to understand and appreciate the culture of the other is doubly compounded by a failure to stand in solidarity with others in their struggle for liberation. Thus in their eras, both of the Niebuhr brothers were opposed to outright racism in America. Yet neither brother engaged in a dialogical relationship with Blacks to gain some insight into the depths of their suffering or their need for others to stand in solidarity with them. This failure was surely unremarkable; as for empowered selves, the oppressed were more objects for mission and pity than moral exemplars trying to change the world.

H. Richard Niebuhr's older and more-famous brother Reinhold Niebuhr's position on the issue of race is aptly examined in a recent essay. Therese DeLisio insightfully identifies the privileged world that formed Reinhold:

> There were also cultural limitations in Niebuhr that may have subdued his ardor. As a white, Protestant, European, heterosexual male in America, he never experienced powerlessness in society. The fullness of his humanity and richness of his culture were never called into question, nor was the absolute right to participate in all the privileges of society ever denied him. Sympathy is not as powerful as empathy born of one's own experience. Niebuhr himself resignedly acknowledged that try as we will we cannot feel the pain of others as vividly as they do.[6]

Where such experience is lacking, however, work has to be done in some effort to compensate. Yet Reinhold does not seem to have gone out of his way to learn about the Black experience and perspective, nor does he seem to have engaged the thought of Black theologians.

A further and most fundamental cultural limitation is that Reinhold does not seem to have ever critically examined his own Whiteness. This seems to have been a complete blind spot for him. Everything Reinhold had to say about the "race problem" was from the White perspective: he saw racism as primarily a White sin but also as a White problem that Whites were primarily responsible to solve. His attitude seems patronizing at times, a remnant of the liberal

Protestantism, perhaps, that he never quite shook. Reinhold suffered from a clear case of privileged White myopia. This limitation is made stunningly evident in a comment he once made that "poverty is a peril to the wealthy but not to the poor."[7] So too his consistent suggestion that Blacks suffer from historically conditioned "cultural backwardness" certainly demonstrates a complete lack of consciousness of his own culturally conditioned Whiteness. Reinhold believed that Blacks were fully human in a spiritual and biological sense, but White culture was the superior norm to strive for. Operative throughout the whole of his thought on the race issue is the unacknowledged presupposition that progress for Blacks means becoming more and more "White." In this regard, Reinhold may have been no more limited than any other racially unconscious White man of his day. However, for purposes of determining what is worthy and useful in Reinhold for a theological and ethical understanding of racism in our own time, this is a limitation that every White theologian must consider and continually examine in themselves.

Finally, Reinhold may have been limited by circumstances in his personal life. In his early public life, he was responsible for the support of his mother and sick brother, Walter. Reinhold was a young, severely underpaid pastor hustling as a writer to make ends meet and to support a family. This may account, in part, for his hesitancy to integrate his own church. Reinhold often pointed out that Catholic clergy had far more freedom in this regard, because they could not be fired by their congregations. In his later years, just as the civil rights movement was gaining national steam, Reinhold's steam was running out.

This assessment of Reinhold comes from a twenty-first-century European American, not a Black scholar. Assuming, for the sake of argument, that DeLisio's observations are a fair and accurate depiction of the cultural conditioning of Reinhold Niebuhr, do these observations have any import for his younger brother Richard? It would not be unfair to say that Richard was similarly conditioned and had similar but by no means identical understandings on issues of race. It is also historically true that much of the consciousness-raising of Reinhold occurred in the later years of his life, at a time when views on race were being revisited by Whites. Unfortunately for Richard, he did not live as long as his brother, dying in 1962 at a time when more-progressive views on race had not coalesced for most Americans. It is not unfair for an evaluation of him and his work to assert that Richard's thinking on these issues would have changed if he had lived longer and interacted with more diverse people. That he did not does not condemn him as a racial primitive but does characterize him as representative of a less-progressive White society and culture.

Again, of what importance is the inescapable conclusion that Richard's ethical responsibilism is to be understood as emerging from an empowered "White" perspective? Furthermore, this empowered perspective is one that was fully engaged in oppressing Blacks.

Reinhold's remarks on the cultural backwardness of Negroes sound so ridiculous now primarily because we live in a world in which Martin Luther

King Jr. is not simply a controversial idealist and struggling civil rights activist, but instead is a superior moral theologian, national hero, and martyr. It is not just the personal accomplishments of King that matter in this discussion. We live in a world in which the field of Christian social ethics has been transformed by James Cone, Katie Cannon, Rosemary Radford Ruether, Gustavo Gutiérrez, José Míguez Bonino, Peter Paris, Sharon Welch, and Cornel West, among others. In this world, theology is no longer the queen of the sciences. Theologies and ethical systems are assumed by many to come properly out of the experiences of peoples rather than just the inspiration of a single brilliant scholar. For many, furthermore, proper ethics must be concerned with liberation and not just order and justice. Our ethical systems now assume that moralists must employ a hermeneutic of suspicion for the powerful and for the powerless. Our Christian social ethics assumes that a moral person must stand in some way in solidarity with the weak and vulnerable, regardless of the prejudices of upbringing. In fairness to Richard, he was aware of God's preferential option for the poor. Rather, what he did not fully understand was the ability of the oppressed to engage in superior moral reasoning and action. And furthermore, he overlooked their ability to correct the ethical systems and approaches of the empowered selves that he sought to change and of which he was himself an exemplar.

This is why legitimate and thoroughgoing correctives are needed of Richard's work. If he had lived a long life, it is not overly speculative to assume that he might have seen such correctives not as rejections of his work, but as attempts to adapt his work to the field of ethics.

One such corrective is the thesis that oppressed people who are locked in a struggle for survival have a perspectival advantage over empowered selves in understanding a more morally defensible understanding of responsibility. This corrective makes sense in the twenty-first century. It makes even more sense in a global village in which the knowledge of the suffering of the oppressed is well understood by those who are oppressed and even by those who are not. Individuals like King, and perhaps even more importantly Nelson Mandela, are much more profound exemplars of the inclination to peacefulness, justice-seeking, and commitment to forgiveness than the moral leaders of Richard's era.

One such moral contemporary of Richard's, Albert Schweitzer, is illustrative. Although he was a phenomenally accomplished individual and dedicated his life to humanity before his death in 1965, he did not challenge the colonial system in equatorial Africa, where he did unselfish work to aid the oppressed. (For example, when he received the Nobel Peace Prize in 1952, he used the money to open a hospital for lepers.) He and others like him were moral exemplars; but like many saints, Schweitzer helped the oppressed cope with their oppression rather than overthrow it. This contrasts with figures such as King and Mandela, who joined in the struggle for justice and improved morality rather than simply serving the suffering like Schweitzer or, later, Mother Teresa. As many have observed, when responsible selves do not simply help the suffering with some aid and alms, but further ask why there are so many suffering, they come into conflict with oppression and oppressors. Dom Helder Camara is rightly famous for having stated, "When I give food to the poor, they call me a saint. When I ask why the poor have no food, they call me a Communist." Empowered selves who seek to come into solidarity with disempowered selves and to join in the struggle for justice—such are demonized as communists, bleeding hearts, or nigger-lovers (or laughingly, for some, community organizers).

If he had he lived a long life, Richard may well have redeveloped his views and his moral approaches, becoming friendlier to newer understandings of theology, ethics, and justice. What ethical responsibilism lacked in Richard's time is an understanding of both the moral competency of the oppressed to fight for the liberation of all and the underappreciation of the moral requirement of empowered selves not to simply desist from supporting systems of oppression, but also to join in the struggle to dismantle oppression and to establish reparative, compensatory, and commutative justice. Contemporary ethicists seek this broader vision and want to put ethical responsibilism in action.

H. Richard Niebuhr's genius was that he understood the struggle for justice as always for God's justice and that God always calls to us to participate responsibly in this process. This understanding that we are all in covenant with God and with each other in a never-ending process of trying to be responsible for right action in a divinely created and sustained community allows those of us living in the twenty-first century to develop Richard's work in cooperation with others in more effective and responsible ways.

In this view, Richard's racism is not merely an expression of twentieth-century evil; it is also a sobering reminder that our social conditioning makes us blind to others in the twenty-first century. Our attempts at ethical responsibilism are made with a clearer understanding of our own complicity with systems of oppression. We may be, therefore, more aware of the mistakes of our own moralizing. At least this is the hope that the application of a hermeneutics of suspicion applied to our own efforts should generate. Hopefully, with the grace of God.

Notes

1. H. Richard Niebuhr, *The Responsible Self: An Essay in Christian Moral Philosophy* (New York: Harper & Row, 1963).
2. For a thoroughgoing analysis of *The Responsible Self*, see Darryl Trimiew, *Voices of the Silenced: The Responsible Self in a Marginalized Community* (Cleveland: Pilgrim Press, 1993), which is written explicitly from an African American experience. This is an unremarkable approach since my book, written in the 1990s, is postliberationist and postmodernist to the extent that it refuses to pretend to represent a universal theological ethic that is useful in any direct application to people of other ethnicities. I am also an African American scholar deeply influenced by James Cone, Paulo Freire, Katie Cannon, and José Míguez Bonino. My book does not try to represent more than an interpretation of responsible selves from the African American experience, historical and existential.
3. H. Richard Niebuhr, *The Social Sources of Denominationalism* (New York: H. Holt & Co., 1929), 262.

4. H. Richard Niebuhr, *The Purpose of the Church and Its Ministry* (New York: Harper & Row, 1956), 31.
5. Albert Raboteau, *Slave Religion: The "Invisible Institution" in the Antebellum South* (New York: Oxford University Press, 1978).
6. Therese B. DeLisio, "Did Reinhold Niebuhr Care about Racism in America?" *Union Seminary Quarterly Review* 61, nos. 3–4 (2008), 14.
7. Reinhold Niebuhr, "Grace and Sin," in *Reinhold Niebuhr: Theologian in Public Life*, ed. Larry Rasmussen (Minneapolis: Fortress Press, 1988), 144.

15

Dietrich Bonhoeffer
on Discipleship

ANTHONY B. PINN

Born in Germany into a well-established family and trained as a church theologian, Dietrich Bonhoeffer (1909–45) demonstrated a theo-ethical orientation that was a natural result of his environment, marked by a "Christian, humanitarian and liberal tradition."[1] His promise with respect to the academy was apparent early on: by the age of twenty-four he had completed his training at Tübingen University and Berlin University and had been offered a position at Berlin University. But first he would visit the United States and study at Union Theological Seminary in New York City (1930–31).

While not impressed with most of the theological work being done in the United States, he did believe the African American Christian tradition, particularly the spirituals and the sermonic articulation of biblical ideals and theological necessities, was of tremendous vitality and importance.[2] He spent much of his time in New York experiencing this tradition as presented at Abyssinian Baptist Church in Harlem.[3] It was there that he first encountered the idea of "cheap grace" from the sermons of ABC's pastor Adam Clayton Powell; the contrast between "cheap" and "costly" grace would figure prominently in Bonhoeffer's later writings. After his year at Union Theological Seminary and in Harlem,

Bonhoeffer returned to Germany, was ordained, and began his duties within both the academy and the church. His strong theological and religious commitments and his political sensibilities resulted in his critique of Hitler's rise to power in 1933 and his eventual participation in a plot against Hitler. After the plot was discovered and its conspirators arrested in 1943, Bonhoeffer was executed in 1945. He would leave behind a variety of authored volumes outlining his brand of theology and "Christian humanism."

In the face of the Nazi Party's warping of humanity through the destruction of human life, undertaken with great pride and not a little religiotheological support, Bonhoeffer's writings wrestled with the meaning of the Bible, Christ, and the church within the context of a troubled world. A simple but deeply poignant set of questions frames some of this work: "What did Jesus mean to say to us? What is his will for us to-day? How can he help us to be good Christians in the modern world?"[4] This set of questions is drawn from the introduction to Bonhoeffer's *The Cost of Discipleship* (1937), one of his last publications before he was banned from publishing and public speaking. With an ethos of profound responsibility and sacrifice, it outlines the implications of the Beatitudes, an element of the gospel message that Bonhoeffer was encouraged to consider by the pacifist Jean Lasserre while at Union.[5]

Bonhoeffer frames much of the discussion in this book around the fundamental distinction between "cheap grace" and "costly grace." Cheap grace paid attention to sin without making strong demands on the one who was committing sin; costly grace required following Christ through the surrender of one's life. Hence, "costly grace" requires discipleship.[6] Placed within the context of struggle to find the relevance of Christianity and the church within the context of racism and disregard for human life, this sense of discipleship places strong demands on the one who would be called a Christian. According to Bonhoeffer, "Christianity without the living Christ is inevitably Christianity without discipleship, and Christianity without discipleship is always Christianity without Christ."[7] It necessitates obedience to Christ. Such a stance involves surrender of one's very life, a profoundly existential and ontological connection to sacrifice. "As we embark upon discipleship," writes Bonhoeffer, "we surrender ourselves to Christ in union with his death—we give over our lives to death." This is not the end of our process of Christian conduct, but rather it is the place we start our followership. In the boldest of terms: "When Christ calls a man, he bids him come and die."[8]

The church and "Christians" are only authentic to the extent that they represent and embody this surrender to Christ through discipleship; and this surrender to Christ brings both the church and individual Christians in contact with suffering through gospel-demanded work on behalf of others. This is concrete, physical ministry, without which we develop "barriers between" God and ourselves.[9] The call to service is first and foremost an individual response to the call of Christ. Once this call is embraced with all the uncertainty of its end, we participate in the fellowship (true community) founded by and on Christ.[10]

While in the world, the disciple has a different set of priorities and concerns; rather than greed for power (as exemplified by Hitler), the disciple delights in the "coming of the kingdom."[11]

AFRICAN AMERICANS AND BONHOEFFER'S DISCIPLESHIP

What I have offered above involves reflection on certain dimensions of Bonhoeffer's sense of discipleship; in this way it does not provide full attention to the various layers of that 1937 text, as well as the connections between that text and his writings during imprisonment. Nonetheless, even a brief overview provides enough to suggest the ways in which Bonhoeffer's sense of Christian commitment and obligation might gain the attention of communities concerned with the meaning of Christ within, for example, other contexts of racism.

In recent writings by J. Deotis Roberts and Josiah Young, some dimensions of African American religious thought have both explicitly and implicitly related Bonhoeffer's theology and religious praxis to their own theo-ethical context.[12] This connection typically is presented first as common racial sensitivity and shared appreciation for religious geography marked by an overlap of cultural expression and religious commitment. "I wager," writes Young, "that Bonhoeffer's ongoing commitment to obey Christ concretely—which landed him in prison, in fact—was related to the 'visible emotion' for the black worship that he experienced."[13] Further unpacking this shared geography, one might observe that his centering of suffering as theologically and existentially significant and connected to relationship with Christ harkens back to the framing of suffering that one finds within spirituals and even more recent modalities of African American theological argumentation. Furthermore, this connection might be appealing within the context of African American theological thinking that has for so very long centered on Christology:

> I must go and stand my trail,
> Nobody else can stand it for me,
> I got to stand it for myself.
> Jesus walked his lonesome valley,
> He had to walk it for himself,
> Nobody else could walk it for him,
> He had to walk it for himself.[14]

One could also make a reasonable argument that African American scholars within church settings found relevance in Bonhoeffer's framing of the church's struggle with matters of theological and practical importance. His appeal to religious integrity above institutional form and commitment appeared to be shadowed by the old claims of African American Christians: "Everybody talkin' 'bout heaven ain't going there." From the 1970s (with the numerical decline experienced by some Black churches) to the present, an implicit and explicit concern lodged in much scholarship on African American religion has involved anxiety regarding how to understand and express the future of the Black Church within the (post) modern world, and in light of the implications of the mega-church phenomenon and the "prosperity gospel."[15]

Bonhoeffer's clear commitment to engaging the problems of the time as a matter of Christian faithfulness should be appreciated; this strong sense of praxis found within Bonhoeffer's *The Cost of Discipleship* is significant and can lend itself to a foundational presence in the world as the marker of African American Christian engagement—the this-worldly orientation of faith writ large. Ultimately, Bonhoeffer, in *The Cost of Discipleship*, appears to wrestle with one of the fundamental questions confronting Black churches in crisis: What does it mean to become the representation of the new fellowship framed by the teachings of Jesus Christ?[16]

CALCULATING THE COST: REFLECTIONS

In spite of the above, there are ways in which Bonhoeffer's theological articulation of Christian commitment does harm when the effort is made to apply his principles to the African American context. His appreciation for the cultural realities and his sensitivity to the existential plight of African Americans is not enough to avoid such dilemmas, although Bonhoeffer possessed a complex sense of race or racism. An explanation is warranted.

First, Bonhoeffer's theo-ethical critique of nationalism holds certain possibilities—including the merits of the individual as historical actor. Clearly, Bonhoeffer worked across national lines and thought in terms of "civilization" over against the German nation-state as a way of criticizing power and its arrangement of collective identity. Yet is power, the collective, always so problematic? And what should we make of this language of spiritual individualism within the context of systematic oppression? Nationalism and Bonhoeffer's sense of discipleship both entail a challenge to human thought over and against unquestioned obedience, favoring instead complex and overlapping notions of the good enacted. Nonetheless, how does a sense of calling, of discipleship, suggest or support the liberation struggle as marked out in contemporary theological movements, movements deeply connected to liberal religious sensibilities? And how does Bonhoeffer's concern with nationalism and its implications jibe with what appears to be a somewhat unchallenged assumption of stewardship as a framing of Christian commitment?

Necessary for African Americans is a larger questioning of the nation-state as the proper geography of meaning and power, within the context of cartographies of right thinking and conduct. Thus full appreciation for and action to safeguard African American humanity requires, at the very least, recognition of the intersections and connections between the various components of the American hemisphere (Africa, Asia, and Europe). In addition, attention to the nation-state

alone does not allow for proper consideration of the manner in which sociopolitical and socioeconomic realities are couched in developments across and between
national borders and boundaries. In the study of African American religion, we
have been slow to explore the nature and meaning of religious commitment and
experience as a hemispheric development based on cultural and historical con-
nective "tissues." Attention to this more geographically expansive framework is a
vital turn, one that promises to enrich the comparative dimensions of our work
and conduct; but it is not a conceptual shift offered by Bonhoeffer's notion of
nationalism within *The Cost of Discipleship*.

Beyond his framing of nationalism and collective identity, the manner in
which Bonhoeffer's discipleship does not ignore but rather embraces embodiment
is a worthy consideration. Yet the ways in which embodiment is felt within the
context of proper relationship to the call of Christ prevents strong appreciation
for the actual workings of the body. The fact that Bonhoeffer does not entirely
vanquish the body/mind split presents quite a dilemma for African Americans
who reside in despised flesh. Related to this, the felt response to Christ's call as
outlined by Bonhoeffer also reinforces some of what I would consider the worst
theological thinking by African Americans: redemptive suffering. In short, the
manner in which African American Christian thought centers on the notion of
suffering as theo-ethically important is given ample (but unfortunate) support
through Bonhoeffer's notion of discipleship's cost.[17] He does not suggest that
disciples seek suffering; yet suffering is not only a result of proper conduct but
also a marker of Christian engagement.

Whereas Bonhoeffer criticized the church in Germany, Black theologians
have rebuked the White church in the United States; and in spite of differing
contexts, the theo-ethical consequences are similar. Thus James Cone writes:

> The real Church of Christ is that grouping which identifies with the suffer-
> ing of the poor by becoming one with them. We should be careful in draw-
> ing the line; the line must nevertheless be drawn. The Church includes not
> only the Black Power community but also all men who view their humanity
> as inextricably related to every man. It is that grouping with a demonstrated
> willingness to die for the prevention of the torture of others, saying with
> Bonhoeffer, "When Christ calls a man, he bides him come and die."[18]

For Cone, the presence of suffering for the other is an undeniable marker of
one's proper religious orientation. Josiah Young presents a similar perspective,
but with even more passion:

> The suffering to which the world's people are heir brings to light the reality
> of Bonhoeffer's suffering God [and by extension the suffering of Christians
> committed to the world]. So much is this the case, that I feel bound to say
> that Christians who would dispense with the cross are living in a fantasy
> world (and forfeiting their identity). . . . Too much death and dying abound
> for persons to act as if redemption were won through some virtue (minus
> the suffering).[19]

What results from the framing of suffering offered by Cone and Young, and through the theological discourse offered by Bonhoeffer, is muddy theology and questionable ethics. It becomes difficult, for example, to articulate a vision of liberation outside the workings of human suffering. All is bound up in the ability to welcome suffering.[20]

While Bonhoeffer and some within Black and womanist theologies arrive at redemptive suffering as the outgrowth of progressive Christian commitment, they do not necessarily take the same path to that theo-ethical position. For example, whereas both promote the principles of the Gospel as the venue for engaging the world, Bonhoeffer seems to reject ethics vis-à-vis anthropological considerations. Cone's formulation, on the other hand, promotes synergy between Christology and a form of theological anthropology that Bonhoeffer would find troubling. And Cone suggests formulation of suffering that is much more restrictive in scope than Bonhoeffer's (e.g., Cone does not envision a surrender of material goods).

Bonhoeffer found little of merit within U.S. theological formulations; instead, he embraced the recognition of sin and so forth that he recognized in African American preaching and song. But can one hold in creative tension Bonhoeffer's Christology and the human Jesus that is so prevalent in African American Christian thought? Participation in the suffering of Christ has embodied consequences for African Americans, lodged within a structure of newly arranged "safety" of life through Christ.[21] This is the implication (if not content) of "costly grace" and the presence of the cross—a metasymbol and pronouncement of an ethical posture toward the world *from within* the world. In a certain way, Bonhoeffer's discipleship and the suffering involved promote a framing and quality of life met through a willingness to die as a concrete commitment to Christ. This take on suffering (which is a bit muddy in *The Cost of Discipleship*) does not entail surrender to evil in its various forms. Rather, "suffering love" has a very different effect in that "evil becomes a spent force" when approached through the model of Christ and within the context of discipleship.[22] Although Bonhoeffer's opposition to Hitler and his appeal to the humanity of the Jews are noteworthy, the manner in which he frames his response to Christ highlights destruction over against gospel-centered progress.[23] This is a troubling framing when borrowed by African Americans in that African American life has been marked by the feel and smell of death. What is less familiar is encounter with affirmation, the safeguarding of their humanity, and theo-ethical support of "health" as sign of proper Christian commitment. If "suffering and rejection sum up the whole cross of Jesus," and discipleship is marked by the same summing up,[24] what of transformation, a push for the integrity of life—in other words, the resurrection, which is of such great importance to the African American Christianity Bonhoeffer so appreciated? What of the push for social transformation as the "coming of the kingdom" that marks so much of the African American Christian tradition he found appealing, a tradition that gives some attention to worldly ambitions consistent with the call of Christ?[25]

Bonhoeffer's formulation does not appear to allow for a detailed understanding of the many ways in which (and the various reasons for which) African American Christians are rejected. The history of the United States would suggest that it is for reasons extending beyond their discipleship. Furthermore, is Bonhoeffer's sense of discipleship as suffering for the Other a version of the surrogacy that womanist theologian Delores Williams rightly rejects? Is the proper body only the body rendered docile, albeit through the call of Christ?[26] And if so, what does one make of the Black body in this context of multiple docilities (i.e., Black, gendered, sexed, classed, and so on) and its visibility? Such questions are important, but their importance in part requires a push beyond the theo-ethical framing offered by Bonhoeffer. Perhaps there is some truth in the old blues tune:

> Them that's got shall get.
> Them that's not shall lose.
> So the Bible said and it still is news.
> Mama may have, Papa may have,
> But God bless the child that's got his own,
> That's got his own.[27]

Notes

1. Gerhard Leibholz, "Memoir," in Dietrich Bonhoeffer, *The Cost of Discipleship*, rev. ed. (New York: Collier Books, 1963), 11.
2. J. Deotis Roberts, *Bonhoeffer and King: Speaking Truth to Power* (Louisville, KY: Westminster John Knox Press, 2005), 45.
3. Alain Locke, "The New Negro," in *The New Negro: Voices of the Harlem Renaissance*, ed. Alain Locke (1968; repr., New York: Touchstone, 1997), 3–18, http://us.history.wisc.edu/hist102/pdocs/locke_new.pdf.
4. Bonhoeffer, *Cost of Discipleship*, 37.
5. David N. Field, "Dietrich Bonhoeffer," in *Empire and the Christian Tradition: New Readings of Classical Theologians*, ed. Kwok Pui-Lan, Don H. Compier, and Joerg Rieger (Minneapolis: Fortress Press, 2007), 391.
6. Bonhoeffer, *Cost of Discipleship*, 45–53.
7. Ibid., 63–64.
8. Ibid., 99. This death involves not simply physical demise, but can also be a surrender of all that is familiar, a denial of what one perceived as one's mission or function, a surrender of one's control over one's life.
9. Ibid., 144.
10. Ibid., 112.
11. Ibid., 121.
12. See Roberts, *Bonhoeffer and King*; and Josiah Ulysses Young III, *No Difference in the Fare: Dietrich Bonhoeffer and the Problem of Racism* (Grand Rapids: Wm. B. Eerdmans Publishing Co., 1998).
13. Young, *No Difference in the Fare*, 8.
14. http://www.negrospirituals.com/news-song/i_must_must_my_lonesome_valley.htm.
15. Bonhoeffer, *Cost of Discipleship*, 60; Roberts, *Bonhoeffer and King*, 45, 101–2.
16. Bonhoeffer, *Cost of Discipleship*, 60.
17. See Anthony Pinn, *Why, Lord? Suffering and Evil in Black Theology* (New York:

Continuum, 1995); and idem, ed., *Moral Evil and Redemptive Suffering* (Gainesville: University of Florida Press, 2002).

18. James Cone, *Black Theology and Black Power*, 20th anniversary ed. (Maryknoll, NY: Orbis Books, 1989), 80–81.

19. Young, *No Difference in the Fare*, 19. Young's theo-ethical understanding of suffering is a bit difficult to follow in light of what he says on page 24: "It is not that suffering is good. To the extent that sin is involved, suffering occurs because people seek a truncated happiness, a crown, at the expense of others." How does one describe suffering when Christians encounter it as part of their discipleship?

20. Recently Victor Anderson, for example, has tried to reposition theological discourse on suffering, but not in ways that satisfy the critique of redemptive suffering. See Victor Anderson, *Creative Exchange: A Constructive Theology of African American Religious Experience* (Minneapolis: Fortress Press, 2009).

21. Bonhoeffer, *Cost of Discipleship*, 62–63.

22. Ibid., 158.

23. Ibid., 99.

24. Ibid., 96.

25. Ibid., 212–13.

26. Delores Williams, *Sisters in the Wilderness: The Challenge of Womanist God-Talk* (Maryknoll, NY: Orbis Books, 1993), chaps. 2–3; Bonhoeffer, *Cost of Discipleship*, 185.

27. http://www.jazzblueslyrics.com/lyrics/billie-holiday/god-bless-the-child-1068.html.

16

John Rawls on Justice

ADA MARÍA ISASI-DÍAZ

Since 1971, when *A Theory of Justice* was published, until his death in 2002, John Rawls worked at developing an understanding of justice that could be a regulating principle for the structures of a democratic society. His work was and continues to be widely critiqued, and Rawls conscientiously responded by refining and changing his proposals throughout his life. In 1999 he published a revised edition of *A Theory of Justice*, and in 2001 Erin Kelly edited yet another revision of Rawls's project, titled *Justice as Fairness: A Restatement*. Undoubtedly Rawls, with great thoroughness and with intellectual and moral honesty, pursued the development of his theory of justice.

Rawls's work is marked by humility. He did not have an inflated sense of self and, "unlike other philosophers in history, Rawls regarded his work neither as a revolutionary new beginning nor as the definitive treatment of a topic area."[1] Therefore, though I do not agree with everything he proposes, I approach Rawls's work with respect, taking into consideration different elements of his theory of justice as fairness in my own work on justice, which is grounded in a *mujerista* worldview that takes the reality and experience of Latinas living in the United States as its source; uses liberation, feminist, and Latina/o understandings; and has as its goal the liberation of Latinas and of all oppressed peoples.[2]

My approach to assessing Rawls is marked by a deep distrust of the fashionable academic way of tearing down, showing every shortcoming, disagreeing with as many arguments as possible, and even reading less than forthright intentions into the work of others. These critiques are often more about what authors do not say or should have said than evaluations of what is actually written. Some of them would be worthwhile if at least they sought to correct what is considered faulty or proposed different understandings. However, this rarely happens, and critiques seem to be valued for their severity instead of for their contributions.

The academic practice of deconstructing what others have proposed before presenting different ideas does not liberate one from the canon but rather obliges new proposals to be constructed in reference to it; this is true because in deconstruction the canon continues to operate as a necessary point of reference. Deconstruction, therefore, makes it impossible for new proposals to respond to the author's community of accountability—in my case, Latinas in the United States—or to envision new questions that arise from a different hermeneutics or even a different epistemology. To unveil flaws and inconsistencies in Rawls's theory is not a necessary preamble to new proposals. Hence, I approach Rawls by engaging what I consider important in his work, while not using elements that are irrelevant or contrary to a *mujerista* worldview.[3] In this chapter I engage four elements of Rawls's theory of justice: (1) the "intuitive ideas of the political culture of a democratic society," which play an important role in grounding his theory; (2) one of the "fundamental ideas"[4] of his theory, "overlapping consensus"; and (3) "reflective equilibrium." These two latter elements are ones I use, mutatis mutandis, in a *mujerista* elaboration of justice.[5] Finally, (4) the "veil of ignorance," which has served as a foil against which to insist on hermeneutical disclosure in *mujerista* ethics and theology.

RAWLS'S THEORY OF JUSTICE

Rawls's goal was to present "a political conception of justice that . . . [would] not only provide a shared public basis for the justification of political and social institutions but also help ensure stability from one generation to the next"; it would do this by elaborating "a regulative political conception of justice that can articulate and order in a principled way the political ideals and values of a democratic regime."[6] Rawls insisted that his theory of justice as fairness was not offered as a general and comprehensive view but rather as a moral conception "worked out for a specific kind of subject, namely, for political, social, and economic institutions."[7] This "political conception" of justice needs to gain "the support of an overlapping consensus . . . in which it is affirmed by the opposing religious, philosophical and moral doctrines, likely to thrive over generations in a more or less just constitutional democracy, where the criterion of justice is that political conception itself."[8]

For Rawls, this overlapping consensus is moral because its aim is to achieve "stability and social unity" of the basic structures of a "modern constitutional democracy," and because it is based on justice and not on self- or group-interest.[9] An overlapping consensus is necessary since pluralism is "not a mere historical condition that will soon pass away . . . [but] a permanent feature of the public culture of modern democracies."[10] An overlapping consensus has to be achieved in order to have a free and willing agreement on justice as fairness, a political conception that is not derived from a general and comprehensive doctrine but instead depends on "certain fundamental intuitive ideas viewed as latent in the public political culture of a democratic society," which "articulate and order in a political way" the basic institutions of such society.[11] Examples of these ideas are "liberty and equality, fair equality of opportunity, and the efficient design of institutions to serve the common good, and the like."[12] Rawls argued that an overlapping consensus can be achieved despite "opposing religious, philosophical and moral doctrine,"[13] since different premises may lead to the same conclusions.

It is this overlapping consensus as well as elements of the second principle of his theory—dealing with distributive justice, which he called the Difference Principle—that are of importance and can be used by those struggling against oppression.[14] Though particulars of overlapping consensus, distributive justice, and other aspects of Rawls's theory are problematic for minoritized and marginalized peoples, the goal of his theory can be read as an attempt to reconcile those who have with those who do not have. The greatest challenge to Rawls's theory from racial/ethnic minorities could well be his insistence on basing overlapping consensus on the "basic intuitions" of U.S. society: appreciations and understandings developed by the dominant group in society, but without taking into consideration oppressed peoples. Liberty, equality, and the common good are indeed important values. However, the issue is, What do they mean in the twenty-first century in a heterogeneous society integrated by others besides Euro-American males? These basic intuitions in fact do not mean what they meant in 1776, or even more recently, in the second half of the twentieth century, when Rawls elaborated his theory of justice. These basic intuitions need to be reformulated to include understandings that arise from the Latina/o reality in this country, from African American, Asian American, Native American, feminist, gay and lesbian, and other minority cultures. From these other perspectives, liberty does not mean autonomous individualism, equality is not characterized by blindness to differences,[15] and the common good trumps private property. The centrality of Rawls's original basic intuitions in elaborating a theory of justice is indisputable. It is also indisputable that their present operative meaning responds only to a certain sector of the United States—one that will be less than 50 percent of the population in two decades at the most—while ignoring and being prejudicial for those whose understandings are not taken into consideration in defining the culture of this country.[16]

Two concepts linked to overlapping consensus in Rawls's theory of justice are "public justification," which is tied to "public reason," and "reflective equilibrium." Public reason refers to "the principles of reasoning and the rules of evidence in the light of which citizens are to decide" whether the principles of justice apply, when are they satisfied, and what laws and policies are needed to fulfill them, given the existing social conditions.[17] This public reason has to do with "ways of reasoning and inference appropriate to fundamental political questions" and operates "by appealing to beliefs, grounds, and political values it is reasonable for others also to acknowledge."[18] Public reason is used to reach public justification, which "proceeds from premises [that] all parties in disagreement, assumed to be free and equal and fully capable of reason, may reasonably be expected to share and freely endorse"[19] from within their own ideological stances. Public justification results in an overlapping consensus regarding justice as fairness, which is "affirmed in reflective equilibrium." There are two kinds of reflective equilibrium. Narrow reflective equilibrium results from bringing in line with what one thinks whatever understandings call for the fewest possible revisions of one's own understanding and without considering alternative concepts of justice. Wide reflective equilibrium, which is more important, considers and weighs the force of different philosophies of justice and the reasons for these, and in doing so, makes it possible to "free ourselves from biases and prejudices."[20]

Undoubtedly Rawls's theory takes into consideration the links that exist between moral principles and deliberative procedures. From a *mujerista* perspective, although Rawls did not seem to have thought of it along these lines, the emphasis on procedure opens the door to dealing with contingencies, historical reality, and subjectivity. However, the question that minoritized and marginalized peoples must raise is whether our ways of reasoning—our epistemological understandings—can operate within Rawls's deliberative procedures. Rooted in very different life experiences from those of the dominant group, and insisting on the intrinsic role of experience in knowledge and ways of reasoning, Latinas and oppressed people in general continue to have to go "out of our minds" to survive in a world that does not take us into consideration. It is true that Rawls made clear that he was proposing a theory of justice for a democratic society and that in doing so he was mainly thinking of the United States. But his concept of the United States as a liberal democracy is detrimental to those of us who are not of the dominant group. It is precisely the goal of *mujerista* ethics to have Latinas' reality actually influence what is understood as the United States and how it operates as a society and a nation. The way Rawls limited his enterprise makes it possible to conceptualize his proposals in ways that correct the blind spots we find in the understanding he had of his own nation.[21]

Rawls's "wide reflective equilibrium" is an important concept in the process of dialogue, a process intrinsic to his theory and to a *mujerista* understanding of justice. It makes clear that dialogue is a reciprocal engagement of all those involved in society, which can yield shared meanings and understandings, without which there is no possibility of justice. A wide reflective equilibrium respects the moral agency of all those vested in the process of bringing about justice. By requiring consideration of other understandings than one's own, which exposes personal prejudices, a wide reflective equilibrium makes possible the equalization of power among those participating in the dialogue. From the perspective of oppressed peoples, however, what must be added to the process in order to achieve a wide reflective equilibrium is the demand that, for any theory of justice, the starting point must be the cries of the poor and oppressed. The reality of injustice—made explicit in the vindications demanded by the oppressed, and not via "intuitions" that respond to a liberal understanding of democracy—ought to ground the process that leads to a wide reflective equilibrium and to an overlapping consensus necessary for justice to become an operative reality at the personal as well as at the structural level.

Rawls's idea of the "veil of ignorance," which deprives those involved of information regarding their own particular characteristics such as gender, ethnicity, race, social status, and even their own concept of the moral good, has been widely criticized and even ridiculed without considering that he proposed it as a mere heuristic device and not as an actual event. In *mujerista* ethics the "veil of ignorance" has been helpful in prodding us to consider that elements need to be at play when talking about justice, even if such considerations arise as we argue against Rawls's proposal. In arguing for a veil of ignorance—again as a hypothetical situation, in order to uncover the most reasonable principles that would lead to fairness—Rawls was emphasizing three ideas central to his theory: the need for social cooperation, all persons as free and equal citizens, and the need for a well-ordered society.[22] For Rawls, the idea of mutual advantage necessitates social cooperation, without which we cannot secure social goods. The original position was conceived "as an alternative to the state of nature and . . . as the appropriate initial situation for a social contract." The original position, with the veil of ignorance as its central idea, was an attempt to describe a fair situation for all those involved in the social contract. Rawls's attempted to find a solution for biased judgments. His goal was to provide a "position of equality," which would make it possible for those involved to be represented solely as free and equal moral persons.[23]

In critiquing Rawls's "veil of ignorance," *mujerista* ethics, as a liberation ethics, takes into consideration two interconnected ideas. In *mujerista* ethics our starting point is the lived experience of Latinas at the level of *lo cotidiano*, "the everyday." This immediately makes evident that it is not possible for us to embrace an understanding that, to bring about justice, one starts by neglecting to consider "knowledge of any particular facts about their own lives or other persons' lives, as well as knowledge of any historical facts about their society and its population, level of wealth and resources, etc."[24] It is dangerous for minoritized and marginalized people not to take into consideration facts about themselves, their communities, and their societies. Precisely by being keenly aware of the situation in which we live, we manage to survive despite very negative circumstances. Furthermore, *mujerista* ethics rejects notions of objectivity that we consider to be but the "subjectivity of those who have the power to impose it as objective."[25] What is operative in our struggles and understandings is a claimed subjectivity that seeks resonance with other subjectivities, a nonexclusive subjectivity that looks for shared understandings operative not only in our own community but also in others, particularly in communities of struggle. This claim of the centrality of subjectivity seeks to unveil the prejudices in favor of dominant groups that validate the present political and economic arrangement while ignoring the reality of well over one-third of the U.S. population and 80 percent of the world population.[26]

Though I am willing to concede that perhaps postmodern understandings of objectivity/subjectivity came too late in Rawls's life for him to take it into consideration in his theory, the same cannot be said of the second understanding of *mujerista* ethics, which is antithetical to the veil of ignorance: the importance of hermeneutics. In our work of liberation for Latinas, one element that is important yet not often considered when discussing hermeneutics is that of the social construction of reality, elaborated by Peter Berger and Thomas Luckmann about the same time as Rawls was working on his theory.[27]

The importance of the social construction of reality in *mujerista* ethics has to do with its focus on "what everybody knows" about institutions and systems,[28] which makes it impossible to ignore the knowledge of the U.S. systems and institutions that Latinas have as well as validating the importance of *lo cotidiano*.[29] Of key importance also is the central thesis of Berger and Luckmann: our concepts of reality are made up of concepts we have that have become institutionalized as we act on them. The realization that oppressive understandings and structures are not basic reality, but just the way operative reality has been constructed, sets in motion for Latinas and other marginalized communities the unveiling of the givenness of reality. What is oppressive has been humanly constructed, and it can be changed.

Mujerista ethics' insistence on the prima facie importance of *lo cotidiano*, requiring no verification because it is simply there, finds important allies in Berger and Luckmann. Their insistence on the "intersubjective world" also finds enormous resonance with Latinas' deep sense of community. At the same time, their pointing out how their "natural attitude to this world corresponds to the natural attitude of others" immediately makes it obvious to Latinas how we must struggle to have our perspectives, ideals, and vision influence what is considered "natural," not only for our sake, but also for the sake of society at large.[30]

I am indeed respectful of Rawls's attempt to deal with prejudices by suggesting the veil of ignorance as a central element of the original position from which what is fair for all was to be determined. However, his lack of consideration of the impossibility of escaping subjectivity and of the social construction of reality not only invalidates his attempt to deal with prejudices but also makes his proposal dangerous for minoritized and marginalized groups. One of our most important tools in the struggle for liberation is precisely to validate our specificity, to take seriously our subjectivity, and to continue to ground ourselves in the struggles of *lo cotidiano*.

Notes

1. Thomas Pogge, *John Rawls: His Life and Theory of Justice*, trans. Michelle Kosch (New York: Oxford University Press, 2007), viii–ix. Pogge was a student and teaching fellow of Rawls.

2. For more on the *mujerista* worldview, see Ada María Isasi-Díaz, *En la Lucha: Elaborating a Mujerista Theology*, 2nd ed. (Minneapolis: Fortress Press, 2004).

3. Among other elements of Rawls's theory that I explore in my own work (ibid.) are "wide reflective equilibrium," "reasonable citizens" and "reasonable pluralism," "the difference principle," and "realistic utopia."

4. John Rawls, *Justice as Fairness: A Restatement*, ed. Erin Kelly (Cambridge, MA: Belknap Press of Harvard University Press, 2001), 14.

5. For excellent articles on the different elements of Rawls's theory of justice, see the *Stanford Encyclopedia of Philosophy*, available online. It includes over 100 scholarly essays on the main elements of Rawls's theory and how it intersects with other theories of justice. They are written by some of the leading experts on Rawls, such as Samuel Freeman and Norman Daniels: http://plato.stanford.edu. For a first articulation of a *mujerista* understanding of justice, see Ada María Isasi-Díaz, "Reconciliation," in *La Lucha Continues: Mujerista Theology* (Maryknoll, NY: Orbis Books, 2004), 219–39; and idem, *Justicia: A Reconciliatory Praxis of Care and Tenderness* (Minneapolis: Fortress Press, forthcoming).

6. John Rawls, "The Idea of an Overlapping Consensus," *Oxford Journal of Legal Studies* 7, no. 1 (Spring 1987): 1.

7. Ibid., 3.

8. Ibid. "Overlapping consensus" was not present in *A Theory* but was elaborated extensively in this 1987 article and was then fully incorporated into his overall theory of justice in *Justice as Fairness*, published shortly before his death in 2002.

9. Rawls, "Idea of an Overlapping Consensus," 1–2.

10. Ibid., 4.

11. Ibid., 6.

12. Ibid., 7, 13.

13. Ibid., 10.

14. Oppression is the most common way those in nondominant groups around the world refer to injustice. Distributive justice is indeed necessary, but Rawls's process for attaining it is highly questionable: the biggest problem is that his process does not start with the cries of the oppressed and that it gives little or no role to them.

15. Rawls seems to ignore differences at the level of these intuitions, though differences are central in his construct of the second principle of justice as fairness.

16. At work here is a rejection of some of the central categories of liberalism, such as the private/public distinction and the trumping of the common good obtained via owning private property. Also highly questionable is the almost constitutive ties of liberalism with market capitalism.

17. Rawls, *Justice as Fairness*, 89–90. Rawls considers that these principles are "found in common sense, and the methods and conclusions of science, when not controversial."

18. Ibid., 27.

19. Ibid.

20. Pogge, *John Rawls*, 166; Rawls, *Justice as Fairness*, 29–32.

21. One of the best ways to proceed in this regard might well be to take Rawls's eight principles for ordering the international basic structure and to define the main concepts from the perspective of marginalized and minoritized peoples.

See John Rawls, *The Law of Peoples* (Cambridge, MA: Harvard University Press, 1999), 37.

22. Rawls, *Justice as Fairness*, 43.

23. John Rawls, *A Theory of Justice*, rev. ed. (Cambridge, MA: Harvard University Press, 1999), 11. See also Samuel Freeman, "Original Position," *The Stanford Encyclopedia of Philosophy*, ed. Edward N. Zalta, Spring 2009 ed., http://plato.stanford.edu/archives/spr2009/entries/original-position/.

24. Rawls, *A Theory of Justice*, 11.

25. I heard this repeated many times by my professor and mentor at Union Theological Seminary in New York City, Beverly Wildung Harrison.

26. Ignoring large parts of the world's population is the reason, for example, behind attempts in the United States to do away with "affirmative action" as a positive permanent feature of society. The lack of realization that affirmative action is "good" for society at large, and not just for marginalized groups, makes it impossible for us to contribute to what is normative, signaling the unwillingness of the dominant group to take Latinas and other minoritized peoples into consideration.

27. When speaking about hermeneutics, the usual points of reference are the works of Martin Heidegger, Hans-Georg Gadamer, and Paul Ricoeur. I am not ignoring their contributions but rather seek to focus on the work of Peter Berger and Thomas Luckmann for their exposition on "the social construction of reality," which is extremely useful in Latinas' struggle for liberation, and which was developed during Rawls's time and in close geographic proximity to him.

28. Peter Berger and Thomas Luckmann, *The Social Construction of Reality: A Treatise in the Sociology of Knowledge* (New York: Doubleday, Anchor Books, 1967), 65.

29. Ibid., 23.

30. Ibid.

17

James M. Gustafson on Virtue

ANGELA SIMS

HISTORICAL BACKDROP

A student of H. Richard Niebuhr, the Reformed theologian, pastor, and preacher James M. Gustafson (1925–) taught at Yale University, the University of Chicago, and Emory University. Beginning in the 1960s, Gustafson established himself, along with Paul Ramsey, as a leading academician in Protestant ethics. For Gustafson, reasoning is based on his theological belief that God's purposes culminate in the embodiment of the common good.[1] Following this view, Gustafson posited that on most occasions the reasons that justify any moral act would justify the moral acts of Christians.[2]

Although Gustafson's body of scholarship reflects understanding regarding the relationship of context and moral decision making, our primary concern here is whether his approach to theological ethical analysis takes into consideration how a normative perspective that emerges from and is influenced by a Eurocentric male dominant viewpoint contributes to constructions of Otherness. This is of particular importance given that Gustafson's theological formation was shaped during a period in the United States characterized by *civil disobedience* by Americans of African descent and persons who stood in solidarity with them. After all, in a nation whose founding documents contradicted the existential reality of indigenous and enslaved persons, as well as females irrespective of ethnicity and social status, consideration must be given to the relationship between the 1960s prophetic outcry demanding that "justice roll down like waters, and righteousness like an ever-flowing stream" (Amos 5:24 NRSV) and Gustafson's proclivity to use social and historical categories as common referents for the disciplines of theology and ethics.[3] Gustafson clearly acknowledged that theologians, pastors, and church members are participants in and affected by the cultures in which they live; thus they must be engaged in interaction with intellectual and other currents of the culture and society in order to address perennial theological issues, such as free will, with more consciousness of our contemporary cultural and scientific interpretations.[4] However, we must discern how his unquestioned acceptance of "church" as a universal construct can and does influence moral decision making in a culture marked by social fragmentations that cut across race, gender, class, orientation, and other sociocultural designators.

THEOLOGICAL THEMES

Gustafson's writings are marked by a concern to ask and to answer an elemental question regarding what constitutes sources for theological ethics and the relationship of said sources to each other, thus highlighting the connection between faith and action. For instance, his *Treasure in Earthen Vessels: The Church as a Human Community* is primarily a social analysis of the church. In the concluding chapter of this 1961 book, Gustafson points to the merits of understanding the church as a social and historical institution in both theological and sociological frames of reference.[5] Since social and historical analyses lend themselves to theological-ethical formulations for both individuals and corporate agents, Gustafson asserts that the church in its totality has both meaning and purpose. Since the church is comprised of persons whose actions point both to an understanding of self as well as to an understanding of the incarnation, Gustafson acknowledges that the common deeds of Christians are of many kinds.[6] Furthermore, he recognizes that these actions call attention to the identity of the church as a distinct human community, with action ultimately being a function of commitment and a confirmation of belief.[7]

In a sense, then, Gustafson contends that the primary purpose of the Christian community in the contemporary world is to function as a community of moral discourse in which Christian perspectives establish a normative cultural standard. He identifies four ways in which the social structure governs human response to moral problems and ethical dilemmas, as well as the manner in which theological perspectives inform Christian social action.[8] Gustafson observes that Christian conviction is not necessarily synonymous with actions that contribute to the common good. In many respects, though, he stresses that it is important to recognize that doctrines promoting justice on behalf of the least of these may not always result in convictions that reflect God's mission in and to the world. However, what Christian moral reflection can do is strive to make the intentions and actions of the church and of Christians consonant with the convictions about God and the needs of humanity.[9]

Like many other scholars, Gustafson opines that sources for theological ethics are multiple and include normative theological claims. Taking it a step further, he presents three considerations for religion and morality and views history as a formative source for theological ethics regardless of whether consideration is given to history's influence on moral discernment.[10] Gustafson also isolates three themes in theological ethics—the interpretation of humankind, the changing use of the Bible, and the procedures of ethical reflection—illustrating that the early 1930s were a crucial turning point in Protestant Christian ethics.[11] Along these same lines, Gustafson sets forth three categories for reflection—the location and nature of the good, the nature of persons as moral agents in the world, and the criteria of judgment needed for the determination of conduct—which are viewed as being intrinsic to ethical inquiry as a framework from which to delineate the task of ethics in general as well as to perceive with greater clarity its relationship to Christian ethics in particular. Attentive to the role that the virtues might play in a moral anthropology, he asserts that we must take seriously the role of character formation as an integral aspect of theological ethics.[12]

Gustafson aims to determine whether a distinctive Christian moral character is manifested in moral actions. He suggests that if persons are religious in the context of the Christian faith, there are certain consequences for their morality. Employing a concrete example as a reality check for the moral theology that emerges, he discusses the problems of individual character, the effect of Christian faith on individual character, Christian faith and the "reasons" for being moral, the interpretation of human situations in religious terms, and religious beliefs and the determination of conduct. In addition, Gustafson identifies three crucial aspects of ethics that are qualified by Christian experience—which he associates with a recognition that it emerges from and is informed by its apprehension of God's reality through the Christian story with compelling clarity.[13]

Turning from anthropocentricism to a more theocentric focus of attention, Gustafson's canon includes significant field-shaping studies in Christology, ecumenical ethics, and the moral dimensions of life in the church. In particular, he argues that theology develops in traditions, and that religious traditions are always in relation to other traditions in a given culture and across cultures. However, Gustafson is not convinced that one can argue from a wide range of particular experiences to a logically necessary conclusion that a powerful Other—a monotheistic God—exists. Yet his discussion does show descriptively how, given affectivity and the ways in which it is engendered not only by common experience but also by participation in a religious tradition, the religious tradition provides warrants and symbols for moving from particular experiences to the experience of responding to an ultimate power.[14]

THEORETICAL AND METHODOLOGICAL
CONSIDERATIONS

Gustafson's work is perhaps best described by a question that is also the title of one of his publications: *Can Ethics Be Christian?* In particular, through the analysis of personal experiences, Gustafson seeks to identify characteristics or attributes that distinguish Christians from individuals who do not self-identify with this group. Convinced that theology is historically conditioned and must begin with experience, Gustafson's illustrations indicate that the response to what on the surface appears to be a relatively simple question is fraught with complexities. This in turn requires a "thick analysis" of a particular situation, which often leads not to definitive answers but to additional questions. One question that emerges is the role of the church in an individual's character development.

In *The Church as Moral Decision Maker*, Gustafson writes with the expressed intent to determine the relevance of the institutional church in increasingly diverse settings. We are asked to consider or maybe even reconsider the purpose of the church, especially as it struggles with identity issues, while we seek at the same time to adapt in a world whose boundaries daily become less recognizable in a global economy characterized by and dependent on technological advances. This requires that we consider the church's viability as a community as it is consciously engaged in ethical discourse on pertinent issues affecting not only the church's significance, but also the lives of those with whom the faith community coexists.

Accordingly, Gustafson suggests a correlation between Christian social action and our understanding of God. In *The Church as Moral Decision Maker*, the question internal to his thought concerns the way in which the "dispositional freedom" of the moral agent is ordered and guided in the world. Yet, based on my reading of Gustafson's *Ethics from a Theocentric Perspective*, if a dominant aspect of a theocentric ethic is based on an understanding of the God who is revealed in Jesus Christ, how is this construction uniquely different from a christological perspective? Also, since the example Gustafson uses in *Can Ethics Be Christian?* indicates that responsible social action is not the sole domain of Christians, how does one determine the relevancy of Gustafson's assertion regarding the link between belief and social response? In addition, what consideration, if any, is to be given to the multiple contexts in which an individual is a member? And in particular, what is the church's role to assist individuals in their attempt to arrive at personal and corporate decisions that reflect the essence of the gospel?

The above questions prompt me to consider whether Gustafson's assessment, made more than thirty years ago regarding the church's ability to effect societal change, is still relevant. In particular, Gustafson's assertion that it is impractical if not almost impossible for the church to use economic and political power as a vehicle for facilitating social action[15] certainly raises concerns for me relative to what appears to be a growing trend among certain megachurches in the United States to partner with the government as recipients of faith-based initiatives. In addition, Gustafson's analysis also prompts me to consider the long-term implications of quasi-political lobbying activities, such as marriages and a recognition of the full humanity of all persons, of certain church-based ministries whose long-term consequences might lead to further polarization in many areas.

On the other hand, if Gustafson's assertion is interpreted to mean that the church should remain neutral, what role if any should faith communities take on social issues? As a second-career pre-tenure faculty member, an ordained National Baptist clergywoman, and a scholar whose primary research on lynching seeks to bring to the fore the voices of black men and women whose historical memories of life in the United States should be recognized as primary texts in their own right, I disagree with Gustafson, though not without some reservation, that churches do not need to form coalitions in order to influence other change agencies. There is certainly a historical basis from the 1960s civil rights movement that would both support and refute my claim. For example, Charles Marsh's *God's Long Summer: Stories of Faith and Civil Rights*[16] contains multiple examples of church-endorsed stances on human rights. Thus it appears that Gustafson is not suggesting that the church remain neutral or silent but that the church become intentional in living out that which makes it a distinct entity. Following this line of thinking, it is possible to conclude that there will be a turning toward something upon which the church's distinctiveness is founded.

To address this concern, Gustafson stresses the duality of the church as a community of both belief and action. In many aspects, Gustafson introduces many of the claims in *Treasure in Earthen Vessels* that he reiterates in *The Church as Moral Decision Maker*. In particular, he highlights the connection between faith and action and calls attention to three forms of common action—worship, witness, and moral action—that reflect the church's distinct character.[17] Yet as Christians seek to make sense of their own lives and events outside their perceived sphere of influence, based on their understanding of the significance of Jesus as a moral exemplar, it is perhaps wise to keep one of the many questions that Gustafson raises—*What is God enabling and requiring us to be and to do?*—as a guide to analyze our motives and subsequent actions.[18] For as Gustafson insists in *Ethics from a Theocentric Perspective*, Christians must remember that God is not in service to us: instead, we are in service to God.[19] Therefore it becomes imperative that we become more conscious and deliberate in increasing our social awareness in order to better discern where and how God is calling us to respond in a manner that bears witness to our relationship with the one in whom God revealed God's self. Thus, an examination of Jesus' interaction with persons from diverse backgrounds provides a basis from which we can assess our own embodied faith. In other words, how do we respond to the gospel's imperative to feed, clothe, visit, and stand in solidarity with others even when such a stand may require that we rethink notions of the common good?

CONTEMPORARY IMPLICATIONS

Theology, to abbreviate Anselm's oft-quoted definition, seeks to provide clarity to that which is central to our understanding of life. Though an abstract concept, I want to suggest that faith, or the expression of our deepest convictions, requires that we at all times consider the implications associated with our actions. Although individuals may share common sources, responses to a particular situation or issue may differ. Thus thought should also be given to the decision-making process. In other words, we are asked to determine, for example, how the Bible, reason, tradition, experience, culture, revelation, and history influence our decisions. In so doing, we may be better positioned not only to analyze different interpretations but also to benefit from alternative viewpoints that may perhaps challenge our understanding of justice.

In particular, these multiple perspectives, emerging from an appropriation of common sources and informed by participation in particular communities, may be a catalyst that will foster conversations on the distinctiveness of ethics as an expression of Christianity. Given the complexity of life in the United States, dialogues on the relationship between the private citizen and the public polis may prompt us to consider ways in which personal decisions sometimes stand in stark opposition to corporate responses. Eventually, as minority voices enter into theological discourse, we might find ourselves uncomfortable when asked to rethink our images of God in light of systemically entrenched poverty, which the church may consciously or unconsciously endorse.

Although Gustafson's social analysis of the church emphasizes the correlation between religious belief and moral response, in *Black Womanist Ethics*,[20] Katie Geneva Cannon presents a defense for using Black women's literary tradition as a resource for ethical reflection. In particular, Cannon supports her thesis through a critical analysis of the life and selected works of cultural anthropologist Zora Neale Hurston. From this examination, Cannon identifies three qualities that she suggests are resources for a constructive ethic. According to Cannon, these virtues reflect Black women's moral tradition. Following this line of thinking, Cannon's exemplification of "invisible dignity," "quiet grace," and "unshouted courage" in Hurston's life and work provide a foundation from which a sociocultural analysis of factors that promote the perpetuation of oppression can be conducted. In particular, Cannon examines the connection between "invisible dignity" and the hierarchies of race, gender, and class analysis as well as identifying examples of "quiet grace" and "unshouted courage" in selected works of Hurston.

Cannon's "excavation" and subsequent naming of virtues operative in the life of Hurston call into question the tendency to apply generally accepted methods in ethics; such questioning is a means of analyzing contexts that are not representative of the traditions to which these academic approaches point. It is not surprising that subsequent conclusions frequently support unquestioned hypotheses articulated by the dominant culture. Ultimately, however, the God of our faith largely influences our intentional commitment to the poor. Thus we must question any normative theological ethical perspective that is not reflective of persons who confront daily situations that push them to the margins of society. In other words, we must embody a theology demanding that we stand with and on behalf of the poor. This stance may require a deliberate act of reorientation whereby we turn from self and toward the Divine, in order to be of service to God when we commit to stand with those who are frequently relegated to real or imagined margins. And it stands to reason that when we start from Christian praxis, the poor and those who stand with them talk about God from a particular vantage point that can, in turn, enlarge theological vocabularies and also challenge images of God and church with which the poor are often unable to identify. When truth in action functions as a starting point for theological inquiry, the possibility exists for a fresh interpretation of classical sources that may, in turn, influence individual and group responses to social issues. Therefore, when considering the relation between theology and social action, we cannot ignore the relationship between experience and its influence in shaping our understanding of a distinctive character of Christian ethics.

Notes

1. David F. Ford, ed., *The Modern Theologians: An Introduction to Christian Theology in the Twentieth Century* (Malden, MA: Blackwell Publishing, 1997), 318–20.
2. Ibid.
3. James Gustafson, *The Church as Moral Decision-Maker* (Philadelphia: Pilgrim Press, 1970), 7–9. At the time this book was written, the 1954 Supreme Court decision to desegregate schools was just being enforced in remaining southern states such as Louisiana. Nearly sixty years after *Brown v. Topeka Board of Education,* there is still an urgency to name correctly and address questions regarding social discipline and the exercise of social power.
4. James Gustafson, "The Vocation of the Theological Educator," in *Theological Education,* Supplement 1987, 53–68. Originally presented as a lecture at Austin Presbyterian Seminary, Austin, TX, November 15, 1985.
5. James Gustafson, *Treasure in Earthen Vessels: The Church as a Human Community* (New York: Harper & Row, 1961), 99–112.
6. Ibid., 93.
7. Ibid., 93–97.
8. Gustafson, *Church as Moral Decision-Maker,* 9–46. The four ways in which the social structure governs human action are (1) the integration of personal existence, (2) the disciplined exercise of group power, (3) representational witness, and (4) cultural ethos. The ways in which Christian social action are governed by one's theological understanding of God's existence are the following: (1) in respect to our personal faith in God, our action is governed in some ways by qualities of our life which may be said to be a consequence of our beliefs; (2) in respect to the order of the world in which we live, our action is governed by our perception of how God orders life; (3) the way in which the dispositional freedom of the moral agent is ordered and guided in the world; and (4) the necessity of formulating and articulating the intentions of the moral agent in the world to provide guidance and illumination for the ways in which persons express their dispositional freedom.

9. Ibid., 97–108.
10. James Gustafson, *Christian Ethics and the Community* (Philadelphia: Pilgrim Press, 1971), 9–12. The three considerations one could give to religion and morality are the following: (1) they constitute autonomous or self-governing realms, each of which is independent of the other; (2) they are categories so integrally related that one must be collapsed into the other; or (3) they are distinct but related categories.
11. Ibid., 10.
12. Ibid. See in particular his discussion of the virtues of faith, hope, and love relative to his descriptions of the various kinds of relationships that exist at both individual and corporate levels.
13. James Gustafson, *Can Ethics Be Christian?* (Chicago: University of Chicago Press, 1975), 169–79.
14. James Gustafson, *Ethics from a Theocentric Perspective*, vol. 1, *Theology and Ethics* (Chicago: University of Chicago Press, 1981), 196.
15. Gustafson, *Church as Moral Decision-Maker*, 33–37.
16. Charles Marsh, *God's Long Summer: Stories of Faith and Civil Rights*, 2nd ed. (Princeton, NJ: Princeton University Press, 2008).
17. Gustafson, *Treasure in Earthen Vessels*, 93.
18. Gustafson, *Theology and Ethics*, 327.
19. Ibid., 342.
20. Katie Cannon, *Black Womanist Ethics* (Atlanta: Scholars Press, 1988).

18

Paul Ramsey on Social Order

KERI DAY

THE AMBIGUITIES OF NEIGHBOR LOVE:
READING "AGAPE" FROM THE MARGINS

Within North America, a central task of Christian ethics in African American perspectives is connecting theological and ethical understandings to wider goals of sociopolitical transformation and individual fulfillment. When speaking of sociopolitical transformation, I refer to the transforming of oppressive sociopolitical institutions that exclude and alienate Black communities as well as other marginalized communities. In speaking of individual fulfillment, I refer to the manner in which society honors each individual's subjective interests, needs, and desires toward fulfillment and thriving. The formation of Christian ethical discourse among African Americans has considered both the quest for social justice and individual fulfillment as integral to society's providing the conditions for the possibility of thriving for all its members.[1]

A significant task of Christian ethics in African American perspectives has also been appraising the theological production of White capitalist hegemony, which has participated (both intentionally and unintentionally) in the subjugation and repression of marginalized communities, often inhibiting social justice and individual fulfillment for these communities.

As an African American Christian ethicist, I narrowly focus on the theological production of one particular White male theologian whose work may inhibit liberation and flourishing for marginalized communities: Paul Ramsey. Though Ramsey's notion of agape as the guiding principle of social order (as well as social transformation) provides a way of grounding moral decisions in an ethics of relationality instead of fixed deontological commitments, his deployment of *agapē* as neighbor love does not consider the ambiguities and contradictions of neighbor love. Hegemonic power relations and authority complicate and even render impossible the execution of this agapic vision within many church communities and the wider social order. Without an account of the ways in which oppressive power and authority subjugate the underside of life, Ramsey's agapic vision is problematic and even dangerous for alienated communities who are locked within systems of domination. Ramsey's principle of agape does not account for the ambiguities and contradictions of neighbor love as practice and regulative ideal; it thus ignores the real force of oppressive power relations and authority within church communities and America's late capitalist social order.

To argue this claim, I return to Paul Ramsey's major works that outline his broad principle of agape and its application to a fragmented social order. After briefly delineating the possibilities of his broad concept of neighbor love, I assess the limitations of his concept for marginalized communities such as Black communities and same-sex loving communities. Stuart Hall's discussion of "dominant codes" addresses the problems of hegemonic power relations and authority for oppressed communities within American society, which complicates and frustrates the ideal and practice of neighbor love. I conclude by returning to my claim that Ramsey's principle of agape as the driving force of Christian communities and the larger social order does not get at the ambiguities and contradictions of neighbor love for those who are alienated.

AGAPE AS NEIGHBOR LOVE: CLUES TO TRANSFORMATION OF SOCIAL ORDER

As a student at Yale Divinity School, I took a course titled "Religious Ethics and Modern Moral Issues." In this course I was introduced to the work and thought of Paul Ramsey. From *Basic Christian Ethics* to *Patient as Person*,[2] Ramsey's texts reflect his eclectic mix of theological traditions. Though his conceptions of agape and human reason employ the language of natural law, his understanding of how agape is applied to concrete social issues such as just war, abortion, and euthanasia reflects the manner in which his thought is influenced by both John Calvin and Martin Luther. Ramsey articulates the possibility that divine love can guide and inform the human condition. Yet he equally maintains a strong reliance on the state to restrain individuals from their "baser" passions and sinful desires.

Augustinian tones of the imperfect earthly city resonate throughout Ramsey's work on agape and a social order in which agape could be present within human communities as an imperfectly perfect solution to the radical division, rampant individualism, and growing disunity of society.

As I continued to read about Ramsey, I learned that the principle of agape is the cornerstone of his thought on how Christian religion can uniquely contribute to America's increasingly fragmented social order. For Ramsey, the contribution of Christian communities in the public square should be governed and guided by the concept of "neighbor-love," which he interprets to be the heart of the gospel. He maintains that love finds its highest manifestation in the sacrificial love of Jesus and is characterized by service to neighbor. Therefore this broad principle of love is not to be construed as deontological. Building his concept of agape on both the Gospels and Pauline Epistles, Ramsey rejects a "rule-bound" ethics:

> Paul counters [rule-bound ethics] with a theme, "'All things are lawful,' but not all things are helpful. 'All things are lawful,' but not all things build up. Let no one seek his own good, but the good of his neighbor" (1 Cor. 10:23, 24 [RSV]). For Paul there is a clear connection between love and doing good works. Paul's principle may be formulated as, "Love and do as you then please"; this by no means implies simply, "Do as you please"; for by definition Christian love will be pleased only by doing what the neighbor needs. In place of rules of conduct, instead of "the law" which Christianity entirely finishes, comes not irregularity but self-regulation, and not merely self-regulation of free, autonomous individuals but the self-regulation of persons unconditionally bound to their neighbors by obedient "faith working through love."[3]

Ramsey sees the principle of love as providing "directives" and "orientations," not fixed rules and procedures. He maintains that there are "always situations in which we are to tell what we should do by getting clear about the facts of the situation and then asking what is the loving or the most loving thing to do in it."[4] For him, Christian ethics should not be interpreted as solely applying rules to each situation.

Instead, Christian ethics, guided by the principle of agape, has a built-in flexibility and freedom by demanding that one's moral actions serve the greater interests and needs of one's neighbor. Ramsey's understanding of agape includes broad principles and rules as well as immediately approaching the concrete situation with a "loving will."[5] Agape means the full freedom to morally act. It means understanding that moral decisions are not made by atomistic individuals but by individuals-in-community who struggle to realize God's love here on earth.

Additionally, Ramsey's description of the social order relies heavily on the presence of natural law. He wants to universalize this agapic possibility by contending that natural law is part of God's foreordained design to transform society through various social institutions and through individual behavior. He believes that there is "some virtue in man's ordinary moral decisions" and that each person has an inclination to "discern the right thing to do."[6] Yet in the case where the "right thing to do" is thrown into question, his notion of "human essence expressed in natural law" must always be "subordinate to agape." Though natural justice and human reason are held as sources of knowledge for Christian ethics, natural justice and human reason are to always serve the higher aims of love. In *Nine Modern Moralists*, he articulates the supremacy of agape as "love transforming natural law."[7] Ramsey measures moral actions against the ideal and achievement of neighbor love.

Consequently, he does not try to fix deontological reasoning in moral situations. For example, in the case of abortion, although he criticizes those who judge the morality of abortion purely on the right of privacy alone, he does hold out that in some cases abortion can be morally permissible when the mother confronts an imminent threat from the fetus. He also assesses euthanasia within the covenant bonds of physician-patient relationship, which allows for multiple moral outcomes insofar as the decision made by physician and patient is informed by love and respect for life. Moreover, his turn to just-war theory acknowledges the complexity of violence among nations and how such evil complicates the desire to use nonviolence. On these points I find Ramsey persuasive. However, I do not find persuasive the manner in which he morally reasons about issues of sexuality. Later in this chapter I will return to his sexual ethics.

To summarize, Ramsey's overarching question for Christian ethics is this: What does the gospel require toward the world? For Ramsey, the gospel requires that Christian communities embody neighbor love, which is able to transform the wider social order. Although Ramsey's thought provides real possibilities within social life by dislodging moral discussion from deontological commitments in favor of a broad principle of agape and its ethics of relationality, his thought also poses real problems, even dangers, for alienated and marginalized communities. As stated earlier, his broad principle does not offer a substantive account of how White capitalistic hegemony and its real power interests frustrate his turn to agape as the governing principle of human relations within church communities and broader society. Because of this absence, this principle could reinforce the conditions that make possible such domination and repression among marginalized persons within Christian communities and the wider sociopolitical order.

POWER, AUTHORITY, AND INTERESTS: A READING OF "AGAPE" FROM THE MARGINS

Ramsey's principle of agape suffers from a specific problem, which poses dangers to the flourishing and fulfillment of marginalized communities (such as Black communities). His interpretation of agape does not substantively consider how hegemonic interests and practices, within Christian communities and America's social order, complicate the flourishing of communities on the margins of society. His notion of agape does not account for the ways in which oppressive power relations exploit and alienate vulnerable members within society.

Black cultural theorist Stuart Hall aids one in understanding how such power relations adversely structure the experiences of alienated communities. Hall argues that "dominant codes" or dominant social norms and values should always be seen as part of a system of power relations wherein dominant groups provide "mappings" of social reality.[8] These mappings of social reality offer preferred meanings of "the social situation," wherein such values and meanings are marked by rank, order, and privilege. Such dominant values are imbued with meaning by the elite and powerful. Consequently, the subjugation of marginalized communities can be understood, in part, by the ideological production and "social mappings" of the elite, who determine what is normative.[9] For instance, the idea of "meritocracy" is a "dominant code" that is imbued with meanings by those who possess socioeconomic power. When turning to poverty, dominant groups provide preferred meanings of what it means to be poor. Interpreted by the philosophy of meritocracy, poor persons are described as indolent, irresponsible, and unwilling to work. Poverty is "socially mapped" as deviance. If poor persons would just work harder, they could rise out of poverty. Yet this understanding of poverty does not recognize how social and economic structures impede and inhibit poor persons' chances in life and quality of living. In this instance, the idea of meritocracy functions as an ideological tool of the wealthy.

When reflecting on Ramsey's "neighbor-love" principle, I am concerned that the interpretation and application of this principle to the social order may function as ideological tools of the elite and powerful. During slavery in America, slaves were taught that obeying their White masters was the highest manifestation of "Christian love." For much of Western history, women have been taught that sacrificing themselves for their husbands and their children is the most "loving" disposition they can exemplify. Ramsey does not give sufficient attention to how oppressive power relations between dominant and marginalized groups complicate and frustrate his agapic vision toward social transformation. Social transformation and change must be seen as a complex process entailing relations of power that oppress and suppress. The achievement or realization of neighbor love in concrete social situations is always challenged by how elites interpret and exploit the content of neighbor love or complicate interpretations of love that are engendered by alienated communities. Because social interpretations are often created and sanctioned by those who possess privilege, an account of hegemonic power relations is necessary.

Ramsey's deficiency in accounting for oppressive relations of power is also disclosed in his discussion of the church's role in relationship to political and policy transformation. Ramsey contends that the church's role is to influence the "political ethos" of society, not participate in political action.[10] His stance makes two assumptions. First, he presumes that the "church" possesses in confession and practice morally upright dispositions in relationship to social problems and political ills. However, church communities have a long history of being complicit with the unjust side of culture when turning to moral dilemmas within social and political life. In the early 1960s, most mainstream White churches proved impotent in addressing race relations in America under the racist system of Jim Crow law. They were unable to influence the political ethos of society because they fueled, perpetuated, and buttressed gross inequalities against Black communities. When I turn to poverty, same-sex unions, health care, living wage, and the like, the church's voice in the public square continues to suffer from impotence due to many faith communities' complicity with oppression and inequality. Christian communities have a long history of perpetuating gross manifestations of unequal and inequitable power, which have led to the oppression and marginalization of persons within their own institutions.

Second, Ramsey assumes that social transformation is largely ideological, in the realm of culture. He assumes that if churches influence societal and political attitudes, transformation will inevitably occur. This ideological turn downplays the material workings of power and therefore what possible strategies can be employed to subvert such hegemony. Social ills are problems of culture and economy. Social problems are products of both ideological hegemony and exploitative economic processes. Because social ills appear in cultural and economic realms, strategies of direct political action alongside strategies of cultural change should be pursued. For example, poor Black women suffer not only from neoliberal ideology, which blames them for their own poverty; they also suffer from economic practices and public policies that regulate and control their material realities. Consequently, strategies toward social transformation involve addressing neoliberal ideology and policies as well as economic systems that vitiate the life chances of these women. Church communities involved in the work of social transformation would do well to address both symbolic and material dimensions of evil and oppression within the social order.

As stated earlier, I am aware that Ramsey articulates a Christian realist position when turning to an array of social issues such as war, death and dying, and abortion. He considers how evil complicates society's ability to act in ways that are just and loving. However, his view that the church should influence the political ethos of society and abstain from political action does not employ this same realism. He does not account for gross abuse and misuse of power within Christian and societal institutions and how such abuse of power affects vulnerable communities.

Ramsey's turn to natural law is also deeply problematic for marginalized persons such as same-sex loving communities. He believes that each human has an inclination to "discern the right thing to do." Yet the "right" and "morally virtuous" are shaped by cultural contingencies that tend to express the interests of those in power. I have already mentioned how slavery and gender discrimination were once considered "right," "natural," and "morally virtuous" here in America, supported by religious institutions and the broader political culture.

Similar to slavery and gender discrimination, heterosexist cultural practices within contemporary religious and political institutions cause one to see how "the right" is often conditioned by larger interests of the elite. Ramsey seems to support notions of sexuality that preclude same-sex loving commitments.

Though he provides the possibility for sex before marriage insofar as sex is within the covenant bonds of love and commitment, his sexual ethics is situated within a heterosexist framework, which poses real dangers for gay and lesbian communities who strive to experience and actualize God's love within their webs of relationality. Because heterosexual relationships are seen as "natural" to the social order, same-sex relationships are rendered abnormal and even pathological. Ramsey's support of natural law has serious implications for social issues such as sexuality because he does not account for the ways in which cultural norms are reified as "given" and "natural."

Thus far I have challenged Ramsey's principle of agape in terms of its potentially destructive effects when turning to hegemonic power relations that marginalized communities confront. Yet I also question the viability of agape as a regulative ideal for marginalized communities. I take "regulative ideal" to mean an ideal that society (or communities) feel(s) should regulate and control our moral actions as members within human communities. Can agape (or unconditional love as the highest expression of neighbor love), even as an ideal, ever be helpful for those who are systemically oppressed and repressed? Might agape reinforce the victimization of oppressed communities by teaching marginalized persons to passively endure inhumane, unjust treatment (as seen during the era of American apartheid)? Can the principle of agape be applied to *institutional* arrangements in which gross imbalances of power are present (within ecclesial institutions as well as other social, political, and economic structures within society)? I am aware that these questions challenge a deeply held belief and core value (agape) of Christian faith. However, I believe that Ramsey's notion of neighbor love does not anticipate the practical force of these questions. The ideal of agape within an oppressive social order may reinforce gross abuses of power and may frustrate actions of social justice and individual fulfillment. His vision of agape misses this dilemma for oppressed communities.

Apart from these criticisms, some vision of neighbor love may hold possibilities for marginalized communities. If so, these possibilities are best expressed when one takes account of hegemony and coercive power between elite and marginalized communities within church institutions and the wider social order in the construction of a "love" directive. While *agapē* might not be the best regulative ideal for alienated communities systemically oppressed and repressed, dialogue over a different kind of love in conjunction with principles of justice and human fulfillment could engender fairness, healing, and reconciliation, which America's social order desperately needs.

Notes

1. Black liberation theology and womanist theology and ethics articulate social justice as central to crafting a liberative ethics for Black communities. Beginning with James Cone and Delores Williams, Black theology and womanist theo-ethical discourse respectively have rebuked White, patriarchal theological production for its lack of attention to racism, sexism, and classism within church spaces and broader society. In the last two decades, Black religious scholars and

cultural critics such as Victor Anderson and Anthony Pinn have broached questions of individual fulfillment and flourishing for marginalized Black people. For discussions on social justice, refer to James H. Cone's *A Theology of Black Liberation* (Philadelphia: Lippincott, 1970) and Delores Williams's *Sisters in the Wilderness: The Challenge of Womanist God-Talk* (Maryknoll, NY: Orbis Books, 1993). For Black religious scholars who articulate visions of social justice as well as individual and human fulfillment, refer to Victor Anderson's *Beyond Ontological Blackness: An Essay on African American Religious and Cultural Criticism* (1995) and *Creative Exchange: A Constructive Theology of African American Religious Experience* (2008), as well as Anthony Pinn's *Why Lord? Suffering and Evil in Black Theology* (1995) and *Terror and Triumph: The Nature of Black Religion* (2003).

2. Paul Ramsey, *The Patient as Person: Explorations in Medical Ethics* (New Haven: Yale University Press, 1970).

3. Paul Ramsey, *Basic Christian Ethics* (New York: Charles Scribner's Sons, 1950), 77–78.

4. Paul Ramsey, *Deeds and Rules in Christian Ethics* (New York: Charles Scribner's Sons, 1967), 5.

5. Ibid.

6. Paul Ramsey, *Nine Modern Moralists* (Englewood Cliffs, NJ: Prentice-Hall, 1962), 15.

7. Ibid.

8. Stuart Hall, "Encoding/Decoding," in *Culture, Media, Language: Working Papers in Cultural Studies, 1972–79*, ed. Stuart Hall et al. (Hutchinson University Library in association with the Centre for Contemporary Cultural Studies, University of Birmingham; London: Unwin Hyman, 1980), 134.

9. Ibid.

10. Ramsey, *Deeds and Rules*, 149, 152.

19

Alasdair MacIntyre
on *After Virtue*

ELIAS KIFON BONGMBA

Alasdair MacIntyre (1929–) is a leading philosopher who has addressed a variety of issues, including Marxism, ethics, and Christian theology. He has held teaching positions in the United Kingdom and the United States, where he has lived since 1969. Author and editor of numerous books on philosophical ethics and theology, MacIntyre has won high acclaim for his systematic retrieval and analysis of Aristotelian ethics and moral virtue, which he has championed to underscore his disenchantment with what he sees as the loss of morality in the post-Enlightenment era. He has employed a critical historical approach to virtue ethics, insisting that modern society has departed from the traditions that provided consensus on moral vision and virtue. In this regard, his most influential and controversial writings (*After Virtue* and *Whose Justice? Which Rationality?* and *Three Rival Versions of Moral Enquiry*) have been widely received even as they have been criticized because MacIntyre seems to undercut his rejection of what he calls the Enlightenment project. MacIntyre's quest for tradition-grounded virtue has also taken him back to Thomas Aquinas and Augustine of Hippo, whose Christian perspectives on morality receive approving discussion from MacIntyre. He remains a leading voice in the revival of virtue ethics, and his work in this area continues to attract dialogue and critique from those who particularly appreciate the gains of the Enlightenment.

In this chapter, I argue that MacIntyre in *After Virtue* and *Whose Justice? Whose Rationality?* has raised significant questions for minority communities on issues of justice and virtue; but by rejecting liberalism, MacIntyre undercuts progress in social and political ethics.[1] MacIntyre has argued that contemporary Western society lost a sense of virtue and lacked a coherent view of justice, which historically emerged as communities examined and appropriated views of virtue and justice that were grounded in a shared narrative. A shared narrative provided a context for thinking about and debating morals and justice. MacIntyre joined ethicists who also rejected liberal approaches to moral theory in favor of a communitarian perspective. When I first read MacIntyre, I reacted strongly against his argument because I thought MacIntyre had moved away from his present into the past, to seek justice which might not be relevant today. It was also clear to me that MacIntyre's historical approach to the question of moral theory and the quest for justice brought a brilliant voice to the communitarian landscape even if all who profess communitarian perspectives do not share MacIntyre's rejection of the Enlightenment.

MacIntyre and critics of the liberal society share a disdain for the quest for justice that is centered on rights. They argue that the foundations of liberalism were and are shaky because they are not anchored in a social narrative or a history of communal reflection that has provided orientation for virtue and justice with a clear teleology.[2] For the communitarians, the liberal tradition overstates its case about the self and virtues of the society grounded on individual rights. Communitarians blame the Enlightenment for this overrated view of the self. According to Michael Sandel, liberalism was constructed on the self and therefore has a faulty anchorage for morality and justice.[3]

MACINTYRE AND JUSTICE

Without doubt, the Enlightenment marked a crucial shift in human thought and action, which affected social relations and perspectives about the rights people have as individuals and members of a political community. MacIntyre's arguments undermined the gains of the Enlightenment, which had created a space for people to think freely without being inhibited by totalizing institutions. These changes affected the way we think of society regarding moral obligations and how we arrive at a consensus on justice.

In past traditions that MacIntyre discusses favorably, such as the Greek tradition of moral discourse, it is clear that they fostered debates about the nature of justice. These debates employed practical reasoning, and such debates today are a "continuation of a history of conflict found in the Athenian social and cultural order during the fourth and fifth centuries."[4] The *polis* (city-state) provided a structured community for moral discourse. Members of the polis followed established norms of behavior that were arrived at through rigorous debates. Ethical questions arose as one was presented with a different way of doing things, a way that departed from the norm. When that happened, people debated the merits of different positions to arrive at a consensus. Such an intellectual adjudication was possible because intellectual traditions like the Homeric poems reminded citizens to pay attention to the forms and structures of their society. These poems also exemplified the *dikē*, what was considered just.[5] The post-Homeric era articulated the view that the good included being good at some activity. The social roles in which these standards of excellence were elaborated were "warfare and combat; seamanship; athletic and gymnastic activity; epic, lyric, and dramatic poetry; farming both arable [land] and the management of animals; rhetoric; and the making and sustaining of the communities of kinship and the household and later of the city-state."[6]

For the Greeks, the achievement of excellence depended on obedience to rules of justice, but the content and binding force of those rules differed because of the contrast between excellence and effectiveness, which were defined according to the performance of the good. Tension in the system happened when the good of one person was compared with that of another person, say a farmer and a poet. Thus there was a need to come up with some standard that would claim *dikaiosynē*, "justice," or "righteousness."[7]

The Greeks' system and structured way of thinking about *dikaiosynē* led MacIntyre centuries later to argue that justice was possible only in such a structured community. The members of that society provided a reasonably articulated tradition over a long time and in a context where members had a common understanding of the "good," perceived as that which prompted and promoted activities and excellence. MacIntyre says:

> The name the Greeks gave to this form of activity was "politics," and the *polis* was the institution whose concern was, not with this or that particular good, but with human good as such, and not with desert or achievement in respect of particular practices but with desert and achievement as such. The constitution of each particular *polis* could therefore be understood as the expression of a set of principles about how goods are to be ordered into a way of life.[8]

Thus the polis provided a context for members to pursue a good end, which would lead members to experience *eudaimonia* (happiness). "The constitution and the life of a particular polity (expressed) . . . a judgment as to what way of life is best and what human flourishing consists in."[9] MacIntyre points out that Aristotle thought the highest achievable form of the good was *theoria*—contemplative understanding. He goes on to say:

> The virtuous activities which enable someone to serve the *polis* well culminate and are perfected in an intellectual achievement which is internal to the activity of thinking. . . . The virtue with which the good man discharges his social roles carries him forward finally to the perfecting of his soul in

contemplative activity. . . . The happiness achieved in political life is purely human; the happiness of contemplative activity moves to a higher level, "divine in comparison with human life."[10]

MACINTYRE AND THE LIBERAL TRADITION

Such vigorous debates about the nature of *dikaiosynē* and the meaning of *eudaimonia* are necessary, but one must not rule out the liberal tradition. To argue that modernity has yielded nothing but confusion, communitarians ignore the concerns of modern societies and look instead to past traditions; in doing so, I believe, they threaten and marginalize the gains of the liberal democratic tradition. Those liberties were articulated by John Locke, who championed human and natural rights; and Immanuel Kant, who argued that people should treat others as an end in themselves; similarly, other modern thinkers like John Stuart Mill and Jeremy Bentham, after the tradition of the Enlightenment, called on all to respect human beings as individuals. These perspectives opened diverse ways of understanding our moral ethos and social responsibilities. These ideas foster the rights and dignity of the individual and the community.

Today one could read MacIntyre's arguments about the loss of focus as a call for each community to reclaim its worldview as an intellectual tradition, which could give inhabitants of a political community a sense of direction.[11] The lesson from the past, then, is that a concept like *dikē* and its justification was embedded in a larger conceptual scheme. Virtues were activities that enabled members of the political community to experience the good. We have a variety of positions today, far more than did the members of the Greek polis. For example, Thucydides separated *aretē* (excellence) and intelligence, and he regarded justice as the wishes of the strong and powerful members of society, who controlled sociopolitical relations inside and outside the polis. Thucydides promoted the interests of the powerful and adopted a stronger version of the Periclean rhetoric as a tool for political action, which governed the relationships of the individual and the polis. Rhetoric then could be used to impose a view of life and course of action rather than a reasoned and deliberative approach, which recognized alternatives. So much of this approach depended on chance and ill fortune.[12]

The claims that MacIntyre makes about the manner in which conflicts are resolved within a tradition is idealistic and removed from real life, especially since he dismisses the liberal tradition. Debates go on about alternative approaches to ethics, but it seems that those who have power can pass on or enforce their views on other communities of discourse. This can be seen clearly from the doctrine of political realism,[13] which holds that nations have to play it tough in international relations and command respects in the "corridors of power." Robert Holmes states that international law "has reserved for international relations, the 'unobtrusive, almost feminine, function of the gentle civilizer of national self-interest.'"[14] When national self-interest is at stake, it is easy to turn to Thucydidean principles. Callicles, like the Athenians, says (in Plato's *Gorgias*,

488c) that the weak are subject to the strong. But he extends this claim to the whole of nature, the animal kingdom as well as human societies. He then makes explicit what is only implicit in the Athenians' speech, which is that this is the way things ought to be: it is natural justice.[15]

MacIntyre is not merely explicating how the Athenians arrived at justice, but also arguing that we are now at a point where we have chaos, and there is no clear moral tradition to guide us as in the past. From this one might imagine that if MacIntyre were talking to communities under siege because of national and global inequities, he might instruct them to return to their own stories and narratives to determine how to become a just society, how to fight injustice. The problem here is that if those besieged communities were to follow MacIntyre, they would have to accept that post-Enlightenment liberalism ignores the community in favor of the individual. According to Sandel, since the liberal tradition is so flawed, we should turn away from the politics of rights and instead embrace the politics of the common good.[16] The liberal response here is that we pursue the common good in a better way when we do not trample on the rights of the individual. Minority communities must insist that the liberal tradition offers important perspectives on justice.

First, rejecting liberalism because it cannot resolve some of its tensions neglects the broad dimensions of that tradition and its capacity to influence both individual and communal practices. MacIntyre denies liberalism a chance to resolve its own conflicts. In dismissing the Enlightenment, MacIntyre also fails to appreciate the view that "a [person] becomes fully human only when, instead of remaining subject to given needs and desires, he [she] shapes his [her] conduct by a law he gives himself, and morality is not only one form of such self-legislation, but also a necessary one for all humanity."[17]

From my perspective, MacIntyre raises some important issues about moral virtue in the liberal state, but that state's political ideals such as "liberty, equality, and fraternity" have contributed significantly to build political communities. In adopting modern liberalism, we have already departed from what MacIntyre considers to be a lofty tradition that existed in the past.[18]

Second, even if one were to accept MacIntyre's argument, it should be remembered that even in the Aristotelian society, individual agency was not destroyed by the community. People excelled in different roles, first as individuals and then by bringing those roles together to make the community function. For communities of color and those dominated for many years by the West, the case for freedom has been made mostly on the grounds of the liberal tradition, rather than conservative practices. The nations of the developing world and communities of color in the West have made their case based on the idea that each person is important as an individual. Minority communities have grounded their quest for justice on the principles that have advanced the rights of people as individuals and as communities.

Third, MacIntyre's case for the recovery of a tradition-based moral inquiry and justice is important, but communities of color would be better served if the gains of the modern liberal society are preserved. The ideals of the civil rights movements in the United States and later movements that expressed the need for justice were articulated successfully because those ideals espoused the views of the liberal tradition. In a global context, people of color ought to remember that when some European intellectuals and leaders have talked about having Africans live according to their own ethical principles, they have aired those views in a colonial context of political and economic domination. For example, General Jan Smuts of South Africa argued that the outcomes of a modern liberal society could not be extended to Africans. In his Rhodes Memorial Lecture presented at Oxford University in 1929, he argued that the need to control the childlike characteristics of the Africans (which clearly stood in the way of Europeans completing their domination in South Africa) meant that the principles of the French Revolution could not be extended to them. Africans, according to Smuts, were a unique race, incapable of accepting liberty, equality, and fraternity. Such a move would "de-Africanize the African and turn him either into a beast of the field or into a pseudo-European."[19]

Smuts lamented the fact that the African traditions had been destroyed to promote equality. Africans were barbarians, and if they were incorporated into the political community as equals with Whites, the basis of the African system would be destroyed. Smuts argued that saving Africa required that Europeans "preserve her [Africa's] unity with her own past." African civilization was to be built on its own foundations. Europeans were urged to practice institutional and territorial segregation and keep the economy of South Africa strong by building a system of migrant labor and barring the wives of the workers from moving into the White areas. While this plot hinged on keeping Africans separate, or promoting their own "traditions" by taking them out of the political system grounded on the principles of modernity, Smut was not promoting virtue or economic and political justice. Since he clearly argued against extending principles of the French Revolution to Africans, his perspective of justice was eventually enforced through apartheid, a regime of social, political, and economic differentiation that on the surface seemed benevolent, but at its core it was unjust and brutal in every imaginable way. My point here is that in calling for Africans to live according to their own past traditions and ignoring principles of the liberal society, Smut called for a radical change of the political landscape. When that social differentiation was firmly established, the White settlers and the Dutch Reformed Church claimed they were simply making it possible for different peoples and nations of South Africa to be governed according to their own cultures and traditions. This distinction was epitomized in the creation of the so-called Bantustan policy in 1951. The Native Lands Act of 1913 stipulated that "[a Black] should only be allowed to enter urban areas which are essentially the white man's creation when he is willing to enter to minster to the needs of the white man, and should depart therefore when he ceases to so minister."[20]

The South African example is instructive because justice was denied on grounds that ideas of the liberal society could not be applied to all South Africans.

This resulted in the fragmentation of South Africa, the establishment of a brutal and a costly system as the White regime established a separate polis for Blacks. That is why communities of color today who reclaim their voices and traditions ought to do so in tandem with the revolutionary ideas that have established the grounds for liberty in the rights of individuals. Change eventually came to South Africa because Whites were challenged to repudiate apartheid, a challenge based on the modern concept of the liberal state, Enlightenment principles, and global protocols embodied in the Universal Declaration of Human Rights.[21]

Fourth, all things considered, the liberal tradition is better prepared to answer or address many moral issues because it does not assume the religious background and values of the traditions preferred by MacIntyre. Although communities of color have called for justice based on Judeo-Christian principles, they have grounded those claims in the liberal tradition, where religion has not been allowed to crowd out liberal doctrines of society and its political ethos. The Enlightenment and its aftermath have created space for a view of society that would not have been possible in the past. In defense of MacIntyre, one could say he correctly asserts that the liberal tradition imposes a certain universalism on different communities of discourse. However, the worlds of Augustine of Hippo and Thomas Aquinas also presented universalizing religious epistemologies and views of justice because they appealed to a supreme God. The liberal tradition has only expanded the basis of justice by also focusing on the individual and individual rights. By focusing on the individual, liberalism does not ignore the community.

UBUNTU AND THE CONCEPT OF COMMUNITY

Some final questions should be considered, even though they cannot be fully explored here. First, in affirming liberal values, does one have to abandon the contextual epistemological perspectives that MacIntyre champions? In other words, should liberalism always champion the individual over against the community? Second, can minority voices and communities of color draw ethical theories from their own background?

Regarding our first concern, the liberal perspective offers a different way of seeing members of the political community. They are individuals, whose rights should not be violated lest individual and communal liberties be compromised. But should individuals and their rights be the sole focus of moral theories? One could think of both individual rights and community priorities without hindering the articulation of justice. Anita Jacobson-Widding has argued that the relationship between one's culture, thought, and the particular individual's lived experience is complex, and that some aspects of personhood relate to the broad cultural areas of an individual's life as well as one's personal experience.[22]

Elsewhere I have argued that Africans establish intersubjective bonds on grounds that individuality is recognized and cherished. In the Wimbum community, people express this individuality when they use the phrase "*Fo Ni Nwe*," which means "pride in a person."[23] Though I support greater emphasis on the individual dimension of life in the African context, one cannot completely rule out the community. Communities share values and beliefs; they develop common practices and obligations, all of which contribute to ethical thought and practices. As members of a particular community, individuals often invest themselves in diverse ways to support the intellectual traditions of the community and pledge themselves to carry out ideas that promote human well-being—both of its individual members and the entire community.

Second, if we have contextual epistemologies that reflect the notions of ethical traditions, as MacIntyre has suggested, those theories cannot ignore liberalism. In the African context, *ubuntu*, "all pull together," is a complex Bantu language group term that refers to a humane way of relating, sharing, expressing hospitality, and doing good toward others inside and outside of the community. Advocates of *ubuntu* argue that the idea sets forth human values of love, support, and respect for one another; it encourages participation in the life of the community. It is also the basis of an interrelated support system, which seeks the good of everyone inside and outside of the community. For that reason, it could serve as a compelling ethical theory.

Ubuntu should be explored further because one cannot describe *ubuntu* as a communitarian perspective only. In order to avoid falling into such a trap, it is worth briefly examining the aspects of *ubuntu* thought mainly through the isi-Zulu (Zulu language) expression "*umuntu ngumuntu ngabantu*," which means "a person is a person through persons." *Ubuntu* as an ethical idea is gaining traction throughout Africa. For example, Bénézet Bujo of the Democratic Republic of Congo describes what could be called the communal dimension of *ubuntu*:

> The human being does not become human by *cogito* (thinking) but by *relatio* (relationship) and *cognatio* (kinship). The fundamental principle in this ethics is not *cogito ergo sum* (I think, so I am), but rather, *cognatus sum ergo sum* (I am related, so I am). Somebody living far from any *cognatio* will never reach the *cogito*. Without communal relationship one can neither find his or her identity nor learn how to think. Self-awareness presupposes somebody opposite to you in human form.[24]

While the analysis that compares it to the Cartesian *cogito* might be helpful, one must be careful of conflating two different concepts. The Cartesian *cogito* introduces methodological doubt as a way of establishing certainty that the doubter must exist to doubt. Although this methodological doubt was clearly articulated by René Descartes, one cannot say that it is mainly a European way of thinking and experiencing life and then assume that the African way of experiencing life must be communitarian. The common replacement of the idea of "I think, therefore I am" with the concept "I am related, therefore I am" should be rejected because it removes the *cogito* from Africans. It might give the impression that Africans do not think.

Ubuntu expresses relatedness, but it should not necessarily be considered a communitarian thesis because it also expresses dimensions of individuality and otherness. *Ubuntu* stresses personhood but also gives us a sense of community to the extent that we can say that one is a person because of other persons. It is implicit in this claim that individuals have subjective, personal identity. One's personhood is confirmed in the presence of another person or other persons. Thus *ubuntu* is a concept that highlights individual subjectivity. The person in relation is already a distinct individual and a part of the community. The relation to the other people only extends the scope of the relations and responsibility. Personhood is intersubjective. *Ubuntu* allows the prioritization of rights with an understanding that intersubjective bonds and demands could undercut those rights. *Ubuntu*, from this perspective, could be a theoretical anchor that supports particularity and communalism. Theologian John de Gruchy has argued that

> [*ubuntu*'s] contemporary reaffirmation is essential for the renewal of democ-
> racy in Africa and more universally. This does not imply the denial of
> individuals or individual political rights. On the contrary, a respect for
> each person as an individual is fundamental. But it is very different from
> possessive individualism. The emphasis is on human sociality, on inter-
> personal relations, on the need which each person has for others in order to
> be herself or himself.[25]

Ubuntu invites theorists to think in terms of realigning intersubjective bonds as a vehicle for a new social vision that is grounded on individual well-being as well as the common good.

Emmanuel C. Eze has argued that *ubuntu* is an inadequate concept to employ in dealing with the problems of contemporary Africa.[26] He insists that reason, or rationality, should be the main criterion for making philosophical judg-ments. *Ubuntu* as an idea "[does not] escape the radical dialectic of that same experience it seems primed to address." *Ubuntu* "as an ideology . . . relies too much on the extraordinary: luck, miracles, and an ambiguous concept of natural goodness."[27] The emphasis on *ubuntu* neglects everyday reason and prefers the extraordinary.[28]

I do not think *ubuntu*, an idea that promotes humaneness, offers any tran-scendental approach to ethics other than stressing a common humanity. I am convinced that *ubuntu* has the potential of returning the community to perspec-tives on justice in a global context, as articulated by the scholars like Emmanuel Lévinas, Simone Weil, Peter Winch, Martha Nussbaum, and Amartya Sen, or political leaders like Nelson Mandela and Václav Havel. They call our attention to what Eze describes as the important task of recovering our common human-ity. In the African context, *ubuntu* can serve as a tradition that requires debate and explication in a liberal democratic context as Africans reflect on justice and its justification. Munyaradzi Felix Murove has argued that African ethics could be described as a "morality of *memoria* in the sense that it is brought into being in the context of *anamnēsis*—remembering one's past within the community of fellowship."[29] The idea of ethics in the African context is also linked to a long tradition. Finding a common consensus on all of these issues is difficult, as MacIntyre has pointed out. Perhaps it is time for the African community to accept the reality of the incommensurability and untranslatability of ideas when it comes to the way we think about the community—in a context where we all agree that *ubuntu* is an important moral concept. We insist that moral discourse after the polis must give liberalism a chance as a viable tradition that is wrestling with its own inner conflicts.

Notes

1. I express my appreciation to Alice Hunt, Anthony Pinn, and the editors, Miguel A. De La Torre and Stacey M. Floyd-Thomas, for their critical feedback.
2. Alasdair MacIntyre, *After Virtue: A Study in Moral Theory* (1981), 2nd ed. (Notre Dame, IN: University of Notre Dame Press, 1984), 52.
3. Michael J. Sandel, *Liberalism and the Limits of the Justice* (New York: Cambridge University Press, 1982), 64–65, 168–73.
4. Alasdair MacIntyre, *Whose Justice? Whose Rationality?* (Notre Dame, IN: University of Notre Dame Press, 1988), 13.
5. MacIntyre indicates that the poems were taught to Athenian boys and were part of the Athenian religion. Justice then was the justice of Zeus.
6. Ibid., 30. MacIntyre says that to this list things like architecture, painting, and sculpture were added as well as the intellectual disciplines of mathematics, philosophy, and theology.
7. Ibid., 33.
8. Ibid., 34.
9. Ibid.
10. Ibid., 107–8.
11. Ibid., 23.
12. Ibid., 66–67.
13. I am indebted to Robert L. Holmes, *On War and Morality* (Princeton, NJ: Princeton University Press, 1989), for his ideas on this subject.
14. Ibid., 51.
15. Ibid., 53.
16. Michael Sandel, *Public Philosophy: Essays on Morality in Public* (Cambridge, MA: Harvard University Press, 2005), 147–55.
17. Charles Lamore, *Patterns of Moral Complexity* (London: Cambridge University Press, 1987), 31.
18. Richard J. Bernstein, *Philosophical Profiles: Essays in a Pragmatic Mode* (Philadelphia: University of Pennsylvania Press, 1986), 140. Bernstein argues that MacIntyre appropriates his reconstruction of the virtues from the Enlightenment tradition, as is evident in his defense of the freedom of every participant to share in some communal life necessary for the good life, and in his demand that each person should be treated with respect and each individual be granted the ability to act rationally.
19. Jan C. Smuts, *Africa and Some World Problems: Including the Rhodes Memorial Lectures Delivered in Michaelmas Term, 1929* (Oxford: Clarendon Press, 1929), 76–78. I am indebted to Mahmood Mamdani for this discussion and citation. Mahmood Mamdani, *Citizen and Subject: Contemporary Africa and the Legacy of Late Colonialism* (Princeton, NJ: Princeton University Press, 1996), 4–5.
20. Christopher Hill, *Bantustans: The Fragmentation of South Africa* (New York: Oxford University Press, 1979), 5.

21. One wonders if MacIntyre's rejection of universals would allow him to accept the principles embodied in the Universal Declaration of Human Rights (http://www.wunrn.com/reference/pdf/univ_dec_hum_right.pdf)—or, for that matter, to accept the preamble of the Constitution of the United States (http://www.usconstitution.net/const.html#Preamble) and statements of other modern states that are patterned after the Social Contract, the idea that people carry out certain obligations because they have agreed to abide by those principles or rules to organize their moral and political lives.

22. Anita Jacobson-Widding, "The Shadow as an Expression of Individuality in Congolese Conceptions of Personhood," in *Personhood and Agency: The Experience of Self and Other in African Cultures; Papers Presented at a Symposium on African Folk Models and Their Application, held at Uppsala University, August 23–30, 1987,* ed. Michael D. Jackson and Ivan Karp, Uppsala Studies in Cultural Anthropology 14 (Uppsala: S. Academiae Ubsaliensis; Washington, DC: distributed by Smithsonian Institution Press, 1990), 31–58. See also Michael D. Jackson's studies of similar phenomena in Sierra Leone: Michael D. Jackson, "The Man Who Could Turn into an Elephant: Shape-Shifting among the Kuranko of Sierra Leone," in *Personhood and Agency,* 59–78.

23. Elias Kifon Bongmba, "Beyond Reason to Interdisciplinary Dialogue on Morality and Politics in Africa: Comments on E. C. Eze's 'Between History and the Gods: Reason, Morality, and Politics in Today's Africa,'" *Africa Today* 55, no. 2 (2000): 98–104.

24. Bénézet Bujo, *The Ethical Dimension of Community: The African Model and the Dialogue between North and South* (Nairobi: Pauline Publications Africa, 1998), 54.

25. John W. de Gruchy, *Christianity and Democracy: Towards a Just World Order* (Cambridge: Cambridge University Press, 1995), 191.

26. See also Bongmba, "Beyond Reason," 98–104.

27. Emmanuel Chukwudi Eze, *Achieving Our Humanity* (London: Routledge, 2001), 230. Eze is also critical of ideas like *negritude* and authenticity.

28. Ibid.

29. Munyaradzi Felix Murove, "Beyond the Savage Evidence Ethic: A Validation of African Ethics," in *African Ethics: An Anthology of Comparative and Applied Ethics,* ed. Munyaradzi Felix Murove (Pietermaritzburg: University of KwaZulu-Natal Press, 2009), 26–27.

20

Joseph Fletcher on Situation

ROBYN HENDERSON-ESPINOZA

In 1967 the Beatles performed their song "All You Need Is Love" on the program *Our World* in the first live global television link. Broadcast to twenty-six countries and watched by over 400 million people, this John Lennon tune changed the way people considered life, love, and the Absolute. In addition to the live performance, this song also debuted on the album *Rubber Soul*,[1] a theological statement about the plasticity and tenacity of what many considered as the embodied soul. Lennon's message? Cast everything aside because all you need is love.

Similarly, Joseph Fletcher (1905–91), a White Episcopal priest who later self-identified as an agnostic, continued in Lennon's theological vein of thought. As a mainline Protestant theologian, Fletcher preached and practiced a moral system predicated on "All you need is love." During the intersection of political and cultural difficulties in the West, the 1960s became a time of excess and flamboyance. In its countercultural vitality, this epoch is not often referred to as moral, yet it was during this time that Fletcher pioneered new ways of thinking ethically and morally. His method of moral thought and decision making is referred to as "situation ethics."

Situation ethics states that sometimes other moral principles can be cast aside in certain circumstances if love is best served, or as Paul Tillich once put it, "Love is the ultimate law."[2] This chapter introduces Joseph Fletcher and the main tenets of situation ethics as exemplified in Fletcher's books, ultimately showing how his model of moral reasoning is insufficient for people within communities of color. I do this by assessing one of his six propositions and exposing the individualistic nature of situation ethics.

INTRODUCING JOSEPH FLETCHER

Joseph Francis Fletcher was born in East Orange, New Jersey, on April 10, 1905. Fletcher worked for the Consolidation Coal Company. His experience with the Monongahela coal mines led to his lifelong sympathy for the working conditions of coal miners, which set the stage for a life of social activism and interest in socialism.[3] He entered West Virginia University at Morgantown when he was seventeen. Already a member of the education staff of the United Mine Workers of America, Fletcher was jailed during his first college year for defying an injunction against speaking in public for the miners' union. A self-proclaimed democratic socialist, his interests in philosophy and history led him to study the utilitarian philosophers Jeremy Bentham and John Stuart Mill, and the pragmatists Charles Peirce, John Dewey, and William James.

Two significant events occurred during his second year in college: he met his future wife, fellow student and poet Forrest Hatfield (of the famous feuding Hatfields), and he became an active Christian in the Episcopal Church. Fletcher embraced Christianity because of his social ideals and democratic leanings. Through his work in the church, he hoped to further the cause of social justice, especially economic democracy[4] for workers. An outstanding student, Fletcher was denied a degree by the university because he refused to participate in compulsory military training. Such training was required of male students in land-grant universities by federal law. Ironically, an honorary doctorate was conferred on him by West Virginia University in 1984.

In 1922, after only three years of college, Fletcher entered Berkeley Divinity School. Working the summer of his first year in a program called Seminarians in Industry, he was assigned to the Plymouth Cordage Company factory, where he discovered and exposed a blacklist of union sympathizers that included Bart Vanzetti, the Italian anarchist. During his second summer he volunteered for the Sacco-Vanzetti Defense Committee in Boston. His last year at seminary was spent collaborating on a book with Spencer Miller, education adviser of the American Federation of Labor, titled *The Church and Industry*, published some years later, in 1931.[5]

INTRODUCING SITUATION ETHICS

Situation ethics is a method of Christian moral reasoning highlighting the role of the situation or context of circumstances. Said differently, the situation or context becomes the locus for moral decision making. Fletcher is notable for popularizing situation ethics, a Protestant ethical system, emphasizing the primacy of love as understood from the Christian Scriptures. Fletcher's situation ethics translates the principle of love into a principle of utility. He develops a type of "act-utilitarianism" whereby he applies utility (in this case, love) instead of rules and norms to judgments and decisions, which is then applied to situations or contexts. At root, Fletcher's ethical system or theological morality is consequentialist: an act is considered morally right only if it maximizes the good. He therefore positions utility (love) as the sole imperative for moral decision making. Yet Fletcher's use of love (*agapē*) is categorically an imperative in the Kantian categorical sense.

For Fletcher and his construction of theological morals, the moral codes of Christianity begin with *agapē*. *Agapē* is a Greek word often translated as "love," meaning absolute, universal, unchanging, and unconditional love for all persons.[6] Fletcher believed that love oriented humanity's moral compass and that theological morals rooted in a system of love were the best expressions of the teachings of Jesus, particularly the teaching "Love thy neighbor" (Mark 12:30). An ethical system whose point of departure is Love (*agapē*) sought to be a middle road between legalistic and antinomian ethics, according to Fletcher.[7]

Most theorists locate situation ethics somewhere between legalism and antinomianism, and Fletcher uses Marx's cognition principle to achieve this middle ethical system. Chiefly, Fletcher seeks to provide a unity of theory and practice.[8] This ethical decision-making system recognizes parts of natural law by accepting reason as a tool for moral judgment. Situation ethics, however, rejects the idea that goodness or virtue is inherently given in the nature of things;[9] hence comes Fletcher's consequentialist trajectory. Natural law/theology is not central to Fletcher's theological morals, unless the believer considers love to be naturally revealed. Love is created and furthermore situated in context and therefore is revealed as a result of the said context.

There are six propositions to situation ethics. Each proposition highlights the place and role of love in moral decision making. In order for anything, particularly ethics, to be good, one must consider love (*agapē*) as something that is generated from that which is good. Goodness, in this sense, is not wholly other: it is the sum of many parts. According to Fletcher, the six propositions are these:

1. "Only one thing is intrinsically good, namely, love: nothing else."[10] Fletcher understands God, whom he believes to be revealed in the Christian Scriptures, as being fundamentally good, and he furthermore confesses that God is love. He generates this idea from reading the New Testament. Love, then, becomes the basis for every Christian decision as the Christian believer seeks the good.
2. "The ultimate norm of Christian decision is love: nothing else."
3. "Love and justice are the same, for justice is love distributed."
4. "Love wills the neighbor's good whether we like him or not."

5. "Only the end justifies the means: nothing else."
6. "Decisions ought to be made situationally, not prescriptively."[11]

Fletcher's practice and embodiment of situation ethics combines love and justice; for him, they become synonymous. He understands justice to be a type of event or act-utility, stating, "Justice is love distributed." By probing the church fathers, particularly Augustine of Hippo, he explains the event of justice as a high level of conscience and prudence that can only achieve goodwill. For him, this was Augustine's confession.[12]

Situation ethics retains one command only: "to love God *in* neighbor."[13] According to Fletcher, the imperative to love God *in* neighbor as the basis of moral decision making is not categorical; it is hypothetical. He suggests that the command to love God *in* neighbor is categorically good and accomplishes goodness. Fletcher refers to his ethical system as a means of achieving moral responsibility.[14] To achieve morality, albeit a responsible morality, one must begin and end with Christian love. This idea of Christian love, according to the tradition of Christianity, is understood only within community. However, he does not raise community as something central to his method of moral decision making. This may well be a barrier to his system since, for many liberationists and feminists, Christian theology is predicated on faith seeking love in community. Love and understanding do not emerge in isolation.

RESPONSIBLE MORALITY AND MOVING BEYOND JOSEPH FLETCHER'S SITUATION ETHICS

For Fletcher, situation ethics states that moral decision making should be based upon the circumstances of a particular situation, and not upon fixed and categorical norms or law. The only norm or absolute is *agapē*. *Agapē* should be the impetus behind every decision and, most important, *agapē* mediates the Christian decision. As long as *agapē* is the intention, the end justifies the means. Justice is not in the letter of the law; it is in the distribution of love; therefore, love is justice. Said differently, situation ethics relies on one principle: what best serves love. For Fletcher, Christian love is unconditional and unsentimental; it is ultimately an ideal to be achieved. It may well be a virtue, which Fletcher ignores. If so, an idea of an Aristotelian virtuous love emerges and becomes fundamentally problematic.[15]

Rooted in the New Testament and modeled after the teachings of Jesus, situation ethics is based on the Christian directive "Love your neighbor as yourself," an altruism that puts others before oneself and shows *agapē*, an ultimate love, toward everyone. It agrees on reason being the instrument of moral judgments, but disagrees that the good is to be disconnected from the nature of things. The situationist's approach says that all moral decisions are hypothetical since they depend on choosing the most loving course of action. Does this translate into responsible morality or theological morals? Is situation ethics really just a modernized and Christianized utilitarianism, where one seeks the greatest good for the greatest number of people, all done while using the language of love? Can situation ethics indeed serve the greatest number of people, particularly those who are marginalized and in communities of color?

The task of this article is to detail the main tenets of situation ethics and then show how Joseph Fletcher's situation ethics is insufficient for the marginalized and those in communities of color. Having provided the philosophy behind Fletcher's theological moral system, it is important to turn to pragmatics. Simply put, situation ethics is not a responsible moral system for those who are marginalized and for communities of color.

In both *Situation Ethics* and *Moral Responsibility*, Joseph Fletcher makes the claim that "Love is Justice," and he goes to great lengths to make his argument. He cites the tradition of Christian theology in using the concept of love, which Christianity has taught from the church fathers to modern theologians. He coalesces love with justice, exclaiming that love is justice. This mode of thinking (Love is justice) sounds compelling on the surface, but when combined with the idea of putting others' interest in place of one's own, it then becomes problematic.

In some communities of color, there is a difference between love and justice. They are not the same and are not even related. Love is an interest or concern for the other. Although some Christians teach that love is disinterested, love can be understood differently, as an event of desire or interest. Justice, on the other hand, is an ambivalent term, which may or may not be used by communities of color. For people who are objects of injustice, justice (for many) seems necessary but unattainable. Though many communities of color want a context of fairness or equality, they may construct different language than "justice." So in this sense, love and justice are not connected, and the situational proposition is inadequate for marginalized people and communities of color.

Another flaw of Fletcher's theological moral system is the idea that one should love the neighbor as oneself. One should place the neighbor's interest before one's own interest. For people and communities of color, the Other's interest has always taken precedent over their own. In Chicago, for example, municipal authorities give White communities better roads and quicker responses. During thunderstorms or after rain, White beaches are closed before beaches in communities of color: the city gives precedence to the safety of White residents. It is on the backs of communities of color that White communities rise to power and prestige. Communities of color do not have an opportunity to put love for their neighbor (read: communities of Whiteness) first. Chicago, in particular, is a city that is strangely and radically segregated: the North side is White, while the West Side and the South Side are of color. The communities of color throughout Chicago do not have a chance to love their neighbor or serve their neighbor in love; they are fighting hard to survive in a White, Euro-American-dominated city. And so, when Fletcher argues that theological morals are achieved when love is best served, it is not accomplished in Chicago, or in any other racially or ethnically segregated city. The communities of Chicago's South Side are constantly fighting for justice, and these communities certainly do not see justice as love.

The theologian Paul Tillich, whom Joseph Fletcher uses quite often, speaks of "Love" as being the "ultimate principle of justice."[16] Love is oriented in a particular direction for Tillich, and Fletcher follows his trajectory. Love is the teleological end, where justice is amplified. Love is the isolated impulse toward the good things in life or justice. For situation ethics, love is not ordered by community or engaged by community. It is driven by Christian narratives but individually embodied. Similarly, situation ethics is based upon Christian directives, particularly "God is love" (1 John 4:8 NRSV). However, in the very next chapter of the First Epistle of John the reader contends with: "For the love of God is this, that we obey [God's] commandments. And [God's] commandments are not burdensome" (1 John 5:3 NRSV). While Fletcher holds that any commandment may be broken in good conscience if love is one's intention, the Bible states that the keeping of God's commandments is the practice of loving God. That said, to break the commandments, regardless of one's intentions, is to not love God. Logic thus holds that the breaking of the commandment was not done in love.

For marginalized people and communities of color, love is understood in community and not in isolation. Love is something that is embodied for the Other and for self and not simply understood in the logic of "event" language. Marginalized communities and people of color (within a certain socioeconomic background) have a tendency to be compelled toward one another in a spirit of solidarity. This is true for those on the South Side of Chicago, or any other segregated city in the nation, where people are relegated to live in gang territory. These individuals join with one another in solidarity to make little moves against destructiveness. It is also true for those along the U.S. borderlands. For example, some groups travel together and may even join their efforts to cross borders together. These border crossers, some of whom leave their families in low economic situations in their country of origin, break laws or become illegal in order to find a better way of life. The border crossers do the unjust act (out of love in community) to establish a more just and fair living situation. Said differently, though recognizing the immigration laws of the United States, border crossers act out a justice that defies the nation-state yet honors their own family context. Their situation of poverty and inability to locate sustainable employment catapults them into a very particular and liminal space, a situation chiefly comprised of living between the "already" and the "not yet." It is a lived space that is constantly negotiated—neither for love nor justice, but for a sustainable life. So in this sense, love for one's family does not translate into justice for one's family, considering that the border crosser always is negotiating one's lived space. The border crosser constantly seeks justice in the entered state and is always looking for a more-just livable space. For many, this justice is achieved by unjust acts, and nowhere is love distributed. More appropriately worded, it is suffering that is distributed throughout their crossing narrative. The ongoing task to find livable space is a task that is in search of justice.

While attention to the situation or context is important, one cannot reduce moral decision making to the situation. Ideologies supporting the unjust situation certainly need radical justice and love. Both love and justice should be broadened to deal with the complexities of people and communities of color. When following Fletcher's theological moral system, people are required to put another's needs before their own; there is no liberation for marginalized people or communities of color here. Ultimately, this is not a responsible morality. Love by itself is not a compelling agent of liberation. Systemic issues are keeping marginalized people and communities of color in a particular raced and gendered space. Their situation (as marginalized and colored) provides no context for love, justice, or liberation.

Serious consideration for an ethical decision-making model should look for ways and methods of liberating marginalized people and communities of color. A model and method should fundamentally begin with an intersectional analysis of race, class, gender, sexuality, and earth justice.[17] Beginning with an analysis of the intersections (or the permeability of margins) allows all creation, however it is comprised, to become central to the situation. When the intersections become the situation, a model of liberation can emerge. If these intersections are ignored or avoided, liberation cannot be achieved, and dominant systems remain static. Situation ethics does not consider social and political intersections as a means for understanding or practicing love or justice. As a result, Fletcher's theological moral system is insufficient for marginalized people and communities of color.

Notes

1. *Rubber Soul* is the sixth studio album by the English rock group the Beatles, released in December 1965 and produced by George Martin.
2. Paul Tillich, *Systematic Theology*, 3 vols. (Chicago: University of Chicago Press, 1951), 1:152.
3. Joseph Fletcher, *Joseph Fletcher: Memoir of an Ex-Radical; Reminiscence and Reappraisal*, 1st ed. (Louisville, KY: Westminster/John Knox Press, 1993), 55–60.
4. Fletcher's "economic democracy" is understood as that which is fundamentally oriented toward the democratic and economically sustainable.
5. Ibid., 55–60.
6. It seems as though "situation ethics" only refers to certain animals—in particular, humanity. Other forms of life—such as dogs, cats, cows, and birds—are not mentioned in this system of moral decision making. Surely there is room for broadening a moral system to include all forms of life. Fletcher, however, does not do so.
7. Joseph Fletcher, *Situation Ethics: The New Morality* (Philadelphia: Westminster Press, 1966), 5.
8. Ibid.
9. Ibid., 26.
10. Joseph Fletcher, *Moral Responsibility: Situation Ethics at Work* (Philadelphia: Westminster Press, 1967), 14–15.
11. Ibid., 15–27.

12. Ibid., 17–18.
13. Fletcher, *Situation Ethics*, 26, 30.
14. *Moral Responsibility* is the title of one of his books, in which he uses circumstances to amplify situation ethics.
15. This is a different way of understanding Fletcher's idea of "when love is best served." The deeper one probes into Fletcher's writings, the more intelligible his "love ethic" is. It strangely implies a method of serving an idea of love, which is fundamentally abstract and disconnected from action and community. This idea/method of a "love ethic" is problematic.
16. Fletcher, *Moral Responsibility*, 44.
17. Earth justice is a phrase that is commonly used to speak about the planet's needs and to refer to just ways to care for its environment. This movement among concerned citizens and communities of faith is an intentional effort to protect the natural environment, most particularly in the American West.

21

Michael Novak on Capitalism

DARRYL TRIMIEW

Michael Novak (1933–) is a celebrated and heralded public scholar working at the very center of religion and public policy.[1] He has led the intellectual religious right for many years, defending a number of conservative causes. This fact is odd in that, historically, he came out of a devout Roman Catholic background that was clearly on the liberal left.[2] What is troubling about Novak is his prodigious and popular publication output, which seems to be moving to the political and theological right in direct ratio to a tendency to become less academically stringent and more oriented toward propaganda.

Novak is an important member of the Catholic Social Teachings ethical discourse. For several years he engaged in a long and important debate with David Hollenbach and others over the proper ethical understanding of Roman Catholic moral teachings on the state's responsibilities to intervene on behalf of the poor, and to do so by recognizing and implementing economic rights. My analysis of this debate and its importance for distributive justice and public policy has been fully examined previously, and I will refer to it only when necessary in this article.[3]

NOVAK ON THE ROLE OF GOVERNMENT

Although most of Novak's positions are not openly racist, they do support an understanding of government that hurts minorities and poor people indirectly—people who, admittedly, have benefited by greater governmental intervention. For example, Novak vigorously defended the second Bush administration as well as the Reagan presidency. Such work has some merit, but Novak defended some of George W. Bush's worst mistakes. Even in the post-Katrina era, after George W. Bush's historic dithering and abandonment of American citizens in the Katrina disaster, Novak continued to assert failed Reaganesque political axioms, writing:

> A long-established lesson is that, even in the best of times, government is mightily incompetent—and the bigger government gets, the more incompetent it becomes. Think of how much time it takes to obtain a building permit, to go through vehicle registration, to correct a government mistake on tax forms or on public utility bills, etc.[4]

Clearly, Novak objects to an expanded role for government in society. There is, however, no long-established lesson that more government is worse government; this assertion is merely a fixed plank in conservative ideologies. Proponents of small government highlight the mistakes and excesses of a large interventionist state while downplaying or omitting the successes or benefits—or even attributing those advances to other organizations. Following the American economic collapse and meltdown in 2008, many analysts maintained that the debacle was caused in part by too little regulation of the market by government officials, especially in securities exchanges on Wall Street. Novak recognized these facts but rejected explanations that implicated big business. For him, the primary cause of the economic collapse was bad loans to poor people. As a result, all he could seem to criticize was the failure of both political parties to properly control, supervise, and regulate Fannie Mae and Freddie Mac.[5] Although these federal agencies did contribute to the economic collapse and certainly were not well supervised, most responsible economists attributed the meltdown to an out-of-control Wall Street that gambled on bundled mortgages and insured derivatives.[6]

Furthermore, Novak neglects the important question of who was most hurt in the economic debacle. Although the media focused most frequently on wealthy shareholders and the middle class, it was the poor, many of whom were minorities, who were hurt most.[7] Many lost their jobs, houses, and social services networks—though *they* were not the cause of the crash. Novak effectively called the poor into question while defending the speculating capitalists.

One of Novak's odd positions has been the minimization of Black poverty. He writes:

> It is sometimes suggested that American blacks are poor. But in the year 2002, 24 percent were poor; over 75 percent were *not* poor. Half of all black

married couple households had incomes over $52,000 per year. The total income of America's 26 million blacks over the age of 15 came to $650 billion in 2002. This is larger than the Gross Domestic Product of all but 15 nations.[8]

Even if Novak's statistics are correct, they are misleading in that they do not account for the large gaps in incomes between Blacks and Whites in America, due to racism. In a country as rich as America, even the poor are wealthier than most of the global poor.

Returning to the issue of state intervention, certain historic events have cast doubt on Novak's understanding of "proper" state action. In the 2010 British Petroleum underwater oil disaster, a preventable off-shore oil drilling accident turned into a monumental ecological disaster. This catastrophe reminded many that it is the responsibility of the government, through diligent oversight, to protect the people and the environment. Again, environmental destruction hurts all people and not just minorities, but the most vulnerable portions of American populations suffer first and most severely. Writing for the Southern Poverty Law Center, Julie Weiss observed that the oil spill disproportionately affected low-income people, especially African Americans and Southeast Asian immigrants, who were "heavily dependent on the seafood industry for jobs." Moreover, research showed that "BP—with the government's approval—has been disposing of oil-related debris at landfills in neighborhoods where mainly blacks, Latinos and Asians live."[9] The 2010 oil spill in the Gulf of Mexico was clearly a disaster for the environment. But it has also been a disaster for people, and it did not affect everyone equally.

Similarly, while the 2008–9 economic collapse similarly hurt all, Blacks and Latino/as already had the highest unemployment rates. However, this is precisely the kind of argument that Novak fails to recognize. After the economic collapse and the Gulf oil spill, his writings continued to neglect the moral responsibilities of government in the support of economic rights, and it is this very assumption of government that makes support for the market morally justifiable. This misunderstanding of economic rights stems primarily from Novak's uncritical moral support for capitalism. Of capitalism he writes:

> Yet in our newly dynamic world, Weber's identification of necessary spiritual and moral conditions for successful economic activity continues to be a source of wisdom. Weber rightly teaches us that success in economics is largely dependent on the spiritual and moral qualities embodied in the practice of economic agents. Moral and spiritual flaws, in other words, have economic consequences. In economic transactions, a failure of insight, determination, perseverance, honesty, respect for law, or cooperativeness with one's fellows can be self-defeating.[10]

In this quote we see some of the problems of Novak's argumentative style. It is frequently an admixture of self-evident truth (moral and spiritual flaws, in other words, have economic consequences) attached to bogus generalizations (Weber rightly teaches us that success in economics is largely dependent on the spiritual and moral qualities embodied in the practice of economic agents). It is now accepted by most in modern history that great fortunes have frequently come out of great crimes. Robber barons have not necessarily been the most spiritual or ethical economic agents.[11]

Capitalism does have some morally defensibly qualities, as well as some reprehensible ones. Since the presidency of Franklin D. Roosevelt, however, American government has intermittently sought to address issues of social justice. Roosevelt's Four Freedoms doctrine specifically called for the government to intervene when an economic depression causes widespread suffering.[12] Roosevelt was frequently attacked for supporting governmental action to further social justice. His critics alleged that the government was improperly intervening in the market, and that his policies would make people overly dependent upon government. This same opposition to redefining and humanizing American notions of social justice has been taken up by Michael Novak.

NOVAK ON SOCIAL JUSTICE

As to social justice itself, Novak continues a neoconservative approach:

> Social justice rightly understood is a specific habit of justice that is "social" in two senses. First, the skills it requires are those of inspiring, working with, and organizing others to accomplish together a work of justice. These are the elementary skills of civil society, through which free citizens exercise self-government by doing for themselves (that is, without turning to government) what needs to be done. Citizens who take part commonly explain their efforts as attempts to "give back" for all that they have received from the free society, or to meet the obligations of free citizens to think and act for themselves. The fact that this activity is carried out *with others* is one reason for designating it as a specific type of justice; it requires a broader range of social skills than do acts of individual justice.[13]

In Novak's aforementioned definition of social justice, that it is carried out with others, this observation itself makes sense. His second characteristic—that of "social justice rightly understood"—aims at the good of the city, not at the good of one agent only. Citizens may band together, as in pioneer days, to put up a school or build a bridge. They may get together in the modern city to hold a bake sale for some charitable cause, repair a playground, or clean up the environment. The second sense in which this habit of justice is "social" is that its object, as well as its form, primarily involves the good of others. Novak goes on to declare:

> One happy characteristic of this definition of the virtue of social justice is that it is ideologically neutral. It is as open to people on the left as on the right or in the center. Its field of activity may be literary, scientific, religious, political, economic, cultural, athletic, and so on, across the whole spectrum

of human social activities. The virtue of social justice allows for people of goodwill to reach different—and even opposing—practical judgments about the material content of the common good (ends) and how to get there (means). Such differences are the stuff of politics.[14]

Though these definitions of social justice have some positive points, they go too far toward privatization. Novak disassociates the duties of improving society from governments and the process of governing and confines them to the acts of individuals and private groups. Simply by descriptive fiat, he deceptively limits the actions of government to a few basic duties and reassigns the duties of achieving justice to private groups. This privatization of social justice links it to a virtue, rather than to any of the responsibilities of government, and uncouples the responsibility of citizens to insist that their government engage in any form of distributive or reparative justice for historically oppressed members of society. This definition sacralizes the status quo with the sole proviso that improvement can and should be achieved solely by private groups—while the state simply maintains law and order.

This approach is a morally viable public policy only as long as some virtuous citizens are banding together in a Tocquevellian covenant to intervene in society. Such activities are indeed morally good and worth doing; they are acts of virtue. But such acts constitute civic engagement and organized charity, rather than a national political commitment to achieve a tolerable measure of social justice. The failure to require a government to be responsible for some measure of social justice allows market forces, profiteers, and others to do as they wish. In Novak's approach, the failure to contain unscrupulous and oppressive forces becomes not a failure of government and watchdog citizens, but a failure of virtuous citizens to engage in what subsequently amounts to supererogatory acts. This approach obscures, for example, the causes of the economic collapse that the United States suffered in 2008–9. Virtuous citizens rarely have much oversight over the manipulations in the market. An ethics of liberation would posit that better financial regulatory legislation and a more active and effective SEC (Security and Exchange Commission) offer better and more-effective national protection.[15] However, Novak is committed to limiting governmental intervention, even if wider governmental intervention is the only way of properly addressing widespread injustice and suffering.

Consider his position on health care:

> I do believe that healthcare is a right, in the sense that free speech is a right; no one can take that right away from you. On the other hand, no one else has to build an auditorium for you, or publish a newspaper for you so that you can exercise your right to free speech. Treating health care as a right that others have the duty to supply for you has a great many ill effects. Universal health care sounds good as a dream, but in actual practice it has a great many deficiencies—besides there is always the danger that everybody will be mandated to have but one choice in medical care, supplied by the government.[16]

For Novak, 43 million Americans without health-care security is still a better world than one in which all Americans might be faced with the "danger" of limited choice.[17] Worse, the universal health-care rights systems of many other Western societies (and many non-Western societies) are dismissed as being mere "dreams," attached to a "great many deficiencies" (all unnamed). Further, critics like Novak offer no alternatives to controlling runaway health-care costs. They are facile in decrying social justice alternatives without ever addressing realistic curative public policy.

NOVAK'S DEFENSE OF CAPITALISM

From his humble beginnings, Novak has become a very successful defender of the status quo in a world in which many people are suffering who need not suffer. Novak's conscience is clear; however, that is to say he is more concerned with the so-called loss of dignity that people might suffer when they receive assistance from the government than he is with their actual physical suffering. Accordingly, he continues to champion capitalism and decry any poor people's reliance upon the government for help.

Novak takes this approach primarily because he has an overly optimistic confidence in capitalism, confidence that borders on a state of delusion. Consider what he has written on the moral defense of capitalism; of his ten moral assertions, I list the worst here:

2. It would awaken the poor from isolation and indolence, by connecting them with the whole wide world of commerce and information.

3. It would diminish warlikeness, by turning human attention away from war and toward commerce and industry. It would, as Adam Smith writes, introduce "order and good government, and with them, the liberty and security of individuals, among the inhabitants of the country, who had before lived almost in a continual state of war with their neighbors, and of a servile dependency on their superiors."[18]

5. It would mix the social classes together, break down class barriers, stimulate upward mobility, encourage literacy and civil discourse, and promote the impulse to form voluntary associations of many sorts.

7. It would teach the necessity of civility, since under the pressures of competition in free markets, dominated by civil discourse and free choice, sellers would learn the necessity of patient explanation, civil manners, a willingness to be of service, and long-term reliability.

8. It would soften manners and instruct more and more of its participants to develop the high moral art of sympathy. For a commercial society depends on voluntary consent. Citizens must learn, therefore, a virtue even higher than empathy (which remains ego-centered, as when a person imagines how he would feel in another's shoes). True

sympathy depends on getting out of oneself imaginatively and seeing and feeling the world, not exactly as the other person may see it, but as an *ideal observer* might see it. This capacity leads to the invention of new goods and services that might well be of use to others, even though they themselves have not yet imagined them.

9. It would instruct citizens in the arts of being farsighted, objective, and future-oriented, so as to try to shape the world of the future in a way helpful to as large a public as possible. Such public-spiritedness is a virtue that is good, not merely because it is useful, but also because it seeks to be in line, in however humble a way, with the future common good.

10. Finally, it is one of the main functions of a capitalist economy to defeat envy. Envy is the most destructive of social evils, more so even than hatred. Hatred is highly visible; everyone knows that hatred is destructive. But envy is invisible, like a colorless gas, and it usually masquerades under some other name, such as equality. Nonetheless, a rage for material equality is a wicked project. Human beings are each so different from every other person in talent, character, desire, energy, and luck that material equality can never be imposed on human beings except through a thorough use of force. (Even then, those who impose equality on others would be likely to live in a way "more equal than others.") Envy is the most characteristic vice of all the long centuries of zero-sum economies, in which no one can win unless others lose. A capitalist system defeats envy and promotes in its place the personal pursuit of happiness. It does this by generating invention, discovery, and economic growth. Its ideal is win-win, a situation in which everyone wins. In a dynamic world, with open horizons for all, life itself encourages people to attend to their own self-discovery and to pursue their own personal form of happiness, rather than to live a false life of envying others.[19]

In these moral arguments one can hear fragments of Adam Smith's most optimistic understandings of capitalism. Yet Smith wrote two centuries ago and therefore was more entitled to be optimistic. In particular, the notion that capitalism discourages envy is ludicrous. The whole system of Madison Avenue advertising is founded on the notion of "keeping up with the Joneses," which by definition is predicated upon encouraging, if not generating, envy.

From a Black perspective, Novak writes as if all of the historic American moral depredations of capitalism never occurred. Capitalism in this country capitalized on slave labor and exploited women, migrant farm workers, child laborers, Chinese laborers (the so-called coolies), and many others. It is only with the instantiation of political and economic rights that these latter members of our society were able to "benefit" in any fashion from the great production that our oppressive society has generated. And this wealth and prosperity came and comes at a tremendous price. One need only ask any current migrant farm worker, legal or illegal.

The suffering that oppressed people undergo, however, Novak considers to be primarily their fault, arguing, for example, that "Census Bureau figures show clearly that most poverty in America results from behavior: regarding work, education, and marriage."[20] Yet almost no economists assign the cause of poverty solely to the poor. Many Americans, rich or poor, know some poor people who cannot be characterized as lazy or depraved since they may work at several jobs just to get by. In short, Novak continues to try to limit government intervention on behalf of the poor while simultaneously blaming the poor for their failure to prosper due to their own shortcomings. This scapegoating tendency is the heart of his opposition to the recognition of most economic rights, such as the right to health care.

Scapegoating the poor relieves capitalism and the American government from the responsibility of trying to create a more just society; this is also why Novak tries to characterize social justice as a form of virtue that some high-minded citizens might engage in, but which good government must refrain from addressing. Oppression, from this point of view, is not a problem best addressed by the intervention of the government. Though Novak's approach of characterizing the government as inept has some benefits—it is true that on some occasions governments can do more harm than help—government is not necessarily predestined to make an economically untenable situation worse. Despite Novak's commitment to Christian piety and faith, his legacy is dangerous—one of scapegoating the poor and hindering the struggle for social justice, basic rights, peace, and sustainability.

Notes

1. Michael Novak was a former U.S. ambassador to the U.N. Human Rights Commission and to the Bern Round of the Helsinki Talks on economics. He now holds the George F. Jewett Chair in Religion and Public Policy at the American Enterprise Institute.
2. Novak collaborated with noted and accomplished liberal theologian, Robert McAfee Brown, and the venerated Jewish civil rights activist, Abraham Joshua Heschel, on a text with regard to Vietnam. See Brown, Heschel, and Novak, *Vietnam: Crisis of Conscience* (New York: Association Press, 1967).
3. See Darryl Trimiew, "The Growing End of an Argument: The Economic Rights Debate," *Annual of the Society of Christian Ethics* 11 (1991): 85–108. See also my fuller examination of the issue in my first publication, *God Bless the Child That's Got Its Own: The Economic Rights Debate* (Atlanta: Scholars Press, 1997).
4. Joseph Bottom and Michael Novak, "The Leadership of George W. Bush: Con and Pro," *First Things*, no. 171 (March 2007): 31–35.
5. Novak writes, "It was the federal government that forced banks to make subprime loans to poor families (who were *known* to be unable to pay their mortgages on a regular basis). It threatened banks that did not invest in poisonous packages of mortgages, vitiated by the bad ones. The federal government even guaranteed the work of two huge quasi government mortgage companies— Fannie Mae and Freddie Mac—that wrote more than half of all mortgages

during the fateful years. Of course, when the house of cards fell, government was not there to make good on its guarantees—or even to accept responsibility for its own heavy-handed actions." See Michael Novak, "Economic Heresies of the Left," *First Things*, no. 198 (June 29, 2009), http://www.firstthings.com/onthesquare/2009/06/economic-heresies-of-the-left.

6. In 2009 Ben Bernanke, chairman of the Federal Reserve Board, stated with regard to the economic collapse that saving inflows from abroad can be beneficial if the country that receives those inflows invests them well. Unfortunately, that was not always the case in the United States and some other countries. Financial institutions reacted to the surplus of available funds by competing aggressively for borrowers, and, in the years leading up to the crisis, credit to both households and businesses became relatively cheap and easy to obtain. One important consequence was a housing boom in the United States, a boom that was fueled in large part by a rapid expansion of mortgage lending. Unfortunately, much of this lending was poorly done, involving, for example, little or no down payment by the borrower or insufficient consideration by the lender of the borrower's ability to make the monthly payments. Lenders may have become careless because they, like many people at the time, expected that house prices would continue to rise—thereby allowing borrowers to build up equity in their homes—and that credit would remain easily available, so that borrowers would be able to refinance if necessary. Regulators did not do enough to prevent poor lending, in part because many of the worst loans were made by firms subject to little or no federal regulation. See Ben Bernanke, "Four Questions about the Financial Crisis," speech at Morehouse College, April 14, 2009, par. 7, http://www.federalreserve.gov/newsevents/speech/bernanke20090414a.htm.

7. Blacks and other minorities are frequently hurt more by economic downturns because they have higher levels of unemployment and poverty. Hence those who are perhaps just one slight push from homelessness can easily succumb to economic freefall. The National Poverty Center of the Gerald R. Ford School of Public Policy notes that "poverty rates for blacks and Hispanics greatly exceed the national average. In 2009, 25.8 percent of blacks and 25.3 percent of Hispanics were poor, compared to 9.4 percent of non-Hispanic Whites and 12.5 percent of Asians."

8. See Michael Novak, "Wealth and Virtue: The Moral Case for Capitalism," February 26, 2004, http://old.nationalreview.com/novak/novak200402180913.asp.

9. See Julie Weiss, "The Gulf Oil Spill: An Environmental Justice Disaster," http://www.tolerance.org/blog/gulf-oil-spill-environmental-justice-disaster.

10. Michel Novak, "Max Weber Goes Global," *First Things*, no. 152 (April 2005): 29.

11. Adam Smith once observed, "As soon as the land of any country has all become private property, the landlords, like all other men, love to reap where they never sowed, and demand a rent even for its natural produce." See http://www.brainyquote.com/quotes/quotes/a/adamsmith107425.html.

12. Franklin Delano Roosevelt, "The Four Freedoms," *U.S. Office of War Information* (1942), 3–15; speech delivered January 6, 1941, http://www.americanrhetoric.com/speeches/fdrthefourfreedoms.htm.

13. Michael Novak, "Defining Social Justice," *First Things*, no. 108 (December 2000): 13.

14. Ibid.

15. See Trimiew, "The Growing End of an Argument, 85–108.

16. Michael Novak, "Is Health Care a Right? Only in a Sense," May 16, 2008, http://www.nationalreview.com/corner/163237/health-care-right-only-sense/michael-novak.

17. According to the National Health Interview Survey, "46.3 million Americans, or about 15.4%, did not have health insurance coverage in 2009, representing a slight increase from 2008. Nearly 60 million, or one in five, had gaps in insurance coverage in the course of the year, according to the survey data." See http://www.emaxhealth.com/1506/cdc-number-americans-without-health-insurance-coverage-increases.

18. Adam Smith, *The Wealth of Nations*, books 1–3 in one volume (1776; London: Penguin Books, 1999), book 3, chap. 4, point 3.

19. See http://old.nationalreview.com/novak/novak200402180913.asp.

20. Michael Novak, "The Truth about Poverty," *Forbes*, December 11, 1989, 82.

22

John Howard Yoder on Pacifism

ROSETTA E. ROSS

A central component of liberation theologies is analysis of structures and systems that inscribe and cause subordination. As Christian constructions, liberation theologies are best understood as reminders of a core element of the biblical message: to especially attend to and honor the weak and despised. One way liberation theologies do this is by unmasking systems of subordination to bring change that improves or opens the way for improving quality of life. Issuing from diverse social movements that opposed colonial subordination, liberation theologies are constructed from the standpoint of particular groups who interpret theological documents and traditions through the lens of what is occurring in specific contexts. Through their contextual theologizing, liberationists contribute to larger religious traditions, bringing insight uniquely available to persons who experience particular material and social circumstances. As a type of liberation thought, womanist theology presents a liberation message from the standpoint of African American women who, within and without the tradition of Christianity, analyze structures, interpret particular contexts, retrieve stories, interrogate history, and complete other work as they join the task of attending to and honoring all, but especially the weak and despised.

John Howard Yoder (1927–97), a writer whose work often was outside mainstream ethics, may be identified as an ethicist whose particularity consistently shaped his scholarship. Yoder held on to and helped forge the meaning of an Anabaptist ethic for the twentieth century. In spite of Yoder's very public particularity, one does not find within his work many similarities to the particularity evident in the work of late twentieth-century contextual theological constructions. The purpose of the present chapter is to examine some of Yoder's work from the perspective of womanist liberationist ethics. My goal is threefold: to discern what elements, if any, present in Yoder's work may be identified as also evident in womanist ethics; to identify obvious dissimilarities between Yoder and womanist ethics; and to offer a brief appraisal of why the similarities and dissimilarities exist.

THE CONTEXTS OF YODER'S THEOLOGICAL DEVELOPMENT

John Howard Yoder emerged as a theologian as the U.S. civil rights movement was reaching its stride. Around the same time, liberation movements in former European colonies were cresting, and the complexity of the United States' role in the Vietnam War was unfolding. Yoder's theological development came out of Christian pacifist training as a child (growing up in a Midwestern Mennonite family), work in Europe on the heels of World War II (completing denominational war relief in France beginning in 1949), and efforts as a relief worker in Algeria (where he served in 1955, during the Algerian-French war). While employed in Europe, Yoder began theological study at the University of Basel and completed doctoral work under the direction of Karl Barth in 1962, five years after he and his family returned to the United States.

As a representative for a Christian pacifist denomination who was confronting the ravages of war while studying for a doctorate in theology, Yoder had fertile ground to develop his perspectives on nonviolence. Before he was thirty, Yoder had "acquired a trans-Atlantic role as a 'peace church' spokesperson on war and peace issues."[1] Moreover, the emergence of his career coincided with the crest of neo-orthodoxy, a movement through which some European and Euro-American theologians confronted the disappointment of two World Wars and came to terms with the reality that goals of the social gospel were overly optimistic. The diverse perspectives within neo-orthodoxy gave Yoder ample conversation partners who reflected on issues of war.

YODER AS A CHRISTIAN ETHICIST

Although some of Yoder's views concurred with thinking in neo-orthodoxy, he is not considered a neo-orthodox theologian. Neither was Yoder a liberal theologian, a movement that was ebbing as Yoder's work was emerging. The waning of liberal theology did not cause Yoder to be outside its theological camp, however. Yoder "was generally regarded as a contrarian thinker rather than as a member of any accepted establishment."[2] His contrariness in some sense derived directly from his Radical Reformation heritage, whereby his theological ancestry conflicted with perspectives on Christian identity and violence held by theological ancestors of most neo-orthodox and liberal Protestant theologians. Though he was outside the norm, Yoder's work was affirmed by colleagues in Christian ethics. He influenced Stanley Hauerwas to "convert" to pacifism, to describe pacifism as what "constitutes the heart of our worship of a crucified messiah," and to adopt a communitarian posture of identifying the Christian church as "God's nonviolent kingdom."[3] In view of broad use of nonviolence as an element of the U.S. civil rights movement, surprisingly little of Yoder's published work reflected on that Christian nonviolent social struggle.

YODER'S THEO-ETHICAL SYSTEM

In addition to situating himself outside established theological camps, Yoder often identified his work in ethics as nonsystematic. By this, he appears to have meant that he did not agree with systems and questions of the Christian ethics establishment, with which he primarily was in conversation. Yoder did have his own method and theo-ethical system. His method may be characterized as ethical historiography because careful historical analysis supported his theological assertions. His historical analysis included biblical study, which Yoder used not as literal history but as a means for examining historical developments in early Christianity. The early church was, for Yoder, the paradigmatic moral context for determining specific and general guides for Christian action. Similar to Anders Nygren, Yoder insisted that Christianity brought something unique into the religiously pluralistic context of Greco-Roman culture. As a consequence, Yoder studied early church identity and actions systematically to discern and to demonstrate the basis upon which he believed Christian ethics should be established.

Yoder's theo-ethical system is a two-pronged foundation for constructing Christian ethics. The system consists of Yoder's insistence on (1) voluntary membership in the Christian community and (2) an understanding of pacifism as seeking to appropriately imitate what Jesus did in going to the cross. Reared as an Anabaptist and later freely committing himself to its tenets, Yoder vigorously held that conscious and voluntary adult confession and devotion are prerequisite to membership in the Christian community. Living out the cross required, Yoder insisted, "voluntary obedience of believers," in which "personal confession and commitment" could be "presupposed."[4] For Yoder, the church is a voluntary society of persons whose identity is against the world.

The ethic of nonviolence, central to the theology of "historic peace churches," also is central to Yoder's work and to his understanding of who Jesus was and the model Jesus presented. The "substance of ethics," Yoder wrote, "consists in the rejection of violence, most categorically . . . of killing one's fellow human beings."[5] Notable, though not exceptional, in Yoder's construal of nonviolence is the exclusive focus on human beings. Though Jesus was nonviolent, Yoder says he was a political messiah who came to bring change to the people of Israel and the world. In the context of his political mission, Jesus chose the nonviolent route of going to the cross instead of waging an Armageddon battle of destruction, which he would have won.[6] Perhaps seeing Jesus as one who sought gradual change, Yoder takes care to state that Jesus was not a "violent" insurrectionist; though having "legions" of divine angels at his disposal when he was accused, arrested, and convicted, Jesus "chose" to avoid violence and instead go to the cross as a consequence of his sociopolitical identity and intentions. Yoder says the call to the Christian community is to follow Jesus' example of seeking to bring sociopolitical change to the world nonviolently, fully bearing the cross of rejection and temporal failure, in the company of Jesus.

YODER AND WOMANIST ETHICS

Yoder's understanding of Jesus' politics of nonviolence presents both a point of affirmation and a site of tension for womanist theology. Jesus faced the cross, Yoder writes, "not as a ritually prescribed instrument of propitiation but as the political alternative to both insurrection and quietism."[7] Yoder's assertion that Jesus went to the cross not as a voluntary sufferer, but voluntarily as a result of his political views, is precisely the point made by some womanist (and other) theologians who oppose understanding the atonement as intentional suffering. Delores Williams, for example, argues that Jesus is not "the ultimate surrogate figure" who "stands in the place of . . . sinful humankind." Instead of passive acceptance of "the exploitation that surrogacy brings," Williams says, "redemption had to do with God, through the *ministerial* vision [of Jesus], giving humankind the ethical thought and practice upon which to build a positive, productive quality of life."[8] Both Williams and Yoder see the cross as resulting from Jesus' sociopolitical vision, notwithstanding Williams's distinction from Yoder in her insistence on attention to quality-of-life concerns when discussing atonement. In spite of the similar interpretation of the atonement found in womanist ethics and Yoder's ethics, there are several areas of concern and tension between womanist thought and Yoder's ethics.

Understanding quality-of-life issues as central to womanist ethics helps shed light on one womanist tension with Yoder's thought. Consistent with Williams's rejection of the crucifixion as exploitative surrogacy, womanist ethics spurns uses of subordination as an ethical model for socially and economically marginalized persons. Womanist theologian Jacquelyn Grant says the suffering-servant model reinscribes the subordinated status of actual servants because "servants have never been properly remunerated for their services." Moreover, Grant continues, "certain people are more often than others relegated to such positions," and "these positions are more often than not relegated to the bottom (or at least the lower end) of the economic scale."[9] Womanist ethics requires identification of methods and ethical constructions that are inclusive enough to analyze the relationship of such temporal realities to the meaning of being a member of the Christian community, and also to develop models of practice that seek to overcome alienating social hierarchies. "The kind of wholism sought in womanist theology," Grant writes, "requires that justice be an integral part of our quest for unity and community."[10]

By contrast, while Yoder opposes defining the cross as "prescribed" suffering, he asserts that subordination can be revolutionary.[11] Yoder says the "reciprocity of relationship" in the Christian calling, as evident in the "apostolic" *Haustafeln* (household rules), overcomes a "one-sided" subordination that otherwise might be read as maintaining the structures of society and as demonstrating complacency or withdrawal, which he abhorred.[12] "Thus there is in the ethical admonition of the *Haustafeln*," Yoder writes, "the possibility of community discipline, of common insight and standards, around which it is possible for a whole group of persons, and not simply a meditative elite, to develop a shared moral commitment."[13] Although Yoder says the "shared moral commitment" of early Christianity included "reciprocity," his description of the shared commitment in practice negates reciprocity: "To accept subordination within the framework of things as they are," Yoder writes, "is not to grant the inferiority in moral or personal value of the subordinate party. In fact, the opposite is true: the ability to call upon the subordinate party to *accept that subordination freely* is, as it was in the *Haustafeln*, a sign that this party has already been ascribed a worth that is fundamentally different from what any other society would have accorded."[14] Although he says the call of the *Haustafeln* is to overcome one-sided subordination, Yoder interprets the *Haustafeln* as calling for acceptance of subordination—which, from the perspective of womanism, offers no improvement in temporal quality of life.

Another tension of womanist and liberationist thought with Yoder's work is evident in his interpretation of choice in subordination in the *Haustafeln*. Ironically, in his discussion of subordination in the *Haustafeln*, Yoder overlooks an element that he identifies as central to Christian identity: free choice. While he disqualifies a person's participation in the community of Christians from being authentic if it is not by choice (e.g., via believer's baptism), Yoder does not see lack of choice in regard to social status as contradicting his ethical theory. But is it possible to "presuppose" that subordination has been "freely" accepted if one has not chosen to take up the subordination? Yoder's identification of accepting "subordination within the framework of things as they are" suggests being complacent about the hierarchal structures of the status quo. Moreover, since the early church is paradigmatic for Yoder and since, presumably, persons who embraced early Christianity did so within statuses prescribed by the prevailing social order over which subordinated persons (especially enslaved persons) had no control, the possibility of making choices about social status was absent.

Yoder asserts mutuality and reciprocity in the *Haustafeln*'s call to subordination; yet without addressing the need to overcome ongoing temporal subordination of all enslaved persons and free women in the early church era, the mutual subordination to which Yoder refers is substantially spiritualized.

Because of the tendency to spiritualize Christian service, Grant calls for a moratorium on Christian servant speech because it causes "institutionalization of oppressive language," especially for persons who support themselves as servants.[15] "As critical components to Christianity," Grant writes, "the notions of 'service' and 'servanthood' [represent contradictions] when viewed in the light of human indignities perpetrated against those who have been the 'real servants' of the society."[16] From this standpoint, Yoder's celebration of Christianity's contribution through the *Haustafeln*, as allowing "the subordinate party to *accept that subordination freely*," reinscribes temporal subordination. An alternative model for Christian ethical practice may be gleaned from Grant's call for a moratorium on use of servant language for already-subordinated persons: Applying the language of servant and giving preferential options of serving others to Christians in social and religious positions of authority would compellingly evoke the "reciprocity of relationship" to which Yoder refers. The shifting of roles could provide useful new insights for all involved.

A final tension of womanist ethics with Yoder's work relates to moral agency. The complex conflict of Yoder's interpretation with womanist theology (as well as with elements of his own thought) is particularly evident in his discussion of subordinated persons' moral agency. This conflict appears to emerge because Yoder's historical analysis of subordination is confined by (or to?) his focus on initial Christian documents and practices in early churches. Interestingly, for issues such as the welfare state, the meaning of property in industrial society, and dilemmas of modern medicine, Yoder concedes that there are no "specific biblical ethical" insights and that generalizations should be made that include a "longer hermeneutic path, and insights from other sources."[17] But with regard to contemporary subordinated persons, Yoder infers that Scripture offers specific content, suggesting that the status of all socially and economically subordinated persons has not changed or is not influenced by issues such as industrialization, the welfare state, and dilemmas of modern medicine.

Yoder argues that moral agency of subordinated persons in the early church community emerged as a result of Christianity. He sees the "early Christian style of ethical thinking" as particularly unique because the

> *subordinate* person in the social order is *addressed as a moral agent*. He [*sic*] is called upon to take responsibility for the acceptance of his [*sic*] position in society as meaningful before God. . . . Here we have a faith that assigns *personal moral responsibility to those who had no legal or moral status* in their culture and makes of them decision-makers. It gives them responsibility for viewing their status in society not as a simple meaningless decree of fate but as their own meaningful witness and ministry, as an issue about which they can make a moral choice.[18]

Even though subordinated persons are members of the Christian community whom Yoder identifies as called to socially engaged revolutionary nonviolence, here Yoder limits the moral realm and moral agency of subordinated persons to their household roles and positions. Yoder further says that without the message of Christianity, these persons would not otherwise have understood or known their circumstance as unjust, or felt themselves as having dignity: "Where had they heard such a message if not from Paul? How had they heard it if not in the form of the report that in Jesus' messianity a new age had begun in which men [sic] are freed for obedience by the resurrection of the Crucified?"[19] This interpretation presents an essentialist understanding of subordinated persons in early Christianity. Also, Yoder neglects historical understandings of injustice and assertions of dignity that were intrinsic elements in actions that opposed enslavement through means such as the Roman Servile Wars, which occurred in the period of 135 to 71 BCE. Yoder's confined historical analysis is further evident in assertions that spiritualize freedom in the present and advocate eschatological freedom as overcoming challenges of temporal subordination. The freedom to which Christ calls a Christian, he writes, "can already be realized within his [sic] present status by voluntarily accepting subordination, *in view of the relative unimportance of such social distinctions* when seen in the light of the coming fulfillment of God's purposes."[20] Although he notes that early church leaders recommended maximizing temporal freedom if occasions arose to do so, here Yoder recommends complacency in subordination and spiritualization of freedom.

In contrast to Yoder's understanding of subordinated persons' agency, womanist ethicist Katie G. Cannon explains how Black women determine ways to exercise moral agency in spite of challenges that often circumscribe their efforts. Ideally, womanist ethics envisions social contexts without subordinating issues that circumscribe moral agency. In the meantime, as Cannon argues, it is necessary to take account of Black women's (and others') subordinated realities to develop ethical methods that discern how subordinated persons exercise moral agency in the face of subordination while also presenting models that emulate Jesus' efforts to bring change to the world. "In order to work toward an inclusive ethic," Cannon states, "the womanist struggles to restructure the categories so that the presuppositions more readily include the ethical realities of black women."[21]

PRIVILEGE AND STANDPOINT IN ETHICAL CONSTRUCTION

The standpoint of Black women, as represented in work of persons such as Williams, Grant, and Cannon, makes it possible to recognize some challenges within Yoder's work. As sociologist Patricia Hill Collins observes, "A Black women's standpoint" derives from "those experiences and ideas shared by African-American women that provide a unique angle of vision on self, community, and society."[22] Arguing that authentic evaluation of ideas requires engagement with groups *and* material conditions that produce ideas, Hill Collins identifies a Black women's standpoint as unique in regard to producing specific knowledge, even though ideas produced are accessible to others.[23] Although she identifies "a black women's standpoint," Hill Collins cautions against the potential to develop essentialist or homogenizing constructions of Black women and notes diverse experiences and perspectives within the "black women's standpoint." Her caution is complicated by the contemporary reality of persons simultaneously occupying different standpoints. As a White male, Anabaptist, Midwesterner, academic, and so forth, Yoder was not excluded from this reality of having a particular standpoint that influenced his ethical constructions.

Liberation ethics recognizes, identifies, and defines ethical perspectives that emerge from distinct contexts, for the purpose of affirming particular groups and knowledge produced by these groups, and to develop ethical theories and methods that model and help envision inclusive, wholistic life together. One womanist ethical view of the vision of inclusive, wholistic life together is over-coming barriers to "reciprocity" (to use Yoder's language). In the case of woman-ists, however, reciprocity means interdependence (including interdependence of persons and of all creation). Within Christianity, from the standpoint of wom-anist ethics, the greater challenge (and calling) may be discerning how to enact reciprocity in the authority to which Jesus calls Christians in the gospels (Mark 13:34; Luke 9:1). In a global culture that historically has ordained hierarchies privileging some and subordinating others (including the earth, on which all creatures depend), those who would construct models of ethical action that help overcome subordination must also interrogate the privileges and structures that sustain our own work as we stand in particularities of the academy, the guild, the denomination, the race, the species, and other points that challenge the ability to define and inclusively live life together.

Notes

1. James McClendon Jr., "John Howard Yoder: One of Our Own, 1927–1997," *Perspectives in Religious Studies* 25, no. 1 (Spring 1998): 22.
2. Ibid., 21.
3. Stanley Hauerwas, "Remembering John Howard Yoder: December 29, 1927–December 30, 1997," *First Things*, no. 82 (April 1998): 15.
4. John Howard Yoder, *The Priestly Kingdom: Social Ethics as Gospel* (Notre Dame, IN: Notre Dame University Press, 1984), 110.
5. Ibid., 110–11.
6. John Howard Yoder, *The Politics of Jesus* (1972; Grand Rapids: Wm. B. Eerd-mans Publishing Co., 1994), 46–47.
7. Yoder, *Priestly Kingdom*, 43.
8. Delores Williams, *Sisters in the Wilderness: The Challenge of Womanist God-Talk* (Maryknoll, NY: Orbis Books, 1993).
9. Jacquelyn Grant, "The Sin of Servanthood: And the Deliverance of Disciple-ship," in *A Troubling in My Soul: Womanist Perspectives on Evil and Suffering*, ed. Emilie M. Townes (Maryknoll, NY: Orbis Books, 1993), 200.

10. Ibid., 214.
11. The succeeding discussion derives primarily, though not exclusively, from a reading of chap. 9, "Revolutionary Subordination," in Yoder's *Politics of Jesus*.
12. Yoder, *Politics of Jesus*, 172. Yoder goes to some length to distinguish the *Haustafeln* as drawn from an apostolic (therefore, a uniquely early Christian) and not Stoic perspective. The basis for his making the distinction is (1) the "literary structure" of the *Haustafeln* as listing persons in pairs and in reciprocal relationship instead of addressing individuals, (2) the use of plural nouns in addressing the community and not individuals in the *Haustafeln*, (3) the *Haustafeln* use an imperative "borrowing—by testimony of syntactic style— . . . not from Hellenistic Judaism . . . but from the prophetic imperatives recorded in the Old Testament *as received from the mouth of God himself* [*sic*]" (*Politics of Jesus*, 173, emphasis added), (4) use of a different, therefore unique, vocabulary in the *Haustafeln*, (5) Yoder's understanding of the *Haustafeln* as focusing on "dignity of the addressee" (e.g., the subordinated), while Stoicism focuses on the male elite, (6) Yoder's understanding of the *Haustafeln* as giving dignity by calling into question subordination of persons on the bottom side of the social order, (7) the inclusion of an explanation in the *Haustafeln* as opposed to Stoicism's expectation that persons will accept the "self-evident appropriateness of giving in to the way things are, and (8) Yoder's understanding of the subordination in the *Haustafeln* as reciprocal. See *Politics of Jesus*, 171–82, passim.
13. Ibid., 119.
14. Ibid., 185, emphasis in original.
15. Grant, "Sin of Servanthood," 210.
16. Ibid., 199–200.
17. Yoder, *Politics of Jesus*, 192.
18. Ibid., 174, emphasis in original.
19. Ibid., 178–79.
20. Ibid., 186–87, emphasis added.
21. Katie Cannon, "Hitting a Straight Lick with a Crooked Stick: The Womanist Dilemma in the Development of a Black Liberation Ethic," in *Katie's Canon: Womanism and the Soul of the Black Community* (New York: Continuum, 1995), 125.
22. Patricia Hill Collins, *Black Feminist Thought: Knowledge, Consciousness, and the Politics of Empowerment* (Boston: Unwin Hyman, 1990), 22.
23. Ibid., 21–22.

23

Richard Mouw
on Divine Command

RODOLFO J. HERNÁNDEZ-DÍAZ

What role should divine commands play in Christian ethics? Richard Mouw, professor of Christian philosophy and ethics and president of Fuller Theological Seminary since 1993, takes up this very question in his book *The God Who Commands*.[1] Mouw tries to identify and elaborate the necessary basis for divine command ethics (DCE), a venerable tradition that has fallen out of favor in the wake of Alasdair MacIntyre's critique of modern moral theory in *After Virtue*.[2] Surveying the moral landscape, MacIntyre concludes that after the Enlightenment moral theory can only proceed along one of two lines: either a Nietzschean secularist-modernist position in which moral utterances amount to nothing more than subjective preferences (emotivism)—or a classical Aristotelian-Thomistic moral framework.[3] Mouw argues that MacIntyre has presented us with a false dilemma. Having drawn the line between Aristotle and Nietzsche, modernist and classicalist, MacIntyre has failed to see a third possibility: a Calvinist, Reformed account of DCE.

In this chapter, I interrogate Mouw's claim that a Calvinist DCE is a viable alternative way of engaging in Christian moral reflection by examining its suitability for communities of color. If we conceive of Mouw's work as a picture, then this chapter endeavors to bring that picture into focus. Each section sharpens the image of the dynamism and complexity of DCE by raising objections and asking questions. As this picture becomes more clear, it reveals that Mouw's methods, subtle style, and claims reflect his training as a philosopher at the University of Chicago, his strong commitments to the evangelical movement and Reformed tradition, and his place of privilege within the dominant culture. Yet, for all the subtlety of Mouw's ethical proposal, it falls short of providing a mechanism for protecting the most vulnerable in society: those living in oppressed and marginalized communities. Although I applaud Mouw's work for reawakening interest in divine command ethics, I cannot accept the overall conclusion that this approach would yield unmitigated positive effects for marginalized communities.

A FIRST GLANCE

At first glance, the image of Mouw's proposal in *The God Who Commands* appears distant, out of focus: who is this God, and what does this God command? One can only make guesses based on semantic associations. The image is brought into focus by briefly describing Mouw's overall project and placing it within the wider mosaic of DCE and Reformed theology. Overall, Mouw's project is an evaluation of Calvinism as DCE, a theoretical position that grounds morality on a conception of the divine and maintains that moral obligation consists in obeying God's commands.[4] Some versions of DCE hold that the commands of God are coterminous with morality. Other, less-restrictive versions maintain that God's commands only inform us about morality.[5] "Reformed" is the label given to the kind of Protestantism and theology that affirms the idea of human depravity while sustaining hope about the ability of human beings to shape the social order. Since John Calvin had more impact on the movement than any other person, the label "Reformed" is used interchangeably with "Calvinism," both in common usage and in this chapter. Thus in proposing a Calvinist DCE, Mouw intends to give an account of morality grounded in obedience to God's commands as a method of social engineering.

QUESTIONS THAT REMAIN UNDERANSWERED

A first glance revealed the contours of the picture, giving shape to the image, without giving it definitive form. A second look refines the resolution of the image and brings it further into focus by raising some questions about Mouw's scheme. Two interrelated questions are immediately suggested by the expression "divine command ethics": Which command(s)? Which God? A third question is suggested by the associations many have with Calvinism: What about the atrocities that Calvin and his followers committed in their leadership at Geneva—what I refer to here as the "Geneva problem"? I examine each question in turn.

WHICH COMMAND(S)?

In advocating for DCE, which command(s) does Mouw suggest we should attend to, and what are their sources? In answer to the second question, Mouw makes it clear that he himself is bibliocentric, holding to a version of the Protestant Reformation emphasis on *sola scriptura*. He believes that the Bible offers "detailed guidance" transmitted through parables, letters, poems, songs, narratives of divine dealings, direct imperatives, and so on.[6] Mouw concedes that there are a variety of sources for divine authority, including natural law, ecclesiastical bodies, individual Christians under the influence of Holy Spirit, or even "dictates of conscience"; yet he argues that these alternative sources are "supplements to, or glosses on, biblical revelation."[7] In answer to the first question, Mouw maintains that there is a plurality of morally relevant commands—in contrast to some who contend that there is only one morally relevant divine commandment, such as love of God and neighbor.[8] This plurality, however, does not include *all* the commandments that are in the Bible. Particular commands—such as God's command to Jonah to preach to the Ninevites or to Abraham to leave Ur of the Chaldees—do not apply. Nor does Mouw wish to promote a fixation around grammatical imperatives. Instead, Mouw proposes a broad understanding of "commands" that are revealed through the various forms of writing cited above. According to Mouw, a person learns about the content of divine commands by gaining familiarity with the character of God as revealed in the context of the biblical text.

Mouw's answer to "Which commands?" is as follows: the commands revealed through evaluation and interpretation by individuals or communities familiar with the "character of the biblical God."[9] For Mouw, the authoritative content of the Bible is the embodied evocation more than an application of biblical propositions.[10] This view of authority has unexpected consequences for ethics. For example, on the eve of the U.S. Civil War, White Southern Christians in the United States, steeped in the biblical narrative, defended the institution of slavery. Priests and pastors of the U.S. Southwest, fearful of mixing between Indians, Africans, and Whites, cited their familiarity with the "character of the Bible God" as the basis of their antimiscegenation stance. Mouw's broad formulation of commands upholds the view of the White Southern slavery advocate and the antimiscegenational minister as divine commands. In trying to avoid the pitfalls of Fletcher's "mono-imperativism" on the one hand, and the hermeneutics of biblical literalism on the other, Mouw has unwittingly subscribed to an evocative ethics that avoids specific commands of Scripture while trying to defend the Scriptures as the source of divine commands.

WHICH GOD?

Our second questions relates to the first: Which God is doing the commanding? This is an important question since historically whenever members of the elite have insisted on obedience to God, the supposed beneficiaries of such obedience have usually paid a horrifying price. For example, at the time of the conquest of the New World, European missionaries, believing themselves to be following God's commands to spread the gospel among American Indians, were unable to perceive any moral or ethical difficulties in actions that led to decimation of the indigenous population and the near destruction of their cultures.[11] European evangelization was no mere expansion of religion, but a violent conquest that forced a complete change of economic, political, and cultural systems.[12] Centuries later, shortly after the mixed-blood descendants of Indians and Europeans had established for themselves a precarious but independent existence in what is now called the U.S. Southwest, a new conquest began. Under the auspices of Manifest Destiny, God's command to expand colonial rule from coast to coast, U.S. invaders raped Mexican mothers and daughters, extorted money from civilians by force, and desecrated churches.[13] When Europeans felt commanded by God to evangelize, they had no qualms about using force to do so.

The actions of people from the dominant social group who believe themselves to be obeying God's commands—interpreted through their understanding of God's character—have often resulted in terrible consequences for minority communities. Therefore members of communities of color should be cautious about uncritical obedience. Communities of color need to interrogate the character of this God. The only God worthy of our obedience is a God who reveals a concern for the weak and powerless, a God who suffers with the disinherited, a God who defends the oppressed, a God who cares for the least of these, a God who liberates. The problem with Mouw's framework is not that it rejects an understanding of God as liberator, but that it allows for an understanding of God as colonial conqueror. A complete philosophical framework for DCE must at the very least set parameters of what is permitted in God's name. Appeals to God's "covenantal fidelity" or the defense of the "voluntarist impulse" or God's absolute sovereignty even over the most powerful of earthly potentates—these are insufficient guarantors of minority rights.

There are perhaps two reasons why Mouw does not provide a fuller description of his God. First, Mouw is writing a defense of the possibility of DCE, not a robust and thorough theology. He leaves to others the task of elaborating a doctrine of God. Nevertheless, for reasons given above, even an apologetic for DCE as a tenable form of moral reasoning must provide a description of the kind of God one has in mind. A DCE that neglects to account for God's character, that provides no further guidance for discerning God's commands other than the principle of "familiarity" with the God of the biblical text, can result in cultural imperialism, exploitation, and oppression.

I am not advancing here the simple argument that Mouw's work is incomplete and thus unconvincing. After all, whose work is complete? Certainly not Calvin's. He completed the first edition of the *Institutes* as a young man but continued to revise and expand on it until his death. Instead, I am suggesting that Mouw's framework is missing crucial elements in order to guarantee the type of ethics consistent with a God who is on the side of the widow, the orphan, and the alien. Second, Mouw's intended audience, the privileged members of society—whether they are evangelicals with Reformed sympathies, conservative Christians concerned with divine commands, or scholars weary with the prevalence of character and virtue theory in Christian moral reflection—have little reason to quibble with an understanding of God as sovereign administrator of the world. As members of the dominant social group, they have a vested interest in dismissing Gustavo Gutiérrez's identification of salvation with liberation from oppressive structures as "ideological captivity."[14] The abstraction of the liberation theme from its biblical setting in the exodus story, they believe, functions as a justification for seizing power from the government. If God is exercising sovereignty over human affairs, then there is no need to try to topple existing governments or change the world order: indeed, this violates the principle of human subordination. As a member of the dominant segment of society, Mouw has the privilege to advocate for a "just" God without adhering to the "ideological baggage" of liberationist thought.[15]

WHAT ABOUT THE "GENEVA PROBLEM"?

The picture of Mouw's Calvinist DCE is now coming into focus. The commands of God are implicit in the practices of people who are familiar with God's character as revealed in the biblical text. We have already given some examples of how this turns out in practice. One key historical example remains: Geneva.

In the minds of most students of the Reformation, the name Calvin is indelibly linked with Geneva, the town in Switzerland that in the mid-sixteenth century gave itself wholly over to his ministrations. In its early years, Calvin's Geneva became a haven for Protestants from all over Europe. The case of Michael Servetus, a Radical Reformer, seriously challenges that characterization. A deeply religious devotee to Christ, Servetus—a Spaniard, physician, and scientist of some note—passionately disagreed with Calvin on several occasions about the doctrine of the Trinity, predestination, and infant baptism. Fleeing from Catholic authorities in Vienne, France, and heading toward Italy, Servetus made the mistake of passing through Geneva, where he was recognized and arrested. At his trial, Servetus demanded the arrest of Calvin on the charges of false witness and heresy. If Servetus had been acquitted, Calvin's influence in Geneva would have been greatly weakened. Servetus was condemned by the civil authorities for having denied the Trinity and rejecting baptism. He was sentenced to death and burned at the stake on October 27, 1553. Above the sounds of crackling flames, he was heard crying "O Jesus, thou Son of the eternal God, have pity on me."[16]

The condemnation of Servetus was a major victory for Calvin. But it raises serious issues in terms of tolerance and inclusion of minority voices and dissenting views. Calvin believed that he was making progress toward his goal to bring about an ideal Christian community. Is Geneva the type of regime envisioned by Mouw's DCE? How does Mouw address Calvin's complicity with state authorities who used their power to persecute other believers, specifically the Anabaptists? Some historians note that Calvin sent private letters from Servetus and manuscript material betraying his identity to the French Inquisition and put in writing that he would not allow Servetus to leave Geneva alive if he should ever set foot in it.[17] Mouw recognizes that Calvinism has been associated with such draconian measures. He calls it the "Hobbesian 'feel' of Calvinism," after the categorization of historian John Neville Figgis, who suggested that Hobbes's *Leviathan* is the political counterpoint to Calvin's theology.[18] Both Hobbes and Calvin conceive of the sovereign as one who confronts and overwhelms the ordinary human will. Mouw concedes that Hobbesian politics and Calvinist soteriology resemble each other on the conception of authority, but this only holds, he insists, if we have a very "rudimentary" notion of Calvin's thought.[19] On Mouw's account, a more complex and complete picture of Calvin's political thought reveals very little of the Hobbesian feel.

For Mouw, the key to complexifying our understanding of Calvin's view of moral and political authority is to recognize the strong voluntarist impulse at work. In contrast to medieval Catholicism's conception of ethical obedience as human adjustment to the natural law, Calvin emphasized the will-to-will character of divine-human interactions. As a voluntarist, Calvin believed that the only proper human response to divine address is surrender. Thus surrender is very much on Calvin's mind as he writes about political authority. But according to Mouw, a simple attempt to ground a claim of uncritical surrender to earthly rulers in the surrender to the will of God violates Calvin's voluntarist framework. There are exceptions to the pattern of submission to human rulers precisely for voluntarist reasons: obedience to the divine will takes precedence over obedience to any earthly ruler. For Calvin, it is a human will, submitted to the will of the divine sovereign, that "must somehow translate" learned "patterns of virtue" into "attitudes and actions appropriate to the political life of the larger society"— including when to disobey civil authorities.[20]

Still, a strict appeal to voluntarism is a long way off from addressing the Geneva problem. Certainly the voluntarist impulse led Servetus to the flames: Servetus was following what he understood to be the commands of God. Ultimately Mouw's efforts to "soften" the Hobbesian "feel" of Calvinist DCE are unsuccessful insofar as they fail to provide adequate protection for minority and dissenting voices.

RECAP AND CONCLUSION

We now have a far sharper and clearer image of Mouw's version of Calvinism as DCE. At first we perceived only the contours of Mouw's scheme: a morality grounded in obedience to God's commands as a method of social engineering. A second look sharpened the picture and challenged these initial perceptions. It revealed that Mouw conceives of commands as an evocative ethic embodied by those familiar with the God of the biblical text. We saw, too, that Mouw's thin description of God amounts to a picture of God made in the image of the dominant social group—which misses crucial elements necessary to guarantee an ethic consistent with concern for the oppressed. Last, we observed that Mouw's DCE fails to adequately protect minority and dissenting voices as seen in light of the Geneva problem.

The preceding analysis of Mouw's work reveals that he is a nuanced thinker, cognizant of the operative value judgments underlying his claims. It also reveals some surprising contradictions. Despite his commitment to the Calvinist doctrine of human depravity, he maintains an unreasonable confidence in the human capacity to discern and act consistently with the morally relevant commands of God. Despite his attention to the Hobbesian character of Calvinist political theory, he assumes the benevolence of the state and fails to provide adequate restraints on state power. Despite its promising title and premises, Mouw's work does not provide a viable way forward for moral reflection for and on behalf of communities of color. It remains unclear that the commands of Mouw's God should play any role in the ethical reflection of minority communities.

Notes

1. Richard Mouw, *The God Who Commands* (Notre Dame, IN: Notre Dame University Press, 1990).
2. MacIntyre, *After Virtue*, 3rd ed. (Notre Dame, IN: Notre Dame University Press, 2007).
3. Ibid., 52–59. According to MacIntyre, the second option (Aristotelian-Thomistic moral framework) has the advantage of containing all three elements necessary for an adequate account of morality: (1) an untutored human nature; (2) human nature as it would be if it realized its telos; and (3) virtues, which mediate between the two conditions.
4. Sometimes also referred to as Divine Command Theory.
5. For anthology with a philosophical approach of DCE, see Janine Marie Idziak, *Divine Command Morality: Historical and Contemporary Readings*, Texts and Studies in Religion 5 (New York: E. Mellen Press, 1979).
6. Mouw, *God Who Commands*, 10.
7. Ibid., 8.
8. This is the position of the once-celebrated and more recently much-maligned Fletcher in *Situation Ethics*.
9. Mouw, *God Who Commands*, 10. We may be able to construe Mouw's position of biblical authority as the interaction of God's written revelation with the Spirit's illumination. That would be closer to a Calvinist position that Mouw

understands himself to be espousing. It is not, however, the language Mouw himself uses.

10. Donald Bloesch notes that it is common to distinguish between the evocative and informative functions of divine revelation. Donald Bloesch, *Holy Scripture: Revelation, Inspiration and Interpretation* (Downers Grove, IL: InterVarsity Press, 1994), 39.

11. For a closer look at American Indian mission history and the role of Christian missionaries in the genocide of American Indians, see George E. Tinker, *Missionary Conquest: The Gospel and Native American Cultural Genocide* (Minneapolis: Fortress Press, 1993).

12. See Enrique Dussel, *The Church in Latin America, 1492–1992*, A History of the Church in the Third World 1 (Maryknoll, NY: Orbis Books, 1992).

13. Moises Sandoval, *On the Move: A History of the Hispanic Church in the United States* (Maryknoll, NY: Orbis Books, 1990), 21.

14. Mouw, *God Who Commands*, 171.

15. "Justice" then becomes a term largely devoid of content.

16. Kenneth Scott Latourette provides a fuller account of Geneva and Calvin's role in it. See his survey, *A History of Christianity: Reformation to Present*, rev. ed., vol. 2 (New York: Harper & Row, 1975), 757–60.

17. Standford Rives, *Did Calvin Murder Servetus?* (Charleston, SC, 2008), 10, xvi.

18. John Neville Figgis, "Political Thought in the Sixteenth Century," in *The Cambridge Modern History*, ed. J. Acton et al., vol. 3, *The Wars of Religion* (Cambridge: Cambridge University Press, 1904), 747, 767; cited in Mouw, *God Who Commands*, 94.

19. Mouw, *God Who Commands*, 96.

20. Ibid., 114.

24

Stanley Hauerwas on Church

MIGUEL A. DE LA TORRE

HISTORICAL BACKGROUND

"Stan the Man," complete with his Texas twang and earthy demeanor, is one of the most influential ethicists at the beginning of the twenty-first century. Born in segregated Pleasant Grove, Texas, on July 24, 1940, he grew up in an economically underprivileged environment. As a young boy of seven or eight, he worked summers beside his father Coffee Hauerwas, who was a bricklayer.[1] Family life was rooted in his local congregation, Pleasant Mound United Methodist Church. His quest for the truth of Christianity led him to books on religion and eventually to Yale Divinity School. By 1970, he was teaching at Notre Dame in South Bend, Indiana. In 1984 he left for Duke, where he has been teaching ever since. According to William Cavanaugh, Hauerwas's theology is learned by placing oneself under the tutelage of the master craftsman: hence comes his opening-day lecture demand: "I don't want you to think for yourselves. I want to make you think like me."[2]

SOCIAL LOCATION

Although Hauerwas is quick to flash his East Texan credentials and low-income humble background as the son of a bricklayer, he falls short of situating himself within the Jim Crow social milieu from whence he came and fails to admit how his moral reasoning is contextualized within his social location. Hauerwas readily admits that he has "no idea how deeply the habits of racism are written into [his] life"; nevertheless, he refuses to use the voices of the marginalized to either raise his own consciousness or inform his ethical analysis. "Still, for me," Hauerwas writes:

> To "use" Martin Luther King Jr., and the church that made him possible, to advance my understanding of "Christian ethics" seems wrong. That is not *my* story, though I pray that God will make that story my story, for I hope to enjoy the fellowship of the communion of the saints. Yet that is an eschatological hope, which, as much as one desires it, cannot be forced.[3]

Because, as Hauerwas acknowledges, he is a "white southerner from the lower-middle classes who grew up embedded in the practices of segregation,"[4] Martin Luther King Jr.'s story *is* Hauerwas's story. As such, he need not wait for the eschaton to enjoy the fellowship of the communion of saints. Praxis can make such communion possible in the here and now. In fact, the lack of such communion serves as testimony that the segregated church Hauerwas privileges may consist of a gathering of people of similar cultural and socioreligious backgrounds, but it is no church—no body of Christ consisting of diverse parts.

Ethicists like Hauerwas, who are not directly harmed by oppressive structures nor interested in solidarity with the dispossessed, have the luxury of pontificating morality. His myopia and/or refusal to consider the social location of the oppressed undermine his entire ethical structure, to the detriment of communities of color. For example, his major proposition—that a narrative ethics based on Jesus teaches him to be a pacifist—is too simplistic. Although he may be advocating pacifism, his dismissal of marginalized voices makes him and his ethics complicit with an institutional violence that, like war, is also responsible for death. Jesus may have taught Hauerwas not to kill, but Hauerwas failed to learn from Jesus that death does not come solely from the barrel of a gun. Death is also caused by economic, social, and political structures, and Hauerwas's refusal to make Martin Luther King's story his own, or to seriously consider the plight of the disenfranchised, negates his advocacy for pacifism. It also negates the Jesus narrative that he holds supreme by not centering it on the "doing to the very least of these" (Mt. 25:31–46).

CONTRIBUTIONS TO THE ETHICAL DISCOURSE

Stanley Hauerwas is credited with developing a narrative theology and is a pioneer in the recovery of virtue within the theological ethics discourse. More important, he has renewed the centrality of ecclesiology. For Hauerwas, Christian ethics must be structured by and grounded in a church of believers, where the Christian "story," as rooted in the biblical text, becomes their story. The task of believers is to be "formed by the kind of community [Jesus] calls into existence."[5] As such, ethics becomes the response of believers who bear witness to the good news by being a "contrast model" of Christian faithfulness to a non-believing world.[6] Ethics is less an action committed within society, and more a character developed within the church. According to Hauerwas, "the primary social task of the church is to be itself. . . . Christian social ethics can only be done from the perspective of those who do not seek to control national or world history but who are content to live 'out of control.'"[7] Hence Hauerwas has been consistent in his critique of political liberalism[8] as a public theologian, strongly reacting to what he perceives to be its predominance within the church.

Not surprisingly, Hauerwas's focus is not on the overall society; rather, he is focused on the believing church. The church, which contains the universal truth of Jesus, must remain distinguishable from wider society, which is not the church; for it is the church that becomes the locus where Christian identity is formed. As such, no basis exists for mutual cooperation for societal justice with those outside the church who do not hold the universal truth of the gospel narrative. He goes on to declare that "the church and Christians must be uninvolved in the politics of our society and involved in the polity that is the church."[9] As problematic for communities of color as Hauerwas's moral thinking may appear, specifically because of his lack of a prophetic ethics, his critique of the Enlightenment Project and liberal individualism along with his emphasis on church community is refreshing and should be applauded.

CONCERNS FOR COMMUNITIES OF COLOR

Hauerwas fails to make justice the underlying characteristic of the kingdom of God. He writes, "The current emphasis on justice and rights as the primary norms guiding the social witness of Christians is in fact a mistake."[10] Elsewhere he writes, "Christian social ethics is not first of all principles or policies for social action, but rather the story of God's calling of Israel and the life of Jesus."[11] The primary task of the church "is not to *make* the world the kingdom, but to be faithful to the kingdom by showing to the world what it means to be a community of peace."[12] Not surprisingly, Hauerwas seems not to advocate prophetic praxes in his recovery of virtue ethics, and he exhibits antipathy toward establishing justice-based principles upon which to foster praxis. For Hauerwas, any attempt to establish social justice is more a response to the Enlightenment Project than it is to the gospel. For Christians to participate in such justice-based praxis is to become complicit with the hegemonic liberalism of the world.[13] Thus, to be a moral agent is more a process in learning how to see reality through a Eurocentric Christian lens than in enunciating praxes that challenge, subvert, or undermine the oppressive structures reinforced within society by the very same Eurocentric Christian lens that Hauerwas wants us to adopt. In short, the Christian must remain aloof from "political change and justice," as well as from "progressive forces."[14]

In *Vision and Virtue*, Hauerwas's first collection of essays, he proposes that ethics is the conceptual discipline that analyzes and imaginatively tests the images most appropriate to score the Christian life. While not denying the importance of action, living a moral life becomes a form of aesthetics concerned with learning how to articulate one's moral visions and notions, or as Hauerwas would say:

> The ethical problem reflects a classical priority in seeking to know the truth rather than to choose or will the good. . . . Such truthful vision, however, does not come without discipline. . . . [Yet] such discipline is not a code of conduct but rather the willingness to stand and accept the reality of the other without neurotic self-regard or the comfort of convention.[15]

Theological ethics for Hauerwas is orthodoxy; it proceeds from the doctrine of the Christian faith. Orthodoxy leads to how the church thinks about, formulates, and/or engages in orthopraxis, the reversal of the liberationist formula insisting that theological and ethical reflections proceed from praxis—the doing of ethics. As he points out, "The first task of Christian social ethics, therefore, is not to make the 'world' better or more just, but to help Christian people form their community consistent with their conviction that the story of Christ is a truthful account of our existence."[16] He confuses an unapologetic conviction of the truth of the Christian narrative with a Eurocentric interpretation of what that truth might be; thus he converts his truth claims into a facade masking a power that reinforces Eurocentric Christian dominance in the discourse as well as the culture. The community becomes the place where "praxis," understood as behaviors or personal piety that emulates the kingdom of God, takes place. Dismantling oppressive societal structures is not as important as developing a Christian character.

For Hauerwas, "Christian ethics is best understood as an ethics of character."[17] Nevertheless, for the U.S. marginalized people, Christian ethics is best understood as an ethics of societal change. Simply stated, there can exist no significant ethics without an emphasis on praxis. Although it is noble to envision how character ought to be seen and intended, and how said character might influence behavior that might bring about change, it is only through praxis geared at dismantling the power and privilege bestowed upon Euroamericans and their churches that character develops. For what good is a virtuous character if oppressive structures remain? Just as "faith without works is dead" (James 2:20 KJV), so too right virtues without right praxis are meaningless.

Hauerwas insists that a moral agent's self-understanding of one's actions (as opposed to how others may interpret those actions) is the foundation of one's morality. Specifically, it is "what kind of agents they think themselves to be in doing what they do."[18] The danger to communities of color is that such a moral vision provides a virtuous way of conduct that ignores the "virtuous" complicity with the structures of empire that cause oppression. This complicity is further masked through his understanding of ecclesiology. He advises that "the church and Christians must be uninvolved in the polity of our society and involved in the polity that is the church."[19] Rather than making a preferential option for the marginalized, as most liberationists do, Hauerwas makes a preferential option for the church of privilege—specifically, the U.S. church, which cannot avoid its complicity with empire, even though Hauerwas may rile against empire.

As Hauerwas often states, "The church does not have a social ethic; the church is a social ethic."[20] When he calls the church "to be the church," Hauerwas intends for the church to serve the world that desperately needs to hear the "truth" of the Christian narrative.[21] But how can communities of color trust a church or the social ethics that the church advocates from a Eurocentric church that historically has been anti-Semitic, racist, sexist, and colonialist, and in many cases continues to be so? Gloria Albrecht asks a similar question, pointing out how Hauerwas's church is patriarchal and authoritarian, ignoring those whom it has disenfranchised. Hauerwas fails, as Albrecht correctly notes, to seriously consider how power operates within the church to the detriment of those marginalized by the church. She writes:

> Hauerwas [does not] question the power relations that actually exist within church communities and the effective silencing of voices that might challenge the views they assume. Essentially, the authority-of-clergy vs. the authority-of-community debate . . . conceals the reality that authority in either case lies within the hands of (predominately white) male clerical or (predominately white) male communal leadership. The obvious problematic consequence for women and men of color is that an authentic understanding of scripture requires submission to the authority and discipline of a (white) male dominated institutional church, its self-defined traditions, its seminaries, and its professional disciplines. Nonetheless, Hauerwas . . . argue[s] that only by this authority and under this discipline, Christians learn to "see" their world. Without this authority, we do not "see" as Christians.[22]

If, as Hauerwas claims, "the primary social task of the church is to be itself,"[23] then all people of color need to be *very* concerned; for this is a church whose ethics has historically accommodated and justified every immoral form of human exploitation—from massacres to war, from slavery to colonialism. Just as Hauerwas, while attending the church as he was growing up in segregated Texas, assumed that oppression in the form of segregation was normal, he still continues in failing to recognize how oppression of people of color is normalized today by his Euroamerican churches.[24] Centuries of White supremacy cannot be washed away simply because Hauerwas envisions what the church of Christ ought to be. Regardless of how progressive Hauerwas's vision of the church may be, his failure to deconstruct the power dynamics embedded in the type of church attended by Euroamericans of relative privilege like him provides little or no hope for the salvation of people of color.

For Hauerwas, the proper response to world hunger and neighborhood poverty is to reclaim the significance of the trivial—to enjoy a walk, to read novels, play sports, or worship God. To indulge in the trivial affirms God's patience.[25] But claiming God's patience in the face of hunger is definitely a middle-class privilege. It is obvious that his church is not the church on his margins; those whose congregants work multiple jobs to avoid hunger have no time to take a walk, read novels, or play sports. And I can assure you, they worship God very differently. Saving lemurs, as an example of a trivial act suggested by Hauerwas, may be a way that peace becomes concretely embodied in Euroamerican lives,[26] but it is not how it is embodied in the lives of those who exist on society's underside, who are more concerned with physically saving their families and themselves. Liturgy may be an effective social action for Hauerwas,[27] but dispossessed communities of color need something more than just liturgy.

In spite of Hauerwas's limited engagement with liberative ethics or theology, we should not be surprised when he dismisses Gustavo Gutiérrez's work on liberation theology as "profoundly anti-Christian," an inadequate theological and sociological expression of liberal theology.[28] Hauerwas seems to think that Gutiérrez's approach to liberation is Kantian, and as such, "does not sufficiently guard against" the Enlightenment Project, which seeks freedom "from all servitude" in the hopes of becoming "artisans of our own destiny."[29] More disturbing is his argument against the hope of salvation from oppression by reminding the marginalized that salvation is, in fact, "a life that freely suffers, that freely serves, because such suffering and service is the hallmark of the Kingdom established by Jesus."[30] All people of color should be concerned when Euroamerican ethicists tell them why their suffering, caused by Euroamericans in the first place, makes them better saved Christians! It is obvious to those excluded from the churches of the dominant culture that the church Hauerwas writes of is not their church. Because Christian churches continue to be segregated in terms of race, ethnicity, and class, the Eurocentric church that Hauerwas seems to privilege remains embedded within the power structures of empire so that he need not freely suffer—only abstractly; nevertheless, those same structures that protect him from such suffering are paid for with the actual suffering and death of those on society's underside.[31] Since the normative U.S. church is White and middle class, a type of sectarian ecclesiology is created, as James Gustafson points out, to which Hauerwas can retreat.[32] Unfortunately, this retreat leads to civil irresponsibility.

CONCLUSION

The sectarian ecclesiology that Hauerwas constructs leans toward abstraction, where his vision supersedes contextualized praxis, thus reinforcing the Eurocentric ability to control the discourse and thereby reinforce empire. By separating his vision of what is virtue from the everyday experiences of communities of color in need of liberative praxis, he sets up an intellectual world where the validity of his propositions can never be validated. Focusing on how the church is to *be* rather than to *have* a social ethics—this moves the discourse to the abstract of what it means to *be*. Such abstract discussions have little or no value for those whose very survival depends on the church *doing* a social ethics. His pronouncements on ethics are therefore legitimized even if they fail to provide any liberative praxis for those residing on the underside of Euroamerican culture.

Ethicists of color can find more in common with Muslims, Hindus, or Jews who are faithful to their sacred texts' calls for justice than with Hauerwas's brand of Christianity, which argues "why justice is a bad idea for Christians."[33] Hauerwas's ethical pronouncements, along with other Eurocentric ethical paradigms that focus on the abstract rather than contextualized praxis, can have no standing within dispossessed communities, specifically because such praxis is too anemic. Ironically, the church that Hauerwas tends to privilege ceases to be the church because it lacks the types of praxis consistently called for by God as recorded within the biblical narrative, the same narrative that Hauerwas seems to privilege. For only through Christian praxis is the Christian church established. Any church lacking praxis is not a Christian church, but a collective of individuals with common traits, no different from an exclusive country club.

Notes

1. Stanley Hauerwas, *Hannah's Child: A Theologian's Memoir* (Grand Rapids: Wm. B. Eerdmans Publishing Co., 2010), 27. Portions of this essay appeared in Miguel De La Torre, *Latino/a Social Justice: Moving beyond Eurocentric Moral Thinking* (Waco, TX: Baylor University Press, 2010). These portions are reprinted with permission of Baylor University Press.
2. William Cavanaugh, "Stan the Man," in *The Hauerwas Reader*, ed. John Berkman and Michael Cartwright (Durham, NC: Duke University Press, 2001), 26.
3. Stanley Hauerwas, *Wilderness Wanderings: Probing Twentieth-Century Theology and Philosophy* (Boulder, CO: Westview Press, 1997), 225–26.
4. Ibid.
5. Stanley Hauerwas, *A Community of Character: Toward a Constructive Christian Social Ethic* (Notre Dame, IN: Notre Dame University Press, 1981), 40.
6. Ibid., 50.
7. Ibid., 10–11.
8. However, Hauerwas's concern with liberalism is its questioning of the truthfulness of the Christian narrative and its proclivity toward a civil religion.
9. Hauerwas, *Community of Character*, 74.
10. Stanley Hauerwas, *After Christendom? How the Church Is to Behave If Freedom, Justice, and a Christian Nation Are Bad Ideas* (Nashville: Abingdon Press, 1991), 45.
11. Stanley Hauerwas, "The Gesture of a Truthful Story," *Theology Today* 42, no. 2 (July 1985): 181–82.
12. Stanley Hauerwas, *The Peaceable Kingdom: A Primer in Christian Ethics* (Notre Dame, IN: Notre Dame University Press, 1983), 103.
13. Hauerwas, *After Christendom?* 190–91, 195.
14. Hauerwas, "The Gesture of a Truthful Story," 185.

15. Stanley Hauerwas, *Vision and Virtue: Essays in Christian Ethical Reflection* (Notre Dame, IN: Fides Publishers, 1974), 2.
16. Hauerwas, *Community of Character*, 112.
17. Stanley Hauerwas, *Character and the Christian Life: A Study in Theological Ethics* (San Antonio, TX: Trinity University Press, 1975), vii.
18. Stanley Hauerwas, "Learning to See Red Wheelbarrows: On Vision and Relativism," *Journal of the American Academy of Religion* 45 (1977): 649.
19. Hauerwas, *Community of Character*, 74.
20. Hauerwas, *Peaceable Kingdom*, 99.
21. Stanley Hauerwas, *Performing the Faith: Bonhoeffer and the Practice of Nonviolence* (Grand Rapids: Brazos Press, 2004), 231.
22. Gloria Albrecht, *The Character of Community: Toward an Ethic of Liberation for the Church* (Nashville: Abingdon Press, 1995), 49–50.
23. Hauerwas, *Community of Character*, 10.
24. Hauerwas, *Wilderness Wanderings*, 225.
25. Stanley Hauerwas, "Taking Time for Peace: The Ethical Significance of the Trivial," in *Christian Existence Today: Essays on Church, World, and Living in Between* (Durham, NC: Labyrinth Press, 1988), 256–57.
26. Ibid., 260.
27. James Gustafson, "The Sectarian Temptation: Reflections on Theology, the Church, and the University," *Proceedings of the Catholic Theological Society* 40 (1985): 87.
28. Stanley Hauerwas, "Some Theological Reflections on Gutiérrez's Use of 'Liberation' as a Theological Concept," *Modern Theology* 3, no. 1 (1986): 69.
29. Ibid.; Hauerwas, *After Christendom*, 50–52.
30. Hauerwas, "Some Theological Reflections," 69–70.
31. John B. Thomson's book *The Ecclesiology of Stanley Hauerwas: A Christian Theology of Liberation* (Burlington, VT: Ashgate, 2003) tries to argue that Hauerwas's theological work is in fact a distinctive kind of liberation theology. Thomson masterfully demonstrates what a liberation theology constructed from the social location of the privileged and powerful, as opposed to the disenfranchised and oppressed, would look like.
32. Gustafson, "Sectarian Temptation," 83–94.
33. Justice is a bad idea for Christians, Hauerwas argues, because "a theory of justice" that provides the means to know in principle what justice entails does not exist. To ground justice in some abstract right or contractual agreement distorts the moral capacity of Christians. Not having a definition for justice means that such discourse is really more a product of the Enlightenment Project than the witness of the Christian church. Hauerwas, *After Christendom*, 45–68.

Bibliography

Alarcón, Enrique. *S. Thomae de Aquino Opera omnia*. Pamplona, Spain: University of Navarre, 2000.

Albrecht, Gloria. *The Character of Our Communities: Toward an Ethic of Liberation for the Church*. Nashville: Abingdon Press, 1995.

Anderson, Victor. *Creative Exchange: A Constructive Theology of African American Religious Experience*. Minneapolis: Fortress Press, 2008.

Aristotle. *Nicomachean Ethics*. Translated by H. Rackham. Cambridge, MA: Harvard University Press, 1999.

———. *Politics*. Translated by H. Rackham. Cambridge, MA: Harvard University Press, 1998.

Armitage, David. "John Locke, Carolina, and the Two Treatises of Government." *Political Theory* 32, no. 5 (2004): 602–27.

Arneil, Barbara. *John Locke and America: The Defence of English Colonialism*. Broadbridge, UK: Clarendon Press, 1996.

Augustine. *City of God*. New York: Penguin Books, 2003.

———. *Political Writings*. Edited by E. M. Atkins and R. J. Dodaro. Cambridge: Cambridge University Press, 2007.

Bainton, Roland H. *Yale and the Ministry: A History of Education for the Christian Ministry at Yale from the Founding in 1701*. New York: Harper, 1957.

Baker-Fletcher, Karen. "Providence, National Destiny, and the Knowledge of Good and Evil." *Quarterly Review* 23, no. 3 (Fall 2003): 227–37.

Baldwin, James. *The Price of the Ticket: Collected Nonfiction, 1948–1985.* New York: St. Martins Press, 1985.

———. "The White Man's Guilt." *Ebony* 20, no. 29 (August 1965). Reprint in his *The Price of the Ticket: Collected Nonfiction, 1948–1985* (New York: St. Martins Press, 1985), 409–14.

Barkai, Avraham. *Branching Out: German-Jewish Immigration to the United States, 1820–1914.* New York: Holmes & Meier, 1994.

Barnes, Jonathan. *The Complete Works of Aristotle.* Princeton, NJ: Princeton University Press, 1984.

Baron de Montesquieu. *The Spirit of the Laws.* Translated by Thomas Nugent. New York: Hafner Press, 1949.

Berger, Peter L., and Thomas Luckmann. *The Social Construction of Reality: A Treatise in the Sociology of Knowledge.* New York: Doubleday, Anchor Books, 1967.

Bernasconi, Robert, ed. *Race.* Malden, MA: Blackwell Publishing, 2001.

Bernstein, Richard J. *Philosophical Profiles: Essays in a Pragmatic Mode.* Philadelphia: University of Pennsylvania Press, 1986.

Bloesch, Donald G. *Holy Scripture: Revelation, Inspiration and Interpretation.* Downers Grove, IL: InterVarsity Press, 1994.

Bogues, Anthony. "John Stuart Mill and 'The Negro Question': Race, Colonialism, and the Ladder of Civilization." *Race and Racism in Modern Philosophy.* Edited by Andrew Valls. Ithaca, NY: Cornell University Press, 2005.

Bongmba, Elias Kifon. *African Witchcraft and Otherness: A Philosophical and Theological Critique of Intersubjective Relations.* Albany: State University of New York Press, 2001.

———. "Beyond Reason to Interdisciplinary Dialogue on Morality and Politics in Africa: Comments on E. C. Eze's 'Between History and the Gods: Reason, Morality, and Politics in Today's Africa.'" *Africa Today* 55, no. 2 (2000): 98–104.

Bonhoeffer, Dietrich. *The Cost of Discipleship.* Rev. ed. New York: Collier Books, 1963.

Bottom, Joseph, and Michael Novak. "The Leadership of George W. Bush: Con and Pro." *First Things*, no. 171 (March 2007): 31–35.

Brown, Robert McAfee, Abraham J. Heschel, and Michael Novak. *Vietnam: Crisis of Conscience.* New York: Association Press, 1967.

Butler, Judith. *Gender Trouble.* New York: Routledge Press, 1990.

Cannon, Katie G. *Black Womanist Ethics.* Atlanta: Scholars Press, 1988.

———. "Hitting a Straight Lick with a Crooked Stick: The Womanist Dilemma in the Development of a Black Liberation Ethic." In *Katie's Canon: Womanism and the Soul of the Black Community.* New York: Continuum, 1995.

———. "Wheels in the Middle of Wheels." *Journal of Feminist Studies in Religion 8,* no. 2 (Fall 1992): 125–32.

Capizzi, Joseph E. "The Children of God: Natural Slavery in the Thought of Aquinas and Vitoria." *Theological Studies* 63, no. 1 (2002): 3–22.

Carter, J. Kameron. *Race: A Theological Account.* New York: Oxford University Press, 2008.

Cavanaugh, William. "Stan the Man." *The Hauerwas Reader.* Edited by John Berkman and Michael Cartwright. Durham, NC: Duke University Press, 2001.

Chappell, David L. *A Stone of Hope: Prophetic Religion and the Death of Jim Crow.* Chapel Hill: University of North Carolina Press, 2004.

Chow, Rey. *The Protestant Ethnic and the Spirit of Capitalism.* New York: Columbia University Press, 2002.

Chrystal, William G. "'A Man of the Hour and the Time': The Legacy of Gustav Niebuhr." *Church History* 49, no. 4 (December 1980): 416–32.

Cohen, Martin. *Philosophical Tales.* Boston: Blackwell Publishing, 2008.

Cone, James H. *Black Theology and Black Power*, 20th anniversary ed. Maryknoll, NY: Orbis Books, 1989.

De Gruchy, John W. *Christianity and Democracy: Towards a Just World Order*. Cambridge: Cambridge University Press, 1995.

De La Torre, Miguel A. *Latina/o Social Ethics: Moving beyond Eurocentric Moral Thinking*. Waco, TX: Baylor University Press, 2010.

DeLisio, Therese B. "Did Reinhold Niebuhr Care about Racism in America?" *Union Seminary Quarterly Review* 61, no. 3–4 (2008): 14.

Deloria, Philip. *Indians in Unexpected Places*. Lawrence: University of Kansas Press, 2004.

Dent, Nicholas. *Rousseau*. New York: Routledge, 2005.

DeWolf, L. Harold. "Martin Luther King, Jr. as Theologian." *Journal of the Interdenominational Theological Center* 4, no. 2 (Spring 1977): 1–11.

Dixon, Valerie Elverton. "From Just War to a Just Peace Paradigm" January 8, 2010. http://justpeacetheory.com/files/From_Just_War_to_a_Just_Peace_Paradigm.pdf.

———. "Torture, Terror, War and the End of Bloodshed Sacrifice." January 8, 2010, http://justpeacetheory.com/files/Torture_Terror_War_and_the_End_of_Bloodshed_Sacrifice.pdf.

Dobbs, Darrel. "Natural Right and the Problem of Arsitotle's Defense of Slavery." *Journal of Politics* 56, no. 1 (1994): 69–94.

Dorrien, Gary. *The Making of American Liberal Theology*. Vol. 2, *Idealism, Realism, and Modernity, 1900–1950*. Louisville, KY: Westminster John Knox Press, 2003.

———. *Social Ethics in the Making: Interpreting an American Tradition*. Malden, MA: Blackwell Publishing, 2009.

Douglas, Kelly Brown. *What's Faith Got to Do with It? Black Bodies / Christian Souls*. Minneapolis: Orbis Books, 2005.

Doyle, Tsarina. *Nietzsche on Epistemology and Metaphysics: The World in View*. Edinburgh: Edinburgh University Press, 2009.

Durant, Will. *The Story of Civilization*. Part 3, *Caesar and Christ*. New York: Simon & Schuster, 1944.

———. *The Story of Civilization*. Part 4, *The Age of Faith*. New York: Simon & Schuster, 1950.

Dussel, Enrique D. *The Church in Latin America, 1492–1992*. A History of the Church in the Third World 1. Maryknoll, NY: Orbis Books, 1992.

Eichhoff, Jürgen. "The German Language in America." In *America and the Germans: An Assessment of a Three Hundred Year History*, edited by Frank Trommler and Joseph McVeigh, vol. 1, *Immigration, Language, Ethnicity*, 223–40. Philadelphia: University of Pennsylvania Press, 1985.

Emerson, Ralph Waldo. "Plato; or, The Philosopher." In *Representative Men: Seven Lectures*, with text established by Douglas Emory Wilson, 21–44. Cambridge, MA: Belknap Press of Harvard University Press, 1996.

Epstein, Steven A. *Speaking of Slavery: Color, Ethnicity, and Human Bondage in Italy*. Ithaca, NY: Cornell University Press, 2001.

Evans, Christopher H. *The Kingdom Is Always but Coming*. Grand Rapids: Wm. B. Eerdmans Publishing Co., 2004.

Eze, Emmanuel Chukwudi. *Achieving Our Humanity*. London: Routledge, 2001.

———. *On Reason: Rationality in a World of Cultural Conflict and Racism*. Durham, NC: Duke University Press, 2008.

———, ed. *Race and the Enlightenment: A Reader*. Cambridge, MA: Blackwell Publishing, 1997.

Field, David N. "Dietrich Bonhoeffer." In *Empire and the Christian Tradition: New Readings of Classical Theologians*, edited by Kwok Pui-Lan, Don H. Compier, and Joerg Rieger. Minneapolis: Fortress Press, 2007.

Figgis, John Neville. "Political Thought in the Sixteenth Century." In *The Cambridge Modern History*, edited by J. Acton et al., vol. 3, *The Wars of Religion*. Cambridge: Cambridge University Press, 1904.

Finnis, John. *Aquinas: Moral, Political, and Legal Theory*. New York: Oxford University Press, 1998.

Fletcher, Joseph F. *Joseph Fletcher: Memoir of an Ex-Radical; Reminiscence and Reappraisal*. Louisville, KY: Westminster/John Knox Press, 1993.

———. *Moral Responsibility: Situation Ethics at Work*. Philadelphia: Westminster Press, 1967.

———. *Situation Ethics: The New Morality*. Philadelphia: Westminster Press, 1966.

Ford, David F., ed. *The Modern Theologians: An Introduction to Christian Theology in the Twentieth Century*. Malden, MA: Blackwell Publishing, 1997.

Fortenbaugh, William W. *Aristotle on Emotion*. 2nd ed. London: Duckworth Publishers, 2002.

———. "Aristotle on Slaves and Women." In *Articles on Aristotle*, edited by J. Barnes, M. Schofield, and R. Sorabji, vol 2, *Ethics and Politics*. London: Duckworth, 1977.

Fotion, Nicholas. *War and Ethics: A New Just War Theory*. New York: Continuum, 2007.

Foucault, Michel. *Discipline and Punish*. New York: Vintage Books, 1977.

———. *History of Sexuality*. Vol. 1. New York: Vintage Books, 1980.

———. *The Order of Things*. New York: Vintage Books, 1970.

———. *Power/Knowledge*. New York: Pantheon Books, 1977.

———. *Security, Territory, Population: Lectures at the College De France, 1977–1978*. New York: Palgrave, 2004.

Fox, Richard Wightman. *Reinhold Niebuhr: A Biography*. 1985. Reprint, Ithaca, NY: Cornell University Press, 1996.

Frank, Jill. "Citizens, Slaves, and Foreigners: Aristotle on Human Nature." *American Political Science Review* 98, no. 2 (2004): 91–104.

Fuchs, Lawrence H. *The American Kaleidoscope: Race, Ethnicity, and the Civic Culture*. Hanover, NH: University Press of New England, 1990.

Grant, Jacquelyn. "The Sin of Servanthood: And the Deliverance of Discipleship." In *A Troubling in My Soul: Womanist Perspectives on Evil and Suffering*. Edited by Emilie M. Townes. Maryknoll, NY: Orbis Books, 1993.

Gustafson, James M. *Can Ethics Be Christian?* Chicago: University of Chicago Press, 1975.

———. *Christian Ethics and the Community*. Philadelphia: Pilgrim Press, 1971.

———. *The Church as Moral Decision-Maker*. Philadelphia: Pilgrim Press, 1970.

———. *Ethics from a Theocentric Perspective*. Vol. 1, *Theology and Ethics*. Chicago: University of Chicago Press, 1981.

———. "The Sectarian Temptation: Reflections on Theology, the Church, and the University." *Proceedings of the Catholic Theological Society* 40 (1985): 83–94.

———. *Treasure in Earthen Vessels: The Church as a Human Community*. New York: Harper & Row, 1961.

———. "The Vocation of the Theological Educator." Lecture, Austin Presbyterian Seminary, November 15, 1985.

Habibi, Don. "The Moral Dimensions of J. S. Mill's Colonialism." *Journal of Social Philosophy* 30, no. 1 (Spring 1999): 125–46.

Hall, Stuart. "Encoding/Decoding." In *Culture, Media, Language: Working Papers in Cultural Studies, 1972–79*. Hutchinson University Library in association with the Centre for Contemporary Cultural Studies, University of Birmingham; London: Unwin Hyman, 1980.

———. *Representation: Cultural Representations and Signifying Practices*. Thousand Oaks, CA: Sage, 1997.

Han, Sora. "Bonds of Representation: Vision, Race and Law in Post–Civil Rights America." PhD diss., University of California–Santa Cruz, 2006.

Hanke, Louis. *Aristotle and the American Indians.* Chicago: Regnery, 1959.

Hartsock, Nancy. "Foucault on Power: A Theory for Women?" In *Feminism and Postmodernism,* edited by Linda Nicholson, 157–75. New York: Routledge, 1990.

Hauerwas, Stanley. *After Christendom? How the Church Is to Behave If Freedom, Justice, and a Christian Nation Are Bad Ideas.* Nashville: Abingdon, 1991.

———. *Character and the Christian Life: A Study in Theological Ethics.* San Antonio, TX: Trinity University Press, 1975.

———. *A Community of Character: Toward a Constructive Christian Social Ethics.* Notre Dame, IN: University of Notre Dame Press, 1981.

———. "The Gesture of a Truthful Story." *Theology Today* 42, no. 2 (July 1985): 181–89.

———. "Learning to See Red Wheelbarrows: On Vision and Relativism." *Journal of the American Academy of Religion* 45 (1977): 643–55.

———. *The Peaceable Kingdom: A Primer in Christian Ethics.* Notre Dame, IN: University of Notre Dame Press, 1983.

———. *Performing the Faith: Bonhoeffer and the Practice of Nonviolence.* Grand Rapids: Brazos Press, 2004.

———. "Remembering John Howard Yoder: December 29, 1927–December 30, 1997." *First Things,* no. 82 (April 1998): 15–16.

———. "Some Theological Reflections on Gutierrez's Use of 'Liberation' as a Theological Concept." *Modern Theology* 3, no. 1 (1986): 67–76.

———. "Taking Time for Peace: The Ethical Significance of the Trivial." *Christian Existence Today: Essays on Church, World, and Living in Between.* Durham: Labyrinth Press, 1988.

———. *Vision and Virtue: Essays in Christian Ethical Reflection.* Notre Dame, IN: Fides Publishers, 1974.

———. *Wilderness Wanderings: Probing Twentieth-Century Theology and Philosophy.* Boulder, CO: Westview Press, 1997.

Heath, Malcolm. "Aristotle on Natural Slavery." *Phronesis* 53 (2008): 243–70.

Henry, John F. "John Locke, Property Rights and Economic Theory." *Journal of Economic Issues* 33, no. 3 (1999): 609–18.

Hill, Christopher. *Bantustans: The Fragmentation of South Africa.* New York: Oxford University Press, 1979.

Hill Collins, Patricia. *Black Feminist Thought: Knowledge, Consciousness, and the Politics of Empowerment.* Boston: Unwin Hyman, 1990.

Hobbes, Thomas, *Leviathan.* Edited by Richard Tuck. New York: Cambridge University Press, 2006.

Holmes, Robert L. *On War and Morality.* Princeton, NJ: Princeton University Press, 1989.

Holmes, Stephen. "Making Sense of Liberal Imperialism." *J. S. Mill's Political Thought: A Bicentennial Reassessment.* Edited by Nadia Urbinati and Alex Zakaras. Cambridge: Cambridge University Press, 2007.

Idziak, Janine Marie. *Divine Command Morality: Historical and Contemporary Readings.* Texts and Studies in Religion 5. New York: E. Mellen Press, 1979.

Isasi-Díaz, Ada María. *En la Lucha: Elaborating a Mujerista Theology.* 2nd ed. Minneapolis: Fortress Press, 2004.

———. *Justicia: A Reconciliatory Praxis of Care and Tenderness.* Minneapolis: Fortress Press, forthcoming.

Jackson, Michael D. "The Man Who Could Turn into an Elephant: Shape-Shifting among the Kuranko of Sierra Leone." In *Personhood and Agency: The Experience of Self and Other in African Cultures; Papers Presented at a Symposium on African*

Folk Models and Their Application, held at Uppsala University, August 23–30, 1987, edited by Michael D. Jackson and Ivan Karp, 59–78. Uppsala Studies in Cultural Anthropology 14. Uppsala: S. Academiae Ubsaliensis; Washington, DC: distributed by Smithsonian Institution Press, 1990.

Jacobson-Widding, Anita. "The Shadow as an Expression of Individuality in Congolese Conceptions of Personhood." In *Personhood and Agency: The Experience of Self and Other in African Cultures; Papers Presented at a Symposium on African Folk Models and Their Application, held at Uppsala University, August 23–30, 1987,* edited by Michael D. Jackson and Ivan Karp, 31–58. Uppsala Studies in Cultural Anthropology 14. Uppsala: S. Academiae Ubsaliensis; Washington, DC: distributed by Smithsonian Institution Press, 1990.

Jahn, Beate. "Barbarian Thoughts: Imperialism in the Philosophy of John Stuart Mill." *Review of International Studies* 31 (2005): 599–618.

James, Joy. *Resisting State Violence.* Minneapolis: University of Minnesota Press, 1996.

James, William. "Dedication of the Germanic Museum." *William James: Essays, Comments, and Reviews, 1842–1910.* 1903. Reprint, Cambridge, MA: Harvard University Press, 1987.

Jefferson, Thomas. "On the Differences between the Races." In *Notes on the State of Virginia.* London: J. Stockdale, 1787.

Kant, Immanuel. *Anthropology from a Pragmatic Point of View.* New York: Cambridge University Press, 2006.

———. *Critique of Practical Reason.* New York: Cambridge University Press, 1997.

———. *Groundwork for the Metaphysics of Morals.* New York: Oxford University Press, 2002.

———. *The Metaphysics of Morals.* New York: Cambridge University Press, 1991.

———. *Observations on the Feeling of the Beautiful and Sublime.* Berkeley: University of California Press, 2003.

———. "Of the Different Human Races." In *The Idea of Race,* edited by Robert Bernasconi and Tommy L. Lott. Indianapolis: Hackett Publishing Co., 2000.

———. "On the Different Races of Man." In *Race and the Enlightenment: A Reader,* edited by Emmanuel Chukwudi Eze, 28–52. Cambridge, MA: Blackwell Publishing, 1997.

———. *Toward Perpetual Peace and Other Writings on Politics, Peace, and History.* New Haven: Yale University Press, 2006.

Kaufman-Osborn, Timothy V. "Capital Punishment as Legal Lynching?" *From Lynching Mobs to the Killing State.* Edited by Charles Ogletree Jr. and Austin Sarat. New York: New York University Press, 2006.

Kazanjian, David. *The Colonizing Trick.* Minneapolis: University of Minnesota Press, 2003.

Kleingeld, Pauline. "Kant's Second Thoughts on Race." *Philosophical Quarterly* 57, no. 229 (October 2007): 573–92.

Kretzmann, Norman, and Eleanor Stump, eds. *The Cambridge Companion to Aquinas.* Cambridge: Cambridge University Press, 1993.

Lamore, Charles. *Patterns of Moral Complexity.* London: Cambridge University Press, 1987.

Latourette, Kenneth Scott. *A History of Christianity: Reformation to the Present.* Rev. ed. Vol. 2. New York: Harper & Row, 1975.

Leibholz, Gerhard. "Memoir." In *The Cost of Discipleship,* by Dietrich Bonhoeffer, 9–28. Rev. ed. New York: Collier Books, 1963.

Locke, Alain. "The New Negro." In *The New Negro: Voices of the Harlem Renaissance,* edited by Alain Locke, 3–18. 1968. Reprint, New York: Touchstone, 1997. http://us.history.wisc.edu/hist102/pdocs/locke_new.pdf.

Locke, John. *An Essay concerning Human Understanding*. Philadelphia: Kay & Troutman, 1847.

———. *Locke's Two Treatises of Government: A Critical Edition with Introduction and Notes*, edited by Peter Laslett. 2nd ed. New York: Cambridge University Press, 1970.

Long, Charles H. *Significations: Signs, Symbols, and Images in the Interpretation of Religion*. Aurora, CO: Davies Group, 1995.

Lützeler, Paul Michael. "St. Louis World's Fair of 1904 as a Site of Cultural Transfer." In *German Culture in Nineteenth-Century America: Reception, Adaptation, Transformation*, edited by Lynne Tatlock and Matt Erlin. Rochester, NY: Camden House, 2005.

MacIntyre, Alasdair. *After Virtue*. 1st, 2nd, and 3rd editions. Notre Dame, IN: University of Notre Dame Press, 1982, 1984, 2007.

———. *Whose Justice? Whose Rationality?* Notre Dame, IN: University of Notre Dame Press, 1988.

Malik, Kenan. *The Meaning of Race: Race, History, and Culture in Western Society*. New York: New York University Press, 1996.

Mamdani, Mahmood. *Citizen and Subject: Contemporary Africa and the Legacy of Late Colonialism*. Princeton, NJ: Princeton University Press, 1996.

Mandela, Nelson. *A Long Walk to Freedom: The Autobiography of Nelson Mandela*. New York: Little, Brown & Co., 1995.

Marsh, Charles. *God's Long Summer: Stories of Faith and Civil Rights*. 2nd ed. Princeton, NJ: Princeton University Press, 2008.

Mattox, John Mark. *Saint Augustine and the Theory of Just War*. New York: Continuum, 2006.

McClendon, James William, Jr. "John Howard Yoder, One of Our Own: 1927–1997." *Perspectives in Religious Studies* 25, no. 1 (Spring 1998): 21–26.

Mehta, Uday Singh. *Liberalism and Empire: A Study in Nineteenth-Century British Liberal Thought*. London: University of Chicago Press, 1999.

Mercer, Kobena. *Welcome to the Jungle: New Positions in Black Cultural Studies*. New York: Routledge, 1994.

Mill, John Stuart. "Civilization." *The Collected Works of John Stuart Mill*. Edited by John M. Robson. 1836. Reprint, Toronto: University of Toronto Press, 1991.

———. "On Liberty." In *On Liberty and Other Essays*. Edited by John Gray. 1859. Reprint, Oxford: Oxford University Press, 1991.

———. *Utilitarianism*. 1861. Reprint, New York: Library of Liberal Arts, 1957.

Miller, J. Joseph. "Chairing the Jamaica Committee: J. S. Mill and the Limits of Colonial Authority." In *Utilitarianism and Empire*, edited by Bart Schultz and Georgios Varouxakis. New York: Rowman & Littlefield, 2005.

Miller, Keith D. *Voice of Deliverance: The Language of Martin Luther King, Jr. and Its Sources*. New York: Free Press, 1992.

Moore, Gregory. *Nietzsche, Biology and Metaphor*. Cambridge: Cambridge University Press, 2002.

Morgensen, Scott Lauria. *Queer Settler Colonialism and Indigenous Decolonization*. Minneapolis: University of Minnesota Press, forthcoming.

Mouw, Richard J. *The God Who Commands*. Notre Dame, IN: University of Notre Dame Press, 1990.

Murove, Munyaradzi Felix. "Beyond the Savage Evidence Ethic: A Validation of African Ethics." In *African Ethics: An Anthology of Comparative and Applied Ethics*, edited by Munyaradzi Felix Murove. Pietermaritzburg: University of KwaZulu-Natal Press, 2009.

Nation, Mark Thiessen. "A Comprehensive Bibliography of the Writings of John Howard Yoder." *Mennonite Quarterly Review* 71, no.1 (January 1997): 93–145.

Nemeth, Charles P. *Aquinas and King: A Discourse on Civil Disobedience.* Durham, NC: Carolina Academic Press, 2009.

Nichols, Mary P. *Citizens and Statesmen: A Study of Aristotle's Politics.* Lanham, MD: Rowman & Littlefield Publishers, 1991.

Niebuhr, H. Richard. *The Purpose of the Church and Its Ministry.* New York: Harper & Row, 1956.

———. *The Responsible Self: An Essay in Christian Moral Philosophy.* New York: Harper & Row, 1963.

———. *The Social Sources of Denominationalism.* New York: H. Holt and Co., 1929.

Niebuhr, Reinhold. *The Children of Light and the Children of Darkness: A Vindication of Democracy and a Critique of Its Traditional Defense.* New York: Scribner, 1944.

———. "The Failure of German-Americanism." *Atlantic Monthly* 118, no. 1 (July 1916): 13–18.

———. *The Godly and the Ungodly: Essays on the Religious and Secular Dimensions of Modern Life.* London: Faber & Faber, 1958.

———. "Grace and Sin." In *Reinhold Niebuhr: Theologian in Public Life*, edited by Larry Rasmussen. Minneapolis: Fortress Press, 1988.

———. *The Irony of American History.* 1952. Reprint, Chicago: University of Chicago Press, 2008.

———. "Justice and Love." In *Love and Justice: Selections from the Shorter Writings of Reinhold Niebuhr*, edited by D. B. Robertson, 27–29. Philadelphia: Westminster Press, 1957. Reprint, Louisville, KY: Westminster/John Knox Press, 1992.

———. *Moral Man and Immoral Society.* 1932. Reprint, New York: Charles Scribner's Sons, 1960.

———. "Yale-Eden." *Keryx* 4 (December 1914): 1–4. Reprint in *Young Reinhold Niebuhr, His Early Writings, 1911–1931*, edited by William G. Chrystal. St. Louis, MO: Eden Publishing House, 1977.

Nietzsche, Friedrich. *The Antichrist: A Criticism of Christianity.* Translated by Anthony M. Ludovici. New York: Barnes & Noble, 2006.

———. *Beyond Good and Evil: Prelude to a Philosophy of the Future.* Translated by Helen Zimmern. New York: Barnes & Noble, 2007.

———. *Human, All Too Human.* Translated by Helen Zimmern. New York: Barnes & Noble, 2008.

———. "On Little Old and Young Women." From *Thus Spoke Zarathustra* and thereby in *The Portable Nietzsche*, translated by Walter Kaufmann. New York: Penguin Books, 1954.

———. *On the Genealogy of Morality.* Translated by Maudemarie Clark and Alan J. Swensen. Indianapolis/Cambridge: Hackett Publishing Co., 1998.

———. *The Will to Power.* Translated by Anthony M. Ludovici. New York: Barnes & Noble, 2006.

Novak, Michael. "Defining Social Justice." *First Things*, no. 108 (December 2000): 11–13.

———. "Max Weber Goes Global." *First Things*, no. 152 (April 2005): 26–29.

———. *The Spirit of Democratic Capitalism.* New York: American Enterprise / Simon & Schuster, 1982.

Painter, Nell Irving. *The History of White People.* New York: W. W. Norton & Co., 2010.

Parekh, Bhikhu. "Liberalism and Colonialism: A Critique of Locke and Mill." In *The Decolonization of Imagination: Culture, Knowledge and Power*, edited by Jan Nederveen. London and New Jersey: Zed Books, 1995.

Pinn, Anthony B. *African American Humanist Principles: Living and Thinking Like the Children of Nimrod.* New York: Palgrave, 2004.

————, ed. *Making the Gospel Plain: The Writings of Bishop Reverdy C. Ransom.* Harrisburg, PA: Trinity Press International, 1999.

————, ed. *Moral Evil and Redemptive Suffering: A History of Theodicy in African American Religious Thought.* Gainesville: University Press of Florida, 2002.

————. *Terror and Triumph: The Nature of Black Religion.* Minneapolis: Fortress Press, 2003.

————. *Why, Lord? Suffering and Evil in Black Theology.* New York: Continuum, 1995.

Plato. *The Dialogues of Plato.* Translated by Benjamin Jowett. New York: Random House, 1937.

Pogge, Thomas. *John Rawls: His Life and Theory of Justice.* Translated by Michelle Kosch. New York: Oxford University Press, 2007.

Popper, Karl. *The Open Society and Its Enemies.* Vols. 1–2. London: Routledge & Kegan Paul, 1945.

Puar, Jasbir. *Terrorist Assemblages.* Durham, NC: Duke University Press, 2007.

Raboteau, Albert. *Slave Religion: The "Invisible Institution" in the Antebellum South.* New York: Oxford University Press, 1978.

Ramsey, Paul. *Basic Christian Ethics.* New York: Charles Scribner's Sons, 1950.

————. *Deeds and Rules in Christian Ethics.* New York: Charles Scribner's Sons, 1967.

————. *The Just War: Force and Political Responsibility.* New York: Charles Scribner's Sons, 1968.

————. *Nine Modern Moralists.* Englewood Cliffs, NJ: Prentice-Hall, 1962.

————. *The Patient as Person: Explorations in Medical Ethics.* New Haven: Yale University Press, 1970.

————. *Who Speaks for the Church?* Nashville: Abingdon Press, 1967.

Rappaport, Roy A. *Ritual and Religion in the Making of Humanity.* Cambridge: Cambridge University Press, 1999.

Rawls, John. "The Idea of an Overlapping Consensus." *Oxford Journal of Legal Studies* 7, no. 1 (Spring 1987): 1–25.

————. *Justice as Fairness: A Restatement.* Edited by Erin Kelly. Cambridge: Belknap Press of Harvard University Press, 2001.

————. *The Law of Peoples.* Cambridge, MA: Harvard University Press, 1999.

————. *A Theory of Justice.* Rev. ed. Cambridge, MA: Harvard University Press, 1999.

Ray, Stephen G. *Do No Harm: Social Sin and Christian Responsibility.* Minneapolis: Fortress Press, 2003.

Rifkin, Mark. *When Did Indians Become Straight? Kinship, the History of Sexuality, and Native Sovereignty.* Oxford: Oxford University Press, 2010.

Riley, Jonathan. "Millian Qualitative Superiorities and Utilitarianism, Part II." *Utilitas* 21, no. 2 (June 2008): 127–43.

Roberts, J. Deotis. *Bonhoeffer and King: Speaking Truth to Power.* Louisville, KY: Westminster John Knox Press, 2005.

Rousseau, Jean-Jacques. *The First and Second Discourses.* Edited by Roger D. Masters. Translated by Roger D. and Judith R. Masters. New York: St. Martin's Press, 1964.

————. *Of the Social Contract, or, Principles of Political Right; and Discourse on Political Economy.* Translated by Charles M. Sherover. New York: Harper & Row, Publishers, 1984.

Russell, Bertrand. *A History of Western Philosophy.* 1945. Reprint, New York: Simon & Schuster, 2007.

Said, Edward W. *Culture and Imperialism.* New York: Vintage Books, 1993.

————. *Orientalism.* New York: Vintage Books, 1978.

Sandel, Michael J. *Liberalism and the Limits of the Justice.* New York: Cambridge University Press, 1982.

————. *Public Philosophy: Essays on Morality in Public.* Cambridge: Harvard University Press, 2005.

Sandoval, Moises. *On the Move: A History of the Hispanic Church in the United States.* Maryknoll, NY: Orbis Books, 1990.

Schneewind, Jerome B., ed. *Moral Philosophy from Montaigne to Kant: An Anthology.* Vol. 1. New York: Cambridge University Press, 1990.

Scott, Jacqueline. "On the Use and Abuse of Race in Philosophy: Nietzsche, Jews, and Race." In *Race and Racism in Continental Philosophy*, edited by Robert Bernasconi with Sybil Cook. Bloomington: Indiana University Press, 2003.

Sheth, Falguni A. "John Stuart Mill on Race, Liberty, and Markets." In *Race, Liberalism, and Economics*, edited by David Colander, Robert E. Prasch, and Falguni A. Sheth. Ann Arbor: University of Michigan Press, 2007.

Shorris, Earl. *New American Blues: A Journey through Poverty to Democracy.* New York: W. W. Norton & Co., 1997.

Shulman, George. *American Prophecy: Race and Redemption in American Political Culture.* Minneapolis: University of Minnesota Press, 2008.

Slatté, Howard Alexander. *Plato's Dialogues and Ethics.* New York: University Press of America, 2000.

Smith, Christopher Upham Murray. "Friedrich's Nietzsche's Biological Epistemics." *Journal of Social and Biological Structures* 9 (1986): 375–88.

Smith, Nicholas D. "Aristotle's Theory of Natural Slavery." In *A Companion to Aristotle's Politics*, edited by David Keyt and Fred D. Miller Jr. Oxford: Blackwell Publishing, 1991.

Smuts, Jan C. *Africa and Some World Problems: Including the Rhodes Memorial Lectures Delivered in Michaelmas Term, 1929.* Oxford: Clarendon Press, 1929.

Spivak, Gayatri. *A Critique of Postcolonial Reason.* Cambridge: Harvard University Press, 1999.

Stoler, Ann. *Race and the Education of Desire.* Durham, NC: Duke University Press, 1997.

Thomas Aquinas. *On Kingship, to the King of Cyprus.* Translated by Gerald B. Phelan. Revised by I. Th. Eschmann. 1949. Reprint, Toronto: Pontifical Institute of Mediaeval Studies, 1967.

————. *Summa theologica.* Translated by Fathers of the English Dominican Province. Allen, TX: Christian Classics, 1981.

Thomson, John B. *The Ecclesiology of Stanley Hauerwas: A Christian Theology of Liberation.* Burlington, VT: Ashgate, 2003.

Tinker, George E. *Missionary Conquest: The Gospel and Native American Cultural Genocide.* Minneapolis: Fortress Press, 1993.

Trimiew, Darryl. "The Growing End of an Argument: The Economic Rights Debate." *The Annual of the Society of Christian Ethics* 11 (1991): 85–108.

————. *Voices of the Silenced: The Responsible Self in a Marginalized Community.* Cleveland: Pilgrim Press, 1993.

Varouxakis, Georgios. "Empire, Race, Euro-centrism: John Stuart Mill and His Critics." In *Utilitarianism and Empire*, edited by Bart Schultz and Georgios Varouxakis. New York: Rowman & Littlefield, 2005.

————. "John Stuart Mill on Race." *Utilitas* 10, no. 1 (March 1998): 17–32.

Viroli, Maurizio. *Jean-Jacques Rousseau and the "Well-Ordered Society."* New York: Cambridge University Press, 1988.

Waldron, Jeremy. *God, Locke, and Equality: Christian Foundations in Locke's Political Thought.* New York: Cambridge University Press, 2002.

West, Cornel. *American Evasion of Philosophy: A Genealogy of Pragmatism.* Madison: University of Wisconsin Press, 1989.

———. *Prophesy Deliverance! An Afro-American Revolutionary Christianity.* 20th anniversary ed. Louisville, KY: Westminster John Knox Press, 2002.

Whitehead, Alfred North. *Process and Reality.* New York: Macmillan, 1929.

Williams, Delores. *Sisters in the Wilderness: The Challenge of Womanist God-Talk.* Maryknoll, NY: Orbis Books, 1993.

Williams, Preston N. "An Analysis of the Conception of Love and Its Influence on Justice in the Thought of Martin Luther King, Jr." *Journal of Religious Ethics* 18, no. 2 (Fall 1990): 15–31.

———. "Christian Realism and the Ephesian Suggestion: Influences That Have Shaped My Work." *Journal of Religious Ethics* 25, no. 2 (Fall 1997): 233–40.

Winchester, James. "Nietzsche's Racial Profiling." *Race and Racism in Modern Philosophy,* edited by Andrew Valls. Ithaca, NY, and London: Cornell University Press, 2005.

Wood, Allen W., ed. *Basic Writings of Kant.* New York: Modern Library Classics, 2001.

Wood, Neal. *John Locke and Agrarian Capitalism.* Berkeley: University of California Press, 1984.

Yoder, John Howard. *The Politics of Jesus.* Grand Rapids: Wm. B. Eerdmans Publishing Co., 1972.

———. *The Priestly Kingdom: Social Ethics as Gospel.* Notre Dame, IN: Notre Dame University Press, 1984.

———. "The Wider Setting of 'Liberation Theology.'" *Review of Politics* 52, no. 2 (Spring 1990): 285–96.

Yolton, Jean. *A Locke Miscellany.* Bristol, UK: Thommes Antiquarian Books, 1990.

Young, Josiah Ulysses, III. *No Difference in the Fare: Dietrich Bonhoeffer and the Problem of Racism.* Grand Rapids: Wm. B. Eerdmans Publishing Co., 1998.

Zagal, Hector. "Aquinas on Slavery: An Aristotelian Puzzle." Paper presented at the International Thomist Congress of the Società Internazionale Tomasso d'Aquino [International Society of Thomas Aquinas], Rome, Italy, September 2003. http://www.e-aquinas.net/pdf/zagal.pdf.

Žižek, Slavoj. *Violence.* New York: Picador, 2008.

Index

CPSIA information can be obtained at www.ICGtesting.com
Printed in the USA
LVOW081911191011

251140LV00003B/1/P